INDUSTRIAL RELATIONS RESEARCH
ASSOCIATION SERIES

Public Sector Employment
in a Time of Transition

EDITED BY

**Dale Belman, Morley Gunderson,
and Douglas Hyatt**

First Edition

Library of Congress Catalog Card Number: 50-13564

ISBN 0-913447-67-6

Price: $24.95

INDUSTRIAL RELATIONS RESEARCH ASSOCIATION SERIES:
    Proceedings of the Annual Meeting
    Proceedings of the Spring Meeting
    Annual Research Volume
    Membership Directory (every fourth year)
IRRA Newsletter (published quarterly)
IRRA Dialogues (published periodically)

Inquiries and other communications regarding membership, meetings, publications,
and general affairs of the Association, as well as notice of address changes should be
addressed to the IRRA national office.

INDUSTRIAL RELATIONS RESEARCH ASSOCIATION
University of Wisconsin–Madison
4233 Social Science Building, 1180 Observatory Drive
Madison, WI 53706-1393 U.S.A.
Telephone: 608/262-2762   Fax 608/265-4591

CONTENTS

Public Sector Employment Relations in Transition

DALE BELMAN
University of Wisconsin-Milwaukee and EPI

MORLEY GUNDERSON
University of Toronto

DOUGLAS HYATT
University of Wisconsin-Milwaukee

Pressures like those that led to the transformation of the private sector industrial relations system of the 1970s and 1980s are now affecting the public sector. Phrases like "reinventing" government (Osborne and Gaebler 1992), "re-engineering" the public sector, and "performance-based" government (Warrian 1995) illustrate the changes that are occurring. These pressures on employers in the public sector have concomitant implications for the employment relationship; they imply reinventing public sector labor relations, re-engineering the employment relationship, and instituting performance-based human resource practices. Issues of downsizing, job security, contingent employment, productivity bargaining, subcontracting, privatization, and succession rights are now prominent in the public sector. Joint ventures and alliances, mergers, separate business units, and internal pricing schemes—concepts that once were largely restricted to the private sector—are now common in the public sector. While the public sector was once regarded as a model for the introduction of progressive employment practices into the private sector, the pressure is now in the opposite direction, with the public sector often being called upon to be a model of restraint. Strategic choices that have been crucial for the development of human resource practices in the private sector will be equally crucial for all actors in the public sector.

Previous IRRA volumes on public sector bargaining focused on the establishment and maturation of collective bargaining in the public sector. Reflecting events of the 1960s and 1970s, the first IRRA public sector volume (Aaron, Najita, and Stern 1979) described the shift away from the doctrine of the sovereignty of the state and toward the establishment of collective bargaining in the public sector. It focused on the rapid upsurge of unionization in the public sector in the 1960s and 1970s and the administrative and legal response to labor's newfound role.

Also reflecting events of the time, the second IRRA volume on the public sector (Aaron, Najita, and Stern 1988) detailed the maturation of the system. It focused on issues such as the legal acceptance of the collective bargaining framework, efforts to develop more effective means of resolving interest disputes (especially as alternatives to the strike), and the stagnation of union membership.

While the first and second public sector volumes dealt, respectively, with the *establishment* and *maturation* of collective bargaining, this third volume focuses on its *transition* and possible transformation to a different system. As well, while the previous volumes focused on collective bargaining, the emphasis in this volume is broader, dealing with the employment relationship in general. Issues of labor adjustment, workplace practices and human resource management policies are prominent, as are alternative dispute resolution procedures and labor-management cooperation in the collective bargaining arena.

While there is no consensus on the ultimate form of the new system, it will be shaped by the two main strategies that are being followed. One involves an emphasis on improving the efficiency of government through innovative practices and a movement away from the bureaucratic, civil service model. Examples of "reinvention" best practices are typically drawn from efficiency-directed reforms.

The other strategy is more sweeping and involves an emphasis on cost cutting—cutting that may well be over and above that which may be regarded as efficient in terms of the provision of public services and infrastructure. Such cost cutting may be regarded as an end in itself, rather than a means to achieve the efficient delivery of public services. The goals may be simply service reduction, downsizing government, privatization of service provision, and reductions in real compensation, irrespective of their impacts on the efficient provision of public services. Given the importance of political factors in the public sector, the process can involve excessive restraint, just as at one time it may have involved insufficient restraint.

The public sector appears to be in the early stages of a transition similar to that which occurred in the private sector in the 1970s and 1980s. The next section inventories those changes that have occurred in the private sector, with the following section highlighting their relevance to the public sector.

The Transformation of Private Sector Employment Relations

Over the 1970s and 1980s, fundamental changes have occurred in private sector employment relations in almost all developed countries. These interrelated changes have involved the inputs of the industrial relations system, the mechanisms for converting inputs to outputs, and the outputs of that system.

On the input side, increased competitive pressures have emanated from various sources including global competition, trade liberalization, and deregulation. Skill-biased technological change, associated with the computer revolution, may also be redistributing the demand for labor among markets. The macroeconomic environment has been characterized by deep and prolonged recessions and "jobless" recoveries. The supply side of the labor market has been affected by pronounced demographic changes, including aging workforces; the dominance of the two-earner family; and increased diversity with respect to such factors as age, gender, and ethnicity.

These changes in the environmental inputs of the industrial relations system have worked through various conversion mechanisms of the industrial relations system. While the conversion mechanisms are generally regarded as converting inputs into outputs, in the industrial relations arena, they are often regarded as ends onto themselves. Industrial restructuring has occurred, usually involving a shift from production of goods to services. Mergers, acquisitions, joint ventures, and business alliances have occurred with many organizations essentially becoming holding companies linked with downstream suppliers and upstream consumers by advanced communications, just-in-time delivery, subcontracting, and offshore production. Deunionization has been prominent, and the legislative environment has often responded as evidenced by changes in collective bargaining legislation and its application, as well as by increased emphasis on protection of individual rights through antidiscrimination and human rights legislation. Workplace and human resource practices have also changed in various interrelated dimensions: job enlargement and enrichment, broader job classifications and multiskilling, part-time and contingent employment, contingent compensation and pay for performance, alternative work-time arrangements, employee involvement and reduced supervision, and an increase in labor-management cooperation and a decline in the strike as a mechanism for solving differences at the workplace.

As indicated, many of these processes are often regarded as ends in themselves and as such are often considered outputs of the industrial relations system. Other outputs also have been dramatically affected. A large share of the workforce have suffered from wage stagnation, and those subject to job displacement often have weathered substantial wage losses and periods of long-duration unemployment. Many countries have experienced increased inflation and unemployment, while job creation has been scant. U.S. labor markets have performed better than those of many other countries along these dimensions but at the expense of increasing wage polarization.

Public Sector Pressures and Changes

In varying degrees, many of these same factors that have affected employment relations in the private sector have begun to play out in the public sector. Furthermore, the public sector itself is subject to additional constraints that have important implications for its employment relations.

The public sector clearly has the opportunity to learn from the private sector practices and to emulate "best practices." There is also considerable pressure to do so. Private sector employers who are under increased competitive pressures want similar forces to be brought to bear on public services supported by tax dollars. Employees in the private sector often have similar feelings, especially when they themselves are subject to layoffs, expanded job assignments, wage stagnation, reduced union protection, and contingent work arrangements and compensation. These forces have been behind the notion of "reinventing government" (Osborne and Gaebler 1992) to facilitate incorporating "best practices" from the private sector as well as efficiency and customer orientation in the delivery of public services.

The public sector is also under severe budget constraints. Political emphasis on reducing budget deficits means that either expenditures have to be curtailed or taxes increased. The latter is not in the "political cards" because of taxpayer pressure. Furthermore, there is fear that high taxes will adversely affect business investment and plant location decisions and the jobs associated with those decisions. With greater global competition and reduced tariff barriers it is easier for capital to flow into countries with low taxes and few regulations and to export into the high-cost countries. Governments are under increased pressure to compete for business investment and the associated jobs, and this interjurisdictional competition may occur in the form of tax reductions and reduced regulations. The tax reductions directly affect the public sector budget constraint and employment relations, especially given the importance of labor cost in the provision of many public services. Reduced regulation indirectly reduces the demand for government services, since such regulation was often provided through the public sector.

Stagnant real incomes and growing income inequality also constrain demand for public services. While the growing portion of the population at the bottom of the distribution may have considerable need for public services, their incomes cannot provide the tax revenues required to support such services. The growing portion of the high-income population has the financial resources to pay for the public services but may see little benefit from taxes for services they are unlikely to access. Instead, they often prefer to opt for higher-end private services, feeling little need for a social safety net or the insurance of transfer payments should their situation deteriorate. Demand from the higher end of the income distribution for public services may come in the form of services to protect their position (e.g., police and prisons), but even these can be purchased privately (e.g., security systems and safe suburbs). In such circumstances, both the stagnant average real income and growing income inequality that are characterizing many economies combine to reduce demand for public services.

While the aging population is likely to lead to an increased demand for health care and pension support, and the increased number of two-earner families leads to an increase in the demand for childcare arrangements, it is unlikely that these will be met by significant increases in public spending on these social services. Rather the emphasis will be on cost saving through such processes as deinstitutionalization and community and family-based care as well as on providing more services by expanding the workload of the existing public sector personnel.

These changing constraints on the public sector have created pressure to emulate the changing workplace practices experienced earlier by the private sector. There will be greater pressure for broader-based job classifications and multiskilling, contingent employment, pay for performance, flexible and alternative work-time arrangements, employee involvement, reduced supervision, increased labor-management cooperation, alternative dispute resolution procedures for solving differences at the workplace, and restructuring away from centralized bureaucratic structures (with rigid distinctions between organizational divisions) and toward reintegration around operations.

Strategic Responses

Just as in the private sector, crucial strategic choices will be involved with respect to employment relations and human resource practices. The cost-cutting, "slash-and-burn" strategy emphasizes cost reductions through such mechanisms as employer-determined layoffs, often accompanied by privatization and subcontracting. The alternative strategy emphasizes labor not so much as a cost to be cut but rather a resource to be effectively utilized and involved in the process of where and how to reduce costs. Efficiency is to be attained through the changing workplace and human resource strategies discussed previously, with involuntary layoffs being a last resort. In unionized environments these issues would be subject to bargaining, with job security being a paramount issue in that bargaining.

Governments also have strategic decisions to make with respect to their role as legislator as well as employer. They can clearly influence public sector bargaining outcomes by changing the legislative environment within which such bargaining occurs. Elements of the legislative environment that can be changed include certification procedures and protections; management rights and the scope of bargaining; dispute resolution procedures (especially with respect to the right to strike and requirements for interest arbitration); the designation of employees who have the right to strike; back-to-work and national emergency legislation; legislative stipulations on criteria to be used by arbitrators, especially with respect to the ability to pay; abrogation of collective agreements and the suspension of bargaining rights; and the imposition of mandatory unpaid leave through legislation or failure to appropriate funds.

Unions will also be confronted with strategic choices in the public sector as in the private sector. Decisions include whether to follow a more cooperative, mutual gains approach or more conventional adversarial distributive bargaining. Furthermore, in the public sector the decision to try to influence the political process is even more important than in the private sector.

Clearly, strategic decisions will be required by all industrial relations actors in the public sector arena. This is even more true in the public sector than in the private sector because of the importance of the political process in public sector employment relations.

Diversity of Public Sector Responses

In the private sector, the imperatives of market forces often dictate the industrial relations response of the different actors. Organizations that do not respond often do not survive, albeit different employment-related responses could be appropriate to the varying circumstances of different organizations.

The public sector has more latitude of response, including no response or over-response. The political constraints of the public sector are less binding than the profit constraint of the public sector in disciplining inappropriate responses, in spite of the imperatives of deficit reduction, taxpayer resistance, and jurisdictional competition for physical and financial capital. Furthermore, different political and institutional conditions will give rise to responses which address the circumstances of a particular jurisdiction but are not readily applied to other public employers.

The public sector responses to changing conditions may also differ from that in the private sector because of other fundamental differences between the two sectors. The public sector labor force tends to be more educated and on the higher rungs of the occupational distribution than the workforce of the private sector. Public sector workers may already have had considerable independent discretion and empowerment at work, albeit centralized bureaucratic control and rigid civil service procedures may have inhibited even greater flexibility. Workers in the public sector may also be covered by broader rights through civil service procedures and even constitutional rights.

Managerial roles also differ between the public and private sectors. Politicians often play a key role, and decision-making authority tends to be more diffuse in the public sector. This can make restructuring more difficult and subject to reversals. Electoral changes, for example, can lead to pendulum-type swings in public sector labor relations policies. The vicissitudes of the political process can be more extreme than the vicissitudes of the market.

The extent of unionization is usually considerably higher in the public sector than in the private sector, and this obviously can give rise to different industrial relations responses to the pressures faced by employers. Collective bargaining can provide a viable arena to negotiate the restructuring and to confront the inevitable trade-offs especially with respect to job security. In contrast, it can also inhibit bargaining over these issues, especially if the adversarial mentality continues and fragmentation of bargaining units inhibits unions speaking with one voice. As well, unions may be wedded to narrow job classifications and seniority principles that may inhibit restructuring.

Attitudes toward the public sector are also changing. There appears to be a loss of faith in the efficacy of government to solve social problems as well as a decreased trust of government and politicians. This can lead to a reduced demand for government services as well as increased pressure to curb public sector compensation and job security, especially as that security is eroded among private sector taxpayers. Rather than looking to government as a model employer, taxpayers may increasingly feel that governments should be emulating private sector practices, especially those that emphasize customer satisfaction. Given the importance of political pressures in public sector labor relations, these changing attitudes can have important implications for employment relations in the public sector.

Clearly, there is no easy answer as to whether public sector industrial relations will undergo a transformation that is similar to that of the private sector. What is clear is that the public sector is under extreme pressure for change and this will have important implications for employment relations in that sector. The exact nature of the transition is less clear, as is the expected structures of the system to come. The various chapters in this volume deal with the transition of public sector employment relations that is currently in progress.

As summarized in more detail in the next section, John Lund and Cheryl Maranto discuss the changing legislative environment, highlighting how it is becoming less favorable to the formation and retention of unions in the public sector. Richard Freeman provides new survey evidence on the attitudes of public sector workers and managers, suggesting that public sector employees are more favorable to unionization than their private sector counterparts and that this helps to explain the higher degree of unionization in the public sector compared to the private sector. Robert Hebdon focuses on the alternative dispute resolution procedures that are evolving to meet the changing pressures in the public sector. Dale Belman and John Heywood focus on wage determination in the federal public sector, with particular attention to the concept of private sector comparability and how it is measured and applied. Peter Doeringer, Linda Kaboolian, Michael Watkins, and Audrey Watson analyze the evolution of the federal public sector from the earlier patronage-spoils system to the merit model and then to the emerging system that involves mixtures of externally imposed cost cutting and downsizing as well as more internally driven reforms which emphasize efficiency through changing human resource and workplace practices (illustrated with case studies). Anil Verma and Joel Cutcher-Gershenfeld also utilize a number of Canadian and U.S. case studies to illustrate the alternative paths to reform, and they identify a number of key ingredients to such reforms. Morley Gunderson and Douglas Hyatt document the evolving employment relationship in the Canadian public sector with respect to such dimensions as legislation, compensation, unionization, dispute resolution, and changing workplace and human resource practices. Phil Beaumont provides a European perspective, with particular attention to alternative paths to reform.

Overview of Chapters

Lund and Maranto: Legal Structure of Bargaining

In the previous IRRA volumes on the public sector, the chapter on the legal structure of public sector bargaining was replete with descriptions of the passage of new bargaining statutes and the increasing sophistication of existing statutes. There were definite trends toward limiting government sovereignty; widening the scope of bargaining; formalizing bargaining structures; and mandating dispute resolution procedures such as fact finding, mediation, and binding arbitration.

This chapter reports both a slower pace of change and signs of retrenchment and reversion since 1987. In the past eight years, only eleven bargaining laws have been enacted: only one is a new law (New Mexico), three are revisions which substantially extend bargaining rights (Texas, Delaware, and Nebraska), while six apply only to educational employees.

There have been a greater number of court decisions which have altered the legal framework of public sector bargaining. Although the courts, mostly at the state level, have not spoken with a single voice, there has been a trend toward reassertion of the sovereignty of the legislature and courts. For example, the Supreme Court of Alaska found that the legislature is free to underfund collective agreements, the Supreme Court of Florida found that the legislature may unilaterally change any monetary item in a contract, and the highest court in Nebraska declared both interest and grievance arbitration unconstitutional because they depose court jurisdiction. Contrary trends may be found in Colorado and Louisiana, where the right to strike of public employees was upheld, and in Iowa, where AFSCME was supported in the enforcement of an arbitration award which the governor refused to fund.

With respect to agency shop fees and current disputes over chargeable expenses, this chapter traces the evolution of decisions of the U.S. Supreme Court, various U.S. Appeals Courts, and various state courts (notably Indiana, Wisconsin, Ohio, and Kentucky).

Numerous tables provide summary pictures of the current provisions of collective bargaining statutes by state and occupational groupings. These are based on various sources: an exhaustive review of state and federal court cases, legislative proposals and attorney generals opinions from 1987 to 1994 using LEXIS, legal periodical data bases, and the BNA Government Employment Relations Reporter. This comprehensive summary of public sector labor law should prove invaluable to practitioners and researchers.

Although the "patchwork quilt" of public sector bargaining laws imparts considerable inertia and stability to the legal structure of public sector bargaining, the pronounced trend since 1987 has been toward circumscription of bargaining and toward support for unilateral action by governments. Continuation of this trend portends harder times for public sector unions, their members, and public employees.

Freeman: Employee Attitudes toward Unionization

While the legal environment may be changing in a direction that is less favorable to unionization, Freeman provides new survey evidence that the attitudes of employees in the public sector are more favorable to unionization than are those of their counterparts in the private sector.

There is notable divergence in the level of organization of the public and private sectors of the United States. While unions represent 11% of the employees in the private sector and unionization is declining by half a percent a year, union membership in the public sector has stabilized at approximately 40% of workers.

What explains this difference? Freeman argues that it is not the demographic composition of the public sector, since that composition is less favorable to unionization in the public sector than in the private sector. Similarly, the legal structure of bargaining is generally less favorable to unionization in the public sector than the private sector, and as discussed by Maranto and Lund (this volume), the legal environment is becoming less favorable for public sector workers (albeit due-process rights and merit-based promotion procedures afford public employees security in organizing, and dispute resolution procedures may make unionization palatable to employees in the public sector). Freeman suggests that much of the difference in unionization is due to more favorable attitudes of both employees and managers in the public sector with respect to the role of unions.

The picture developed in this chapter is drawn from an extensive, but nonrandom, survey of public employee attitudes which parallels a survey by Freeman and Rogers in the private sector. Similar to the private sector, in the public sector there is a substantial "gap" of about 35% between the desired and perceived level of involvement of employees in decisions about their employment. This gap is particularly large for teachers, and it tends to be larger for unionized employees than for nonunion employees. Employees in the public sector, however, express greater satisfaction with their jobs than do employees in the private sector, and this is true for both union and nonunion employees.

One of the more striking differences is the greater perceived willingness of managers to share power in the public sector. While public employees give their managers lower ratings on leadership and pay increases than do private employees, they give them much higher ratings on willingness to share power and authority. This holds true for both union and nonunion employees.

Freeman also reports that public employees, including nonunion employees in the South, have more favorable attitudes toward unions than do their counterparts in the private sector. They also believe that their managers are less likely to oppose union organizing than are private sector workers.

This survey also indicates that employee involvement is alive and well and possibly in somewhat better health in the public sector than the private sector. Compared to the private sector, public employees are 5% to 10% more likely to work where there are "town meetings," open-door policies, or joint labor-management committees. Public employees are also more likely to be in a workplace with an employee involvement program and to participate in that program.

Overall, the attitudes of public employees and managers toward their work, toward employee involvement in the workplace, and toward employee representation provide a strong underpinning for public employee unionism. The underlying factors influencing these attitudes remains a topic of further study.

Hebdon: Dispute Resolution

Public sector dispute resolution procedures are intended to institutionalize conflict and protect the public from the consequences of such conflict, particularly from strikes. The decline in strike activity and the rise of new sources of conflict over issues such as privatization and contingent employment have posed challenges for procedures not intended to address these emerging areas.

The 1990s have seen increased aggression in public sector collective bargaining. Fiscal pressures and a more conservative political environment have combined to create the apparent need for major cost reductions and downsizing of the public sector workforce and have resulted in increased conflict over these issues. Although public sector strike activity has fallen off over the last decade, conflict finds expression in other forms, notably in grievance filing, arbitrations, and unfair labor practice charges against employers.

Dispute resolution procedures are adapting to the changing needs of the public sector, albeit at a slow and uneven rate. Experiments with cooperative approaches to bargaining are being tried, and some state labor relations agencies are providing training in these techniques. There has been an increase in the use of special mediation for settling grievances and unfair labor practices and some use of preventative mediation to improve the relationship of parties away from the bargaining table. Although such methods appear useful when applied to particular issues, they appear less successful in resolving ongoing conflict between the parties.

The other major forms of dispute resolution, fact-finding and arbitration, have proven less adaptive. The use of fact-finding to resolve disputes has increased, but there is considerable dissatisfaction with its performance. Evidence is mounting that its usefulness is declining.

Arbitration is becoming increasingly popular as an alternative to courts through alternative dispute resolution (ADR) procedures, but interest arbitration is coming under increased scrutiny in the public sector because of its perceived inability to handle economic issues. The focus of this scrutiny is the application of ability-to-pay criteria, with arbitrators failing to articulate clear standards to judge the issue and problems arising in the application to a fiscal structure dominated by discretionary expenditures. Criticism has also arisen over the reluctance of arbitrators to make decisions on issues which would fundamentally alter the relationship between the parties, thereby limiting the effectiveness of interest arbitration in addressing emerging issues such as privatization.

Existing evidence is not sufficient to tell whether public sector dispute resolution systems are undergoing a transition or a more fundamental "transformation." The move toward extensive restructuring in the public sector, however, will hasten its evolution by putting new demands on the system.

Belman-Heywood: Compensation

The appropriate level of compensation of public employees is one of the oldest and most contentious issues in public sector employment relations. Issues in the debate include the standards by which public sector wages are determined, the methodology used to measure public and private wages, and the components of pay to be included in the measure of compensation.

One area of general agreement, at least in principle, is that public sector employees should be paid comparably to equivalent employees in the private sector. Although other criteria exist, such as ability to pay or using the public sector to influence trends in the broader economy, comparability is the most widely accepted standard for setting public sector pay.

The practical application of this principle, however, is fraught with difficulties and controversy. Although there is general agreement that comparability should extend beyond wages, it is often difficult to collect data on nonwage compensation and to evaluate benefits like job security. Furthermore, there may be a divergence between the costs of providing fringe benefits and the value attached to them by employees. Difficulties also arise if there are no comparable jobs in the private sector or if comparator wages reflect noncompetitive factors or discrimination.

Comparability has been measured by two main approaches. Wage surveys have been used to compare wages in the same narrowly defined occupation or position in the public and private sectors. Regression analysis has been applied to large cross-sectional data sets to compare the wages of otherwise similar persons in the public and private sectors. The measures emerging from these alternative approaches have been rather different. Occupational wage surveys indicate federal wages are below those paid to equivalent employees in the private sector, while regression approaches generally find the opposite. This pattern is reversed for state and local employees, where regressions indicate underpayment and occupational wage surveys indicate overpayment. More recently, hybrid studies have been employed involving regression approaches which add controls for position, such as firm size and more detailed occupational controls, to the typical human capital characteristics. These studies tend to reduce the discrepancy between the typical regression and occupational wage survey results.

Disaggregate analysis also reveals that aggregate public-private sector wage differentials can mask considerable variability. Comparability in the aggregate often reflects an offsetting "averaging" of large positive and negative deviations from comparability at the disaggregate level.

A clear pattern found in all studies is the decline of wages in the public sector relative to the private sector. Similarly, there is considerable evidence of wage compression, with the upper levels of the civil service being paid considerably less than their counterparts in the private sector. This is consistent with the work of Doeringer, Kaboolian, Watkins, and Watson in this volume, which suggests that the federal sector is having trouble recruiting and retaining an adequately skilled labor force.

Doeringer, Kaboolian, Watkins, and Watson: New Directions at the Federal Workplace

This chapter reviews the performance of the federal government's employment system, with particular emphasis on developments since the 1970s. The current merit model originated in the late nineteenth century as an alternative to the patronage or spoils system. The intent was to ensure a reliable government infrastructure to support economic growth and development. The central features of this system are merit-based employment, the doctrine of sovereignty, the application of scientific management, and private sector pay equivalence.

The reforms in the 1970s could generally be labeled as "progressive." The most notable were the introduction of collective bargaining to provide greater voice to employees, the implementation of equal employment opportunity, and improvement of the quality of federal management by reform and restructuring of the federal civil service system. These reforms have produced important changes in the federal employment system—for example, the federal government has been far more successful than the private sector in closing the gender gap in pay. However, problems arose, including those associated with maintaining pay competitiveness, opportunities for advancement, and recruiting a high quality federal workforce.

Reform proposals since 1980 have been in very different directions. Some have focused on externally imposed cost cutting and a reduction in the scope of direct federal activity through privatization, downsizing, and devolving federal powers to the states. Other proposals have focused on improving efficiency through internal reform. Total Quality Management (TQM) strategies were introduced by the Reagan and Bush administrations, and support for this approach was institutionalized in the Federal Quality Institute in 1988. The National Performance Review, championed by Vice President Gore, advanced earlier initiatives of improving service to citizens, increasing managerial flexibility, and empowering federal employees.

Although many agencies have been more adept at the rhetoric than the substance of these programs, and although an ongoing emphasis on cost cutting and reducing federal employment has, to some degree, undermined the legitimacy of the reforms, there have been notable successes. The Internal Revenue Service has been particularly successful at shifting from a hierarchical organization with adversarial labor relations and extreme problems in meeting its goals to a more productive and less adversarial organization through a TQM program and partnership with the National Treasury Employees Union. The Bureau of Printing and Engraving has also had notable success in transforming its employment structure. Historically, the bureau has had a fragmented craft production structure, a legacy of scientific management, and adversarial relations with multiple unions. The introduction of new technologies and consequent conflict over its effect on the existing employment structure led to a dialogue with the union leadership, the formation of a Joint Partnership Council with the unions, and movement by management toward more strategic assessment and planning of human resources.

These cases, among others, show that there are multiple routes to reform. The authors suggest that the implementation of reform is critically dependent on reducing the unilateral prerogatives of federal management and increasing the scope of employee involvement. They argue that a larger role for collective bargaining is concomitant with such changes. Failing this, efforts at reform are unlikely to produce the efficiency gains sought by reformers.

Verma and Cutcher-Gershenfeld: Workplace Innovations

The public sector employment relationship is dominated by the bureaucratic/civil service model. Although this structure affords employee advantages such as substantive and procedural due process, considerable job security, and hiring and promotion by merit and seniority, it is hierarchical and rule bound and provides employees little power over their work.

In parallel with trends in the private sector, there have been numerous experiments with alternative forms of employment involvement in the public sector. Verma and Cutcher-Gershenfeld review several of these experiments in both Canada and the United States: (1) a socio-technical employment structure at a greenfield site of the Ontario Office of the Registrar General, (2) a socio-technical systems approach to construction engineering employees at a Canadian Armed Forces base undergoing a downsizing, (3) work teams at British Columbia Hydro, (4) continuous quality improvement methods in the Michigan Department of Natural Resources, (5) labor-management partnerships at the U.S. Department of Agriculture and the Norfolk navy yard, and (6) alternative dispute resolution systems at the Lansing Mail Sorting Center of the U.S. Post Office.

The authors highlight the two main motivations behind efforts toward workplace change: a value-added approach which emphasizes harnessing employee energy, effort, and know-how and a cost-based approach which emphasizes the reduction of labor costs. Both are present in most change initiatives, but value-added strategies with their emphasis on employee development, empowering lower-level employees, and the development of cross-functional teams are dominant in the cases studied in this chapter.

The authors conclude that the current stresses and constraints will force the emergence of alternatives to the bureaucratic, civil service model of employment relations. While the emergence of alternative models is driven by crises, their success depends on key ingredients: (1) the crises being neither too severe nor too mild, (2) a compelling case for change, (3) local autonomy among managers, (4) union involvement in the change process, (5) local bargaining that will not destabilize a master agreement, and (6) union and management leaders who are skilled handlers of the change process.

The authors also suggest that efforts at workplace change in the public sector are particularly difficult because of the exposure to the political processes, the glare of publicity, and the instability of political goals. Whether the typical effort at change in the public sector can, under such burdens, emulate the success of some of the cases reviewed in this chapter remains to be seen.

Gunderson and Hyatt: Canada

Public sector labor relations have a longer history and are more varied and extensive in Canada than in the United States. Although Canadian law varies considerably by province and by employee function, it is typically more supportive of collective bargaining, more likely to permit bilateral decision making, and more permissive of strikes and binding dispute resolution procedures than are the comparable U.S. laws. The support for collective bargaining is reflected in the high level of union coverage in the Canadian public sector—between 50% and 80% depending on the level of government and function.

The authors provide considerable evidence that the historic support for collective bargaining in the public sector may be reversing. Canada faces pressures parallel to those bearing on other countries: an aging population which makes costly demands on services, a budget deficit combined with reluctance to raise taxes, a private sector which faces increasing competitive pressures, and a public desire to reduce the cost of government while maintaining services. This combination of forces has led to policies such as the overriding of the collective bargaining process and direct regulation of employment. It may also be leading to a more cooperative and service-oriented approach to labor-management relations; whether this will help preserve the bargaining process remains to be seen.

There have been some notable shifts in strike activity and in methods of resolving interest disputes in Canada over the past ten years. Strike rates are much lower in the public sector than in the private sector. Furthermore, strikes have declined in both sectors, although the decline has been smaller in the public sector so that the public sector accounts for a growing proportion of (declining overall) strike activity. While strikes are less common in the public sector, overall dispute rates (proportion of settlements which end in a strike *or arbitration*) are more similar (14% in the private sector and 11.5% in the public sector), reflecting the much greater use of interest arbitration in the public sector. A notable development in dispute resolution in the public sector has been the increased use of legislated interventions, such as wage controls, back-to-work legislation, and outright abrogation of the collective agreement; they are now the more common ways to conclude negotiations than strikes or arbitration.

As in the United States, comparability is the central principle for public sector wage determination under interest arbitration. Summarizing current research (largely based on regression techniques), the authors report that public employees earn between 5% and 10% more than otherwise comparable private sector employees. This favorable differential is largest for women and low-wage employees. Furthermore, the public sector likely provides somewhat better fringe benefits than the private sector. However, similar to the findings of Belman and Heywood for the United States, the public sector wage advantage is trending downward, particularly for males. There is also evidence that the impact of unions on wages is smaller in the public sector than in the private sector and that arbitrated wage settlements tend to be slightly higher than wage settlements achieved under right-to-strike regimes.

The Canadian system faces a number of challenges brought about by economic, budgetary, and social pressures that are affecting the functions and role of government. These in turn are creating pressures for privatization, subcontracting, performance evaluation, restructuring, and downsizing—all of which are influencing wages and job security. As such, the various actors in the Canadian public sector are facing key strategic choices with respect to such matters as labor-management cooperation and workplace restructuring and the potential for considerable conflict over the directions taken. These strategic choices will determine the shape of the public sector employment relations system for years to come.

Beaumont: Europe

Europe faces financial issues similar to those of the United States and Canada, but their social relations have sent them on different courses than their North American counterparts. With the exception of the United Kingdom, the more extensive role of labor and the strong support for social welfare programs have blunted tendencies toward downsizing, privatization, and internal transformation of government functions.

Relative to the United States, most European countries have a larger proportion of their GDP devoted to public expenditure and a larger share of employment in the public sector. For example, while 15% of U.S. employment is in the public sector and public spending is 36% of GDP, these figures respectively are 19% and 42% in the United Kingdom, 23% and 50% in France, and 32% and 55% in Norway. The European countries also face more severe debt and deficit issues than the U.S. The requirements of the Maastricht Treaty to reduce these debts and deficits and looming increases in social costs as the populations of these countries continue to age have focused attention on reducing government expenditures.

Virtually all European countries have used measures such as pay restraint and pay freezes and reduced indexation to reduce the cost of government. In the Netherlands, nominal pay cuts have occurred. Although these measures have succeeded in reducing public sector compensation relative to the private sector, they have not resulted in substantial reductions in budget deficits.

Efforts at broader reforms, such as privatization and moving the public sector toward a private sector bargaining framework as well as importing private sector human resource practices (e.g., performance-related pay standards), have been adopted to varying degrees by a number of countries, especially the United Kingdom. Driven in part by ideology, the British government has undertaken a wide range of reforms: transferring close to one million jobs to the private sector since 1979, requiring local public sector authorities to competitively bid on many projects and services, market testing many civil service jobs to determine if they can be done less expensively by the private sector, decentralizing public sector collective bargaining, and implementing performance-related pay systems for three-quarters of the civil service labor force. Efforts at reform in other European countries have been far more limited and, in general, based more on consultation and compromise with public sector employees and their representatives. This difference in approach reflects the strength of the public sector unions, their willingness to use strikes to oppose what are perceived as excessive cuts, and a less ideologically driven effort at change on the continent.

Although there is no doubt that all European countries will continue to reform their public sectors, it is far from certain what paths will evolve and whether the British model will be taken up by other European countries. Even more in doubt is whether these reforms will resolve the budget issues faced by these nations.

Concluding Observations

Clearly, employment relations in the public sector are in a time of transition. The public sector is under great pressure for change. Many of these pressures are the same as those faced by the private sector in the 1970s and 1980, but some are unique to the public sector. The emphasis is not simply on collective bargaining (as analyzed in previous IRRA volumes in the public sector) but on the overall employment relationship in general, especially with respect to human resource policies and workplace practices.

The chapters in this volume highlight that, although the pressures facing the public sector are similar, different paths to reform and restructuring are being followed. This applies to different countries, different jurisdictions within countries, different public sector functions, and even different units within the same country and jurisdiction. Clearly, the public sector is now facing crucial strategic choices involving alternative paths to reform. Those choices will shape employment relations in the public sector for years to come. Whether the transition that is underway will lead to a fundamental transformation of the public sector employment relationship will be played out over the next decade.

References

Aaron, Benjamin, Joyce Najita, and James Stern. 1979. *Public Sector Bargaining.*
Washington, DC: Bureau of National Affairs.
_____. 1988. *Public Sector Bargaining.* 2nd ed. Washington, DC: Bureau of
National Affairs.
Osborne, D., and T. Gaebler. 1992. *Reinventing Government.* Reading, MA: Addison-
Wesley.
Warrian, Peter. 1995. "The End of Public Sector 'Industrial' Relations in Canada?"
Toronto: KPMG Center for Government Foundation.

CHAPTER 1

Public Sector Labor Law: An Update

JOHN LUND
University of Wisconsin-Madison

CHERYL L. MARANTO
Marquette University

Law governing collective bargaining rights of state and local government employees continues to be a crazy-quilt patchwork of state and local laws, regulations, executive orders, court decisions, and attorney general opinions. This patchwork is far from static. For labor relations practitioners, academics, and policymakers alike, there is an ongoing need to update the status of these laws. That is the objective of this chapter.

To develop this update, a LEXIS® search of state and federal court cases, laws, legislative proposals, and attorney general opinions for each state was conducted from 1987 (the year the last IRRA research volume on the public sector was published) through 1994. Additionally, several CD-ROM literature databases, including a legal periodicals database as well as the BNA *Government Employment Relations Reporter*, were searched.

This chapter begins with a review of significant state legislative changes as well as selected court decisions, executive orders, and attorney general opinions since 1987 which affected collective bargaining rights in the public sector. We then summarize current legal provisions (the duty to bargain, terminal resolution procedures, and strike penalties) by state and sector (police and fire, state workers, etc.). Finally, we review and analyze two key post-1987 trends: (1) legislative and constitutional limitations on the finality of collective bargaining agreements or interest arbitration awards and (2) procedures for handling nonmember objections to agency shop fees in light of *Hudson*, 475 US 292, 121 LRRM 2793 (1986) and *Lehnert*, 111 S.Ct 1950, 137 LRRM 2321 (1991).

Major Changes since 1987

Major State Legislative Changes

The seven-year period from 1987 to 1994 witnessed a relatively low level of legislative activity with only 11 states enacting laws.[1] Only one state (New Mexico) passed a comprehensive law granting bargaining rights to public employees where no previous bargaining law existed. Nebraska's new law extends bargaining rights to state workers, and Texas law gives localities the option of providing bargaining rights to police and firefighters. The remaining eight states amended existing bargaining laws at the margins, and most (six) of these covered educational employees only.

Given the low level and limited nature of changes in state collective bargaining legislation, it might be tempting to conclude that the legal framework in the public sector is quite stable. However, as Hebdon (this volume) points out, this apparent stability is largely an artifact of the fragmented structure of public sector bargaining law. Our later discussion of limitations on the finality of collective bargaining agreements and "binding" arbitration awards through judicial decisions and fiscal control measures demonstrates that a great deal of flux exists beneath the stable veneer.

Table 1 summarizes these laws. Changes in administrative regulations and proposed legislation are not included. Significant court decisions interpreting *existing* law or regulations, executive orders, and attorney general opinions are reported later.

Significant Court Decisions Affecting Bargaining Rights

Since it is not possible to report *all* significant court decisions here, priority is given to decisions which affected the duty to bargain, terminal resolution steps, the right to strike, and the finality of collective bargaining agreements and arbitration awards. Thirteen significant state court decisions regarding public sector bargaining are reported in Table 2. Five concern the finality of ratified collective bargaining agreements or interest arbitration awards. These are discussed at some length in a separate section on the finality issue. Three decisions relate to the legal status of public employee strikes and are discussed in the summary of current state law provisions. Finally, two decisions concern the legal status of interest arbitration, and the remaining three deal with miscellaneous issues.

Significant Attorney General Opinions and Executive Orders

Perhaps the most significant attorney general opinion since 1987 involves the prohibition of public employee strikes in West Virginia.

TABLE 1
New or Amended State Bargaining Laws since 1987

State	Coverage	Summary of Change
Alaska (1992)	Public school teachers	Allows public school teachers the right to strike after submitting to advisory arbitration. (A 1982 Alaska Supreme Court decision had ruled that teacher strikes were illegal under the old law.)
Delaware (1994)	State, county & municipal, excluding teachers, police & firefighters	Expands mandatory subjects of bargaining to include wages and benefits.
Illinois (1995)	Public school employees, Chicago only	Expands the list of prohibited bargaining subjects (e.g., subcontracting, layoffs and their impact), prohibits teacher strikes for 18 months, exempts educational employers from requirement to submit to binding dispute resolution process, gives principals sole authority to suspend and discipline teachers, position vacancies to be filled by principal without regard to seniority.
Iowa (1991)	Public school teachers	Eliminates fact-finding from available impasse procedures. If mediation fails, dispute goes directly to final offer arbitration.
Michigan (1994)[a]	Public school employees	Imposes fines on employees and unions for striking, prohibits unfair labor practice strikes, requires courts to enjoin strikes and lockouts without finding of irreparable harm, prohibits labor organizations from vetoing contracts, prohibits requiring association ratification, expands the list of prohibited bargaining subjects.
Nebraska (1987)	State workers, excluding university and college employees	Twelve statewide bargaining units defined, contracts must expire with end of biennial budget cycle, all negotiations must be completed by March 15. If no agreement by January 15, parties submit to binding arbitration (special master) who must rule by February 15. Arbitration decisions are appealable to the Public Employment Relations Commission. No right to strike. Also see Appendix.
New Mexico (1992)	All public employees	State workers are automatically covered by the Public Employment Labor Relations Board (PELRB), but nonstate jurisdictions may create a parallel structure which is at least as effective as PELRB. State workers contracts, if not settled by November 15 go to fact-finding, with recommendations

TABLE 1 (*Continued*)

New or Amended State Bargaining Laws since 1987

State	Coverage	Summary of Change
		due by December 10. If no agreement by December 15, unresolved issues are resolved by the appropriations process. Nonstate worker units may develop alternative terminal resolution procedures. Striking unions may be decertified for one year.
Pennsylvania (1992)	Educational employees	Parties negotiate a terminal resolution arbitration procedure which selects from either union, employer, or factfinder final offers or recommendations, either issue by issue, economic and noneconomic packages, or total package. If fact-finding recommendations not totally accepted by both parties, the terminal resolution procedure takes effect, and parties give notification of their intent to proceed to arbitration which is binding unless either party rejects it. If either party refuses to select arbitration, a strike or lockout may occur outside of a ten-day notice period. Rejection of the arbitration award frees them to legally strike or lockout. Strikes are not permitted from the time fact-finding is requested until the report is made. Strikes must cease when the parties agree to arbitration. Selective strikes are illegal, and strikes which prohibit the school board from providing the required number of days in the school year may be enjoined. There are restrictions on the use of outside strikebreakers.
Texas (1993)	Police and firefighters only	Enabling legislation requires cities to adopt the law by referendum. Non-binding arbitration available. Strike penalties include union fines, forfeiture of dues checkoff, and for striking employees, two years probation and no compensation increase for one year after strike.
Utah (1993)	Certificated school employees only	Mediation available after 90 days of negotiations and if impasse occurs. If no mediated settlement within 15 days, parties may submit to a state hearings officer for fact-finding.
Wisconsin (1993)	Certified teaching personnel	A revenue control measure adopted in 1993 (S.B. 16) amended the Municipal Employment Relations Act (MERA) to require that, between 7/1/93 to 6/30/96, if a school district employer offered a "qualified economic offer" to a union representing school district professional employees,

TABLE 1 (*Continued*)

New or Amended State Bargaining Laws since 1987

State	Coverage	Summary of Change
		the parties would be precluded from arbitrating economic issues. A "qualified economic offer" (QEO) applies only to teachers union and must maintain the percentage contribution toward employees' existing fringe benefits and maintain those fringe benefit costs which existed 90 days prior to contract expiration (provided that the costs of doing so are plus or minus 1.7% of total compensation costs during the previous 12 months) and total wage cost increases, including length of service and education increments do not exceed 2.1% of total compensation costs during the previous twelve months.

ᵃ The circuit court has ordered a stay of implementation of the Michigan law, declaring two sections to be unconstitutional (automatic fine of union for strike without determining union authorization and requirement of automatic issuance of injunctions against strikes). At this time, the case is on appeal.

This state currently lacks any legislation establishing the right of public employees to bargain collectively. A 1962 state attorney general opinion advised "public employees may join unions and government officials may discuss wages and hours with such unions, but the final determination . . . rests with the governmental authorities and cannot be delegated away" (BNA SLL 1994, 59:220). A 1990 attorney general opinion to the state superintendent of schools further advised, "[T]here is no right to strike against the state . . , any strike or concerted work stoppage by public teachers in this state is illegal." The attorney general stated that in the absence of state laws, "[I]t is axiomatic that a strike by public employees for any purpose is illegal under common law." In response to the ongoing teachers strike, the opinion further advised that teacher contracts expressly prohibited strikes; any teacher who participates in one is subject to disqualification for one year, may be suspended and forfeits all due process protection (Attorney General opinion, March 8, 1990). The attorney general opinion conformed to a state Supreme Court decision in *Jefferson County Board of Education v. Jefferson County Education Association*, 183 W.Va. 15 (1990), which similarly found the same teachers strike was illegal.

Perhaps the most significant executive order during this period was issued by Governor Bayh of Indiana in 1990. Although the governor had

TABLE 2

Significant Court Decisions Affecting Public Sector Bargaining Laws since 1987

State	Citation	Summary of Decision
Alaska	*Public Employees Local 71 v. State*, Supreme Court of Alaska, 775 P.2d 1062 (1989)	The legislature is free to choose not to fund the monetary terms of a collective bargaining agreement signed by the state, but then the parties may resume negotiations.
Colorado	*Martin v. Montezuma-Cortez School Dist.*, Supreme Court of Colorado, 841 P.2d 237 (1992)	Applies the Industrial Relations Act (initially passed in 1915) to public employees and grants all public employees the right to strike. Under the act, labor disputes are subject to the authority of the director of the division of labor, who "may render a final order settling the dispute." In *Donlon v. Denver Classroom Teachers Assoc.*, Denver Dist. Ct. No. 94 CV 5055 (1994), the district court applied Martin to the Denver teachers strike, ruling that teachers have the right to strike and that the Commissioner of Labor surrendered jurisdiction when he presented a compromise contract which he sought to impose and the union rejected.
Florida	*State v. Florida Police Benevolent Assn.*, Supreme Court of Florida, 613 So. 2d 415 (1992)	Public employee unions requested judicial review of the legislature's unilateral changes in leave policy in a collective bargaining agreement. The court ruled that the legislature is free to underfund an agreement (due to separation of powers) and, in so doing, is then free to unilaterally change any monetary item in the contract. The court rejected the unions' request for renegotiation as being "administratively untenable."
Iowa	*AFSCME/Iowa Council 61 v. State*, Supreme Court of Iowa, 484 N.W. 2d 390 (1992)	Unions brought action to enforce an arbitration award after the governor vetoed an appropriations bill funding the award. The legislature failed to override the veto. The state contended that it could not fund the awards due to budget constraints, and that it was not bound by the award because it is subordinate to the appropriations process (due to separation of powers and the constitutional prohibition against undue delegation of duties). In ordering the state to pay, the court ruled that by passing PERA, the state made itself bound by its labor contracts. The claimed shortage of funds "can be ascribed to discretionary funding choices."

TABLE 2 (*Continued*)

Significant Court Decisions Affecting Public Sector Bargaining Laws since 1987

State	Citation	Summary of Decision
Louisiana	*Davis v. Henry,* Supreme Court of Louisiana, 555 So. 2d 457 (1990)	The court ruled that public sector employees are covered by the state's "Little Norris LaGuardia Act" which protects "all employees in the exercise of their right to engage in concerted activities." The court rejected the school board's argument that public employee strikes are illegal under common law (since Louisiana is not a common law state) and found that the state constitution gives public employees "the same right to engage in collective bargaining as held by their counterparts in the private sector." Except for police strikes which by their nature endanger the public, public employee strikes are legal and not enjoinable absent factual findings of danger to public health and safety.
Michigan	*MEA v. Engler,* Wayne County Circ. Ct., 94-423581-CL	Unions challenged the constitutionality of five provisions of new amendments to PERA dealing with public school employees. The court found two provisions unconstitutional: (1) automatic fines against the union without determination of union knowledge/support or authorization, and (2) requirement of courts to enjoin school strikes without finding of irreparable harm. The circuit court issued a stay of the entire law's implementation. Currently on appeal.
Nebraska	*Nebraska v. Nebr. Assn. of Public Employees Local 61,* Supreme Court of Nebraska 239 Neb. 653 (1991)	This case arose not out of the bargaining law but the state's Uniform Arbitration Act. The union's contract with the state required final and binding arbitration regarding terms and conditions of employment; a similar clause required binding arbitration of grievances. The state supreme court found final and binding arbitration of *both* contracts and grievances to be unconstitutional, because it ousts the courts of jurisdiction.
New Hampshire	*Furlough,* Supreme Court of New Hampshire, 135 NH 625 (1992)	The N.H. Supreme Court was requested by the state House of Representatives to determine whether a pending bill, HB 1058-FN, which would require state employees to take unpaid leaves of absence in response to a state fiscal crisis, would violate the state employee collective bargaining agreement. The court found the proposed law *did* impair the collective bargaining agreements despite the state's assertion that no minimum amount of work was guaranteed. The court also rejected the state's argument that such

TABLE 2 (*Continued*)

Significant Court Decisions Affecting Public Sector Bargaining Laws since 1987

State	Citation	Summary of Decision
		a decision to furlough was within the purview of management rights and finally that this action was within the "emergency" provisions of the contract. The N.H. Supreme Court also rejected the proposed bill on constitutional grounds.
New Jersey	*Hillsdale*, 622 A.2d 872 (N.J. Super, A.D. 1993)	Two police arbitration awards were challenged by two cities on the theory that the arbitrators did not adequately address all eight statutory criteria governing awards (34:13A-16g). The New Jersey Supreme Court vacated both decisions (see below).
Oklahoma	*Del City v. Fraternal Order of Police Local 114*, Supreme Court of Oklahoma, 869 P.2d 309 (1993)	Oklahoma's Supreme Court invalidated Sections 51-65 of the Police and Fire Law which provided for an "evergreen" clause allowing negotiated settlements to "roll over" for an additional year if no contract settlement was reached. The city argued that to continue to pay negotiated salaries and benefits from the previous fiscal year would create a budget deficit which would violate a state constitutional provision requiring a three-fifths referendum to increase indebtedness above revenues. The Oklahoma Supreme Court agreed.
Pennsylvania	*Masloff v. Port Authority*, Pennsylvania Supreme Court, 531 Pa. 416 (1992)	Port Authority transit workers in Pittsburgh struck in 1992, and the *city* of Pittsburgh (not a party to the dispute) obtained an injunction citing a "clear and present danger" to public health and safety. Two issues were involved in the appeal: (1) did the city have standing to file for the injunction; and (2) was a clear and present danger established? The court ruled that the city *did* have standing to file. Relying upon rulings under the PERA, the court found that although "[O]rdinary inconveniences resulting from a strike don't by themselves establish a clear and present danger," there was one in this case. The court ordered the union and the Port Authority into court-supervised negotiations only because binding arbitration had been removed by a 1986 amendment to the Port Authority law.
South Dakota	*Rapid City*, Supreme Court of S. Dakota 522 N.W.2d 494 (1994)	Under §3-18-8.1 of the South Dakota law, school boards may implement their last offer eleven days after impasse is reached, unless state intervention is requested. Following impasse, Rapid City's board of education implemented its final

TABLE 2 (*Continued*)

Significant Court Decisions Affecting Public Sector Bargaining Laws since 1987

State	Citation	Summary of Decision
		offer. A union's unfair labor practice charge alleged one implemented provision of the school board's final offer was even more restrictive than state law. The state supreme court held this action was not an unfair labor practice.
Texas	*Beaumont,* Texas Court of Appeals, 763 S.W.2d 57 (1992)	A city ordinance which originally authorized binding interest arbitration was subsequently repealed by the voters. The union brought suit claiming the repealing ordinance conflicted with state law by removing the provision for binding arbitration. The court of appeals found no conflict, since binding arbitration is not required by the act.

promised to pursue legislation providing collective bargaining rights to state workers, a bill to do so, as well as two other bills (one relating to all public employees and one to police and firefighters only), all failed passage. The state workers' bargaining bill was withdrawn from consideration in the senate, after passing the house, on the grounds that it might necessitate a statewide tax increase. Although the governor lacked the jurisdiction to mandate bargaining rights, the executive order grants state workers the right to elect union representation. An election will be scheduled following a showing of sufficient interest. The order prohibits strikes, strikers are subject to dismissal, and participating unions lose recognition by the state (*Government Employment Relations Reporter,* June 4, 1990, p. 699). Despite the lack of a bargaining duty and the absence of terminal resolution procedures, at least three contracts covering state workers have been negotiated since the order was issued (GERR, June 13, 1992, p. 968).

Current State Collective Bargaining Law Provisions

The Appendix summarizes the variations in state requirements with respect to the duty to bargain, terminal resolution procedures, and strike penalties affecting different public employee groups. Here we present summary tabulations of the prevalence of those legislative provisions. Table 3 reports the prevalence among states of laws which mandate a bargaining duty (as defined in Sec. 8(d) of the LMRA) by sector. Eleven states continue to have no legislation granting public employees bargaining rights, while twenty-three states and the District of Columbia grant bargaining rights to all public employees, and sixteen states grant bargaining rights to only some public employees.

TABLE 3

Number of States[a] with Legislative Bargaining Duty, 1994

Employee Group	Number of States
All public employees	24
All but state employees	3
Police, firefighters, and education	2
Education and municipal	2
Education only	5
Police and firefighters only	4
None	11

[a] Includes the District of Columbia.

The top panel of Table 4 summarizes strike policies governing public employees by sector. Sixteen states have legislation that explicitly prohibits strikes by all public employees, and all but four of these specify one or more penalties for striking. Not surprisingly, police and firefighters are most frequently subject to strike prohibitions (31 states and D.C.). State, education, and municipal employees are fairly equally subject to strike prohibitions (20, 23, and 21 jurisdictions, respectively). Police and firefighter strike prohibitions are most likely to have specified penalties attached (22 jurisdictions), with educational strikes close behind (19 jurisdictions). On the other hand, ten states now permit strikes by all public employees except police and fire with no or minor restrictions.[2] One state (Colorado) permits strikes by all public employees. Three of the states which permit strikes have laws which are silent on the issue (in fact, two lack enabling legislation entirely), but their state supreme courts have ruled that public employee strikes are legal (*County Sanitation Dist. No. 2 of L.A. County v. L.A. County Employees Assoc.*, 699 P.2d 835, 838 [1985], in California; *Davis v. Henry*, 555 So. 2d 457 [1990], in Louisiana; and *Martin v. Montezuma-Cortez School Dist.*, 841 P.2d 237 [1992], in Colorado).

The type of terminal resolution procedure is summarized in the lower panel of Table 4 for each state and sector. (See Appendix for additional detail.) The designations in Table 4 reflect the *mandatory*, explicit, and final step of the statutory bargaining dispute resolution procedure; the format of the terminal step (e.g., what type of arbitration) is not specified here. Unless the statute clearly indicates that the terminal step is mandatory, the next lower and mandatory step (e.g., fact-finding or mediation) is

TABLE 4

Number of States[a] with Various Strike Policies and Terminal Resolution Procedures

	Police & Firefighters	State	Education	Municipal
Number of States with Various Strike Policies[b]				
Allowed without restriction	2	3	3	3
Allowed with minor restrictions	1	8	9[c]	9
Prohibited, no penalty specified	10	6	4	7
Prohibited, with penalties specified	22	14	19	14
Total states with strike policy	35	31	35	33
Number of States by Terminal Resolution Procedure				
Silent	17	23	15	21
Mediation	5	9	9	9
Fact-finding	6	13	19	15
Interest arbitration	22	5	8	6

Notes:

[a] Includes the District of Columbia.

[b] The number of states with a strike policy does not equal the number with a legislated bargaining duty because: (1) some laws are silent on strike policy, and (2) some states which lack a bargaining law have strike policies established via judicial decisions.

[c] A new law in Illinois covering only Chicago schools prohibits strikes for 18 months but is being challenged in the courts. Illinois is still coded as allowing strikes in education with minor restrictions.

reported. In some cases, the law authorizes the parties to jointly agree to a terminal resolution procedure but does not clearly indicate what would happen if the parties fail to reach agreement on a terminal step. In these cases, the next lower mandatory terminal step is reported in this table.

A second definitional problem occurs in determining whether the terminal step is binding. Clearly mediation and fact-finding, by definition, are nonbinding. Interest arbitration is presumed to be binding, but in several states, the legislature or governing body has the ability to override portions of an arbitration award or portions of the award are nonbinding. (For example, in Rhode Island the award is advisory only on all economic issues and is binding on noneconomic issues only if a majority of the arbitration panel concurs.) Rather than seek to resolve this definitional problem, the lower panel of Table 4 indicates whether arbitration is mandatory but not whether the arbitration award is binding. The diversity of arbitration provisions among states prevents adequately capturing such detail in a summary table. The Appendix provides such detail.

As the lower panel of Table 4 indicates, public sector bargaining laws are often silent on the terminal dispute resolution procedure, with that "silence" being most prevalent for state employees and then for municipal employees. When the terminal procedure is specified, it is most often fact-finding, followed by interest arbitration, and then mediation. Mandatory interest arbitration is by far the most common terminal resolution procedure for police and firefighters (22 jurisdictions), whereas fact-finding is the most common procedure for teachers (19 jurisdictions). "Silence" is most common for state and municipal workers, although if a terminal resolution procedure is specified for them, fact-finding is most common for both groups. Interest arbitration is the least common resolution procedure for state, education, and municipal employees.

Finality of Collective Bargaining Agreements and Interest Arbitration Awards: Legislative Overrides and Imperatives

In a period of tightening government budgets and broad public opposition to tax increases, an issue of increasing importance in public sector bargaining is whether and under what conditions the monetary terms of a collective bargaining agreement or an arbitration award are binding on the employer. Presently there is no clear trend among states on this issue. We first review recent court cases and attorney general opinions dealing with the question of whether the legislative body can override voluntary bargaining settlements or arbitration awards. We then examine recent legislation which significantly alters terminal resolution procedures.

Four state courts have found that collective bargaining contracts ratified by the state or arbitration awards do not constitute binding obligations on the state and its legislature, and four state courts and an attorney general's opinion have found that ratified and funded collective bargaining contracts or arbitration awards do bind the state, at least under the fact situations presented in the cases. Since states have different collective bargaining statutes and state constitutions, it is difficult to generalize beyond these cases.

Among the cases in which courts (or the attorney general) found that collective bargaining agreements *are* binding obligations, four are based on the contract clause of the U.S. Constitution. *Association of*

Surrogates v. State of New York, 588 N.E.2d 51 (N.Y. 1992), dealt with a challenge to a new law that would withhold five days' pay from both unionized and nonunionized personnel, to be paid as lump sums when employees quit or retired, in order to offset a state budget shortfall. The court found that this legislation violated the contract clause of the U.S. Constitution, which prohibits states from passing any law impairing the obligation of contracts (U.S. Const., Art. I, sec. 10, cl.[1]). Specifically, the court found that the impairment created by the "payroll lag" was substantial, inasmuch as the payment deferral could be for many years, and that such a measure was not reasonable or necessary to accomplish an important state purpose because the state had many alternative ways to raise or save revenue.

In *Carlstrom v. State of Washington*, 694 P.2d 1 (Wash. 1985), the state legislature initially appropriated sufficient money to fund its collective bargaining agreements, then later canceled the wage increases contained therein after declaring an economic emergency. The *Carlstrom* court found that this law unconstitutionally impaired the collective bargaining agreements. The impairment was unreasonable given that the state was aware of financial problems before entering into the contracts and these problems changed in degree but not in kind during this period. "An economic emergency may be properly considered, but it is just another factor subsumed in the overall determination of reasonableness" (694 P.2d 1, 5). Additionally, the *Carlstrom* court reasoned that the state could have, but failed to, include a clause in the contracts which specifically made wage increases contingent on legislative approval (although the contracts did state that the agreements are subject to all present and future acts of the legislature).

In *Furlough*, 135 N.H. 625, 609 A.2d 1204 (1992), the New Hampshire Supreme Court issued an opinion in response to the legislature's inquiry as to the constitutionality of a proposed law which would have required all state employees, including those covered by collective bargaining agreements, to take unpaid leaves of absence. The New Hampshire court also found that the U.S. Constitution's contract clause prohibits states from enacting such a law since the law does constitute a substantial impairment, unless it is reasonable and necessary to serve an important public purpose. The *Furlough* opinion concluded that such a law was neither reasonable nor necessary, since many alternative means of dealing with the fiscal problem were available (though perhaps less politically feasible), and because a state cannot consider impairing its contract obligations on par with other policy alternatives.

In 1989 the Connecticut attorney general (Conn. AG LEXIS 5) was asked by the senate president and speaker of the house whether a law to decrease or delay COLA adjustments of state employees "notwithstanding existing contracts or pending contract negotiations" would violate state or federal law. The attorney general advised that such an enactment would violate the U.S. Constitution's contract clause unless the state could show severe financial emergency (i.e., an important public purpose), that the emergency was not foreseeable when the contract was agreed to, and that no alternative methods of meeting the fiscal crisis would have less impact on contractual obligations. These four decisions and the attorney general's opinion suggest that, in the absence of specific language in state public sector bargaining laws which conditions monetary items of ratified contracts on sufficient legislative appropriations, the contract clause of the U.S. Constitution provides some protection against abrogation of contractual wage increases and payments for which appropriations had been made during the term of the agreement.

The important role of state public sector bargaining statutory provisions is highlighted by *AFSCME/Iowa Council 61 v. State of Iowa*, 484 N.W.2d 390 (Iowa 1992). This case involved interest arbitration awards for state employees which the legislature funded. The governor line-item vetoed the appropriation funding the awards. The legislature did not override his veto. The unions then petitioned the court for enforcement of the arbitration awards. The state argued it was not bound by the awards because they are subordinate to the appropriations process. Because of the governor's successful veto, the appropriation was never made. The state further argued that the constitutional requirement for separation of powers prevents arbitrators, as members of the judiciary, from spending public money. In rejecting these arguments, the Iowa Supreme Court ruled that when the legislature passed the Public Employment Relations Act (PERA) in 1974, it expressly made itself bound by its contracts. There is no provision in the Iowa law, as there is in other states, which expressly makes the monetary terms of a collective bargaining agreement subject to funding through legislative appropriations. Sec. 20.17(6) of PERA states:

> No collective bargaining agreement or arbitrator's decision shall be valid or enforceable if its implementation would be inconsistent with any statutory limitation on the employer's funds, spending or budget or would substantially impair or limit the performance of any statutory duty by the public employer.

The court rejected the state's claim that Sec. 20.17(6) made the contracts unenforceable, given the budget difficulties the state was facing. The court found that all limitations or impairments suggested by the state were under the control of the state, "[T]he shortage of funds, at least to the extent of liability on these contracts, can be ascribed to discretionary funding choices" (484 N.W.2d 390, 395). Although the governor had the power to veto the appropriations bill, this veto did not erase the state's obligation.

Alliance v. Secretary of Administration, 597 N.E.2d 1012 (Mass. 1992), closely parallelled the fact situation in *AFSCME* but yielded an opposite result. Five collective bargaining agreements were signed by the state secretary of administration; the legislature appropriated sufficient funds to finance the cost items of the agreement, but the governor vetoed the appropriations bill. His veto was not overridden. The Massachusetts Supreme Court found that, in the absence of the governor's signature, no valid appropriation was made, so the contracts were not binding on the state. There are, however, critical statutory and contractual differences between *AFSCME* and *Alliance*. Unlike the Iowa law, Sec. 6 of the Massachusetts bargaining law provides, "[I]f the appropriate legislative body duly rejects the request for an appropriation necessary to fund the cost items, such cost items shall be returned to the parties for further bargaining." All contracts also stated that the cost items would not become effective unless sufficient appropriations were enacted.

In *State of Nebraska v. Nebraska Assoc. of Public Employees Local 61* (Neb. 1991), the Nebraska Supreme Court declared the state's Uniform Arbitration Act unconstitutional. The law authorized binding arbitration of future disputes and contract clauses providing for binding arbitration. The court found that these provisions violated Article 1, Sec. 13 of the Nebraska Constitution, which states that "[a]ll courts shall be open, and every person, for any injury done to him in his lands, goods, person or reputation, shall have a remedy by due course of law." The court cited a long history of cases indicating the Nebraska judiciary's zealous guarding of their jurisdiction. It is unlikely that other states would be influenced by this holding.

Two cases in Florida and Pennsylvania which found that collective bargaining contracts did not bind the public employer have potentially far-reaching implications for public sector collective bargaining in those states. In *State v. Florida Police Benevolent Assoc.*, 613 So.2d 415 (Fla., 1992), the Florida Supreme Court ruled that public employee collective bargaining agreements are subject to legislative appropriations. Further, if the legislature fails to appropriate sufficient monies to fund the monetary items of an agreement, it can unilaterally alter any monetary contract provisions without a requirement to return the issues to the parties. The court said that requiring further negotiations would be "administratively untenable." The *Florida PBA* court effectively skirted the fact that public workers also have a constitutional right to bargain collectively in Florida. Art. 1, sec. 6 of the Florida Constitution states: "[T]he right of employees, by and through a labor organization, to bargain collectively shall not be denied or abridged." The court reasoned that allowing the legislature to unilaterally change contract terms does not abridge collective bargaining rights but instead reflects "an inherent limitation due to the nature of public bargaining itself," given the separation of powers doctrine (613 So.2d 415, 419).

Florida PBA arguably represents a major departure from Florida precedent. In *Dade County Classroom Teachers Assoc. v. Legislature of Florida*, 269 So.2d 684, 685 (Fla. 1972), the Florida Supreme Court held that, except for the right to strike, public employees have the same right to collective bargaining as do private employees. Furthermore, the *Dade County CTA* court "threatened to impose judicial guidelines if the legislature failed to pass" enabling legislation. Thus, historically, the Florida Supreme Court had actively encouraged public sector employee bargaining rights. Dissenting in the *Florida PBA* case, Justice Kogan noted that the court previously ruled that a refusal of a public employer to honor contractual provisions involving money *was* an abridgement of the constitutional right to collective bargaining and, thus, required a showing of compelling state interest to be sustained (*Hillsborough County Governmental Employees Assoc. v. Hillsborough County*, 522 So.2d 358 (Fla. 1988). No such showing was required in this case. However, *Florida PBA* did not explicitly overturn *Hillsborough*, reasoning that *Hillsborough* was inapplicable because the legislative exercise of appropriations power is not an abridgement but an inherent limitation of public sector bargaining. Justice Kogan stated,

> I would hold that Article I, section 6 imposes upon the legislature, at a minimum, a duty to seek renewed negotiations with unions whenever the legislature decides to ignore the governor's negotiated agreement with those unions. . . . To say otherwise would render Article I, section 6 meaningless for public employees (613 So.2d 415, 424).

At least three states have used fiscal control measures to impair the finality of collective bargaining agreements or interest arbitration awards or to block access to interest arbitration. In *Wilkinsburg Police Officers Assoc. v. Commonwealth*, 636 A.2d 134 (Pa. 1993), unions challenged the constitutionality of the Pennsylvania Financially Distressed Municipalities Act, which requires a city so designated to develop a recovery plan which may include changes to existing collective bargaining agreements. The law further prohibits future collective bargaining agreements which violate a recovery plan's provisions. The law does not mention any contracts, other than collective bargaining agreements, in its provisions. The Pennsylvania Supreme Court ruled that this law is constitutional, despite Art. 3, sec. 32(7) of the Pennsylvania Constitution which reads: "The General Assembly shall pass no local or special law. . . . Regulating *labor*, trade, mining or manufacturing" [emphasis added]. The *Wilkinsburg* court ruled that this prohibition simply requires that a statutory classification have a rational relationship to a proper state purpose. It found that the purpose of the law is to "ensure fiscal integrity of municipalities" and that the classification is rationally related to that purpose because only municipalities in poor financial condition are subject to the act. The court justified the selective inclusion of collective bargaining contracts by noting that by passing the Public Employment Relations Act (PERA), the state already regulates labor contracts to the exclusion of nonlabor contracts. Justice Papadakos dissented, noting that the law "effectively permits municipalities to adopt recovery plans which unilaterally determine the limits of future collective bargaining agreements and awards (including the reduction in salaries or benefits) without any meaningful input by the employee organization" (636 A.2d 134, 140). He further suggested the law regulates collective bargaining agreements to the exclusion of any other contracts and should be declared unconstitutional: "[T]he Act effectively suspends collective bargaining and places all union employees in the category of nonunion, at-will employees of the municipality" (636 A.2d 134, 141).

In *Hillsdale PBA Local 207 v. Bourough of Hillsdale*, 622 A.2d 872 (N.J. Super. A.D. 1993), the court found that compulsory public sector interest arbitration will not pass constitutional muster unless arbitrators confine themselves to a very strict reading of all eight arbitral decision-making criteria in the statute. The unions argued that the statute gives arbitrators considerable discretion, as it states that the arbitrator's award must be "based on a reasonable determination of the issues, giving due weight to those factors listed in N.J.S.A. 34:13A–16(g) which are *judged relevant* for the resolution of the specific dispute" (622 A.2d 872, 880) (emphasis added). The court rejected the unions' argument:

Without proper consideration of the legislative standards, public interest arbitration may very well be an undue delegation of legislative authority. It may be that in public sector interest arbitrations the parties fail to present evidence on some factors. . . . However, the public interests at stake in public sector arbitration are and must be paramount and demand more attention to the statutory factors than an unsupported passing reference . . . the interest arbitrators must detail in their opinions the specific reasons why an enumerated factor is not "judged relevant" (622 A.2d 872, 883–884).

The *Hillsdale* court took particular aim at the arbitrators' heavy weighting of comparability and minimal weighting of the Local Government Cap Law (which prohibits cities from increasing appropriations by more than 5% over the previous year). "Indeed, an arbitrator's consideration of a town's Cap situation is mandated by the Constitutional proscription against undue delegation of legislative authority to individuals" (622 A.2d 287, 881). As displeasure with the fiscal impact of interest arbitration awards grows, more states may turn to the courts to impose a stricter adherence to all statutory arbitral criteria, and/or pass revenue control laws that directly constrain interest arbitration awards and collective bargaining agreements.

To our knowledge, to date only Wisconsin has enacted legislation which significantly reduces access to existing arbitration procedures. Initiated temporarily by Wisconsin Act 16 and made permanent by the state budget bill in 1995, school boards can avoid interest arbitration on economic issues for professional school employees by offering a "qualified economic offer" (QEO). An offer is a QEO if it contains combined salary and benefit cost increases 3.8% above the previous year. Step increases must be included in calculating the cost increase. The statute requires the parties to use forms developed by the Wisconsin Employment Relations Commission (WERC) to determine wage and benefit cost increases. This law also put a cap on the amount of increase in school spending, thus, significantly limiting school boards' ability to pay, even in the absence of QEO limits. The 1993 law also contained a sunset provision which would have eliminated interest arbitration for all municipal employees except police departments of large cities, fire departments, and city and county law enforcement agencies. Fact-finding would then become the only terminal resolution procedure. Despite significant sentiment in the legislature and by the governor to allow the interest arbitration provision to sunset, the 1995 budget bill ostensibly removed the sunset provision, thus restoring interest arbitration in those sectors. The bill's final language is so unclear that it can be interpreted as repealing interest arbitration for all municipal employees except teachers, although this was clearly not the intent. Seizing the opportunity, three counties supported by the Wisconsin Association of Counties have filed declaratory judgment actions seeking a judicial determination that the compulsory interest arbitration provision of the Municipal Employment Relations Act no longer applies to any employees except school district professional employees (e.g., *Juneau County v. Courthouse Employees Local 1312 AFSCME, Highway Dept. Employees Local 569 AFSCME, and Professional Employees AFSCME*, Juneau County Circ. Ct., 95 CV 214). While these cases are pending (at this writing), several counties are refusing to submit interest disputes to arbitration. Should the court rule in the counties' favor, it is conceivable that the legislature would refrain from reversing the ruling legislatively.

Agency Shop Fees

Case Law

Unions in the public sector, like their private sector counterparts, have sought to further their financial and institutional stability through union security provisions. Whether referred to as "fair share" or "agency shop," these provisions, once negotiated into a collective bargaining agreement, require individuals to join the union or remain a nonmember but pay some agency fee or fee for service, which generally approximates union dues. While agency shop and fair share clauses have become more prevalent in public sector contracts, at least in jurisdictions which do not outlaw such forms of union security (e.g., the so-called "right-to-work" states), so too have legal challenges from objecting nonmembers who have been required to pay fair share dues.

In this section, the legal framework for challenges by objecting fair share payers is briefly reviewed. Two central issues emerge from these legal challenges: (1) exactly what union expenses beyond the core functions of collective bargaining and representation are "chargeable" to objecting fair share payers, and (2) what procedural safeguards must be established by the union to allow objecting fair share payers to receive the nonchargeable fees and/or to challenge the reasonableness of the union's determination of what is chargeable. We begin with a brief discussion of these substantive and procedural issues through several U.S. Supreme Court decisions. We then review several lower and state court decisions which have applied these precedents to different fact situations. Concurrent with the development of case law, at least eight states have codified many or all of the substantive and procedural requirements developed by the U.S. Supreme Court. It seems likely that such codification will continue as substantive and procedural issues become settled law.

For workers in the *public* sector, the Supreme Court confirmed the constitutionality of agency shop or fair share fee provisions in *Abood v. Detroit Board of Education,* 431 US 209, 95 LRRM 2411 (1977), where several nonmember fair share payers objected that the agency shop provision interfered with their freedom of association rights under the First and Fourteenth Amendments. Relying upon a series of Railway Labor Act cases, the Court held that any such interference was constitutionally justified, as the "desirability of labor peace is no less important in the public sector, nor is the risk of free riders any smaller in the public sector" (431 US 209, 224). However, the *Abood* Court limited the *use* of such fair share fees.

> We do not hold that a union cannot constitutionally spend funds for the expression of political views, on behalf of political candidates or toward the advancement of other ideological causes not germane to its duties as collective bargaining representative. Rather, the Constitution requires only that such expenditures be financed from charges, dues or assessments paid by employees who do not object to advancing those ideas and who are not coerced into doing so *against their will* . . . (431 US 209, 235–36). (Emphasis added.)

The *Abood* Court noted the dividing line between chargeable and nonchargeable activities was "somewhat hazier" in the public sector than in the private sector but declined to draw any distinction between the two types of activities given the lack of evidentiary record. In a later Railway Labor Act case, *Ellis v. Railway Clerks,* 466 US 435, 116 LRRM 2001 (1984), the Court developed and applied two tests to determine whether expense categories were chargeable to objecting fair share payers: (1) Were the expenditures "necessarily or reasonably incurred for the purpose of performing the duties of an exclusive representative of the employees in dealing with the employer on labor-management issues" (466 US 435, 448), and (2) Did they "involve additional interference with the First Amendment interest of objecting employees, and if so, were they adequately supported by government interest" (466 US 435, 456).

The U.S. Supreme Court, in *Chicago Teachers Local 1 v. Hudson*, 475 US 292, 121 LRRM 2793 (1986), then further developed *procedural* safeguards to prevent agency fees being used to subsidize ideological and political activities by objecting nonmembers. In *Hudson* the union automatically rebated to *all* nonmember employees 5% of total dues paid as *nonchargeable* expenses. The union also established an appeals procedure whereby nonmembers could appeal the *amount* or percentage used to determine nonchargeable expenses. The *Hudson* Court held:

> The constitutional requirements for union collection of agency fees include: (1) an adequate explanation of the basis for the fee; (2) a reasonably prompt opportunity to challenge the amount of the fee before an impartial decision maker; and (3) an escrow for the amounts reasonably in dispute while such challenges are pending.

The *Hudson* Court clearly stated that the burden is on the objecting nonmember to challenge the determination of what is chargeable. However, before this objection can be made, the union must first provide adequate information enabling the nonmember to make an intelligent objection.

In *Lehnert v. Ferris Faculty Association*, 111 S. Ct. 1950, 137 LRRM 2321 (1991), the Supreme Court revisited the chargeability determination left open in *Abood* (and partially answered in *Ellis*): What is the dividing line between chargeable and nonchargeable expenses? The majority set forth the following three requirements: (1) the expense must be germane to collective bargaining, (2) the expense must be justified by a policy interest in labor peace and avoidance of free riders, and (3) it must not significantly add to the burdening of free speech that is inherent in the agency or union shop.

Lower Court Cases

A number of federal and state court cases since 1986 have applied *Hudson* and *Lehnert* to applicable state law and collective bargaining situations. In a procedural case, *Mitchell v. L.A. Unified School District*, 140 LRRM 2121 (CA 9, 1992), the Ninth Circuit held that *affirmative* consent of nonmember agency fee payers is not required to protect their First Amendment rights; these rights are adequately protected as long as they are given the opportunity to object to such deductions. The court cited with approval the California Supreme Court's decision in *Cumero v. Public Employment Relations Board*, 132 LRRM 2575, 49 Cal.3d 575 (1989), which stated that it was the objecting nonmember's obligation to object. "It must be affirmatively asserted or else it is waived" (140 LRRM 2121, 2124). In other words, rebates are given *only* to those fair share payers who object.

The *Mitchell* court held the union's notice procedures adequately protected First Amendment rights. The union sent two notices to nonmember agency fee payers advising them that they were obligated to pay the full fee unless they objected in writing within thirty days to paying for nonrepresentational union activities and that the cost of union representational activities accounted for 84.6% of the agency fee.

In *Albro v. Indianapolis Education Association*, 140 LRRM 2406 (1992), the Indiana Court of Appeals dealt with the substantive issue, finding that the teachers union failed to meet its burden of proving the proportion of expenses which were chargeable. The union's method of establishing chargeable expenses did not provide adequate information to enable the objecting nonmember to intelligently challenge the determination, thus improperly shifting the burden to the objecting nonmember. The *Albro* court also made detailed delineations among the types of expenses which are chargeable, relying on *Lehnert*. Lobbying expenses unrelated to collective bargaining are not chargeable, nor are political and charitable contributions, even if they are de minimis in amount. Public relations expenses were also found not chargeable, despite the union's contention that it may charge for internal public relations relating to activities within the bargaining unit. Expenses incurred by state and national affiliates for litigation not brought on behalf of the bargaining unit are not chargeable. "Defensive" organizing also failed to survive *Lehnert's* three-part chargeability standard, as the *Albro* court found no free rider problem associated with defensive organizing and charging for activities to convince members to remain part of the union adds significantly to the burden on free speech. The expenses for providing benefits to union members only are not chargeable, and expenses for affiliation with state and national bodies are chargeable only if these concern activities that the local can prove are otherwise chargeable and will ultimately benefit nonmembers of the union. The court in *Albro* also ruled that *Lehnert* must be applied retroactively.

A hybrid procedural and substantive case was presented in *Browne v. WERC*, 140 LRRM 2647 (1982), where the Wisconsin Supreme Court considered an appeal challenging the Wisconsin Employment Relations Commission's (WERC) finding of an unfair labor practice against several unions for deducting fair share fees without first providing all the procedural safeguards required under *Hudson*. On the substantive issue, the union's notice to nonmembers disaggregated intermediate-level union expenses into 38 separate categories, indicating those which were chargeable and those which were not. The audited statement of the *intermediate* union body was used to derive a percentage of chargeable to total expenses, which was then applied to the *local* union's expenditures. On the procedural question, the notice to nonmembers stated that objecting nonmembers had thirty days following its posting each year to object to the use of fair share funds for the payment of nonchargeable expenses. The objector would receive advance rebate of this amount. Once such an objection was made, 100% of the challenger's fair share payments were put in an escrow account. All challenges were consolidated into a single hearing before an impartial arbitrator. The union paid the cost of arbitration and bore the burden of proof for the accuracy of the chargeability determination. Escrowed amounts were disbursed pursuant to the arbitrator's decision.

Both the nonunion objectors and the union appealed a myriad of procedural and substantive questions. Objectors challenged the determination of the chargeability of certain categories of expenses in light of *Lehnert*. They also challenged the adequacy of procedural safeguards (the notice to members, fairness of the hearing, the escrow account) and the legality of the *employer* deducting the full amount of fair share fees without ascertaining that the union's procedure incorporates the requisite safeguards.

On the (substantive) chargeability issues, the *Browne* court held that public relations expenses, which involved "public advertising of positions on the negotiation of or provisions in the bargaining agreement and representation matters," were chargeable. Lobbying for collective bargaining legislation and regulations was chargeable, but lobbying for other political, charitable and ideological matters was not. Extra-unit litigation dealing with jurisdictional disputes, impasse resolution and concerted activity, and collective bargaining was not chargeable based on Justice Blackmun's reasoning that such activities are more akin to lobbying than bargaining unless they are "germane" to the affected bargaining unit. The *Browne* court also found organizing expenses to be nonchargeable.

The *Browne* court then turned to the procedural issues under *Hudson*. The court did not find any constitutional defect in the union's challenge procedure. But it did take exception with the chargeability determination, particularly the automatic application of the chargeability percentage of the intermediate body to the local union's expenses. The court agreed that a random sampling of expenses by an auditor would be sufficient to create a presumption for the percentage; a full-blown audit would therefore not be necessary to make this determination for the local union. The court also found fault that the escrow for the challengers' fair share fees was totally controlled by the union, ruling that a more independent escrow was required. Finally, the court ruled that the employers did not commit an unfair labor practice by automatically deducting the fair share fees and that the facts of the situation warranted a retroactive application of *Lehnert*.

In *Gwirtz v. Ohio Education Association*, 887 F.2d 678, 132 LRRM 2650 (CA 6, 1989), six nonmember teachers claimed the union's procedure was not constitutionally sound because it failed to provide sufficiently detailed financial information supporting the chargeability of expense categories. The appellants argued that the notice, which contained the Audited Basic Statement and Audited Supplemental Schedule of the intermediate and national bodies showing chargeable expenditures, was insufficient, and that the "highest" available level of auditing service was required by *Hudson*. The Sixth Circuit disagreed, arguing that *Hudson* did *not* require "absolute precision in the calculation of the charge to nonmembers" and that the union "need not provide members with an exhaustive and detailed list of all its expenditures." Rather, adequate disclosure in such cases requires only "the inclusion of major categories of expenses, as well as verification by an independent auditor" (475 US at 307).

The Kentucky Supreme Court in *Housing Authority of Louisville v. Service Employees Local 557*, 93–SC–397–DG, 1994 Ky. LEXIS 119 (1994), let stand an arbitrator's ruling that the employer violated the contract by failing to withhold the full dues amount from nonmembers without specific written authorization from the nonmember. Relying upon *Hudson*, the Kentucky court held that it is the objecting nonmember (and not the public employer) who is responsible for challenging union disclosure regarding chargeable and nonchargeable expenses and that the adoption of such procedural safeguards is a matter between the union and the nonmember employees, not the employer and the union. Indeed, the "concerns expressed by HAL [the employer] about the constitutional rights of its nonunion employees may be well intentioned but lack the legal authority required of standing to bring a lawsuit on that basis alone" (1994 Ky. LEXIS 119 at °4–5). Moreover, the court stated that the record did not establish any indication that the union engaged in any "extraneous political or ideological activity of any sort."

Two central issues have been addressed in this section: (1) what union expenses are chargeable to the objecting fair share payer's dues, and (2) what procedural safeguards must be instituted by the union for objectors. Chargeability challenges will now be resolved by applying a specific fact situation to the three basic principles set forth in *Lehnert*: (1) the expense must be *germane* to collective bargaining, (2) it must be *justified* in terms of labor peace and avoidance of free riders, and (3) it must not *significantly* impair free speech. As can be seen from the Wisconsin and Indiana cases, sometimes the same type of expense is found to be chargeable by one court yet not by another. Clearly, the determination of what is chargeable will turn on the facts in evidence in each case, applying the three-part test of *Lehnert*.

The procedural safeguards required for objectors appear relatively clear. The union must give adequate written notice to all nonmembers, with sufficiently detailed information to make an intelligent decision whether to challenge the chargeability percentage. However, this information need not be the most detailed that is available. Estimates of chargeability from one level of the union applied to another will not meet the standard if *Browne* is applied. Rather, a same-level audit is required. Further, the challenged funds must be escrowed by a third party, a hearing must be held in which the evidence is considered, and a neutral third party must make a ruling. Any awards will probably be applied retroactively. Finally, the employer need not assess the adequacy of the procedural safeguards or the chargeability determination.

State Laws Dealing with Agency Shop Objectors

At least eight states have already codified procedures for how agency fee objectors will recover rebates for nonchargeable expenses under *Lehnert* and *Hudson*. These provisions appear to incorporate the substantive and procedural principles elaborated in the decisions reviewed above, with some variation. Pennsylvania's law, which became effective in June 1993 requires that as

> a precondition to the collection of fair share fees, the exclusive representative shall establish and maintain a full and fair procedure, consistent with constitutional requirements, that provides nonmembers, by way of annual notice, with sufficient information to gauge the propriety of the fee and that responds to challenges by non members to the amount of the fee. The procedure shall provide for an impartial hearing before an arbitrator to resolve disputes regarding the amount of the

chargeable fee. A public employer shall not refuse to carry out its obligations on the grounds that the exclusive representative has not satisfied its obligation under this subsection.

If a challenge is filed, the union must pay for the arbitration, which will be conducted pursuant to American Arbitration Association rules. Moreover, use of this procedure does not preclude constitutional challenge. Finally, the law requires that all materials and reports filed pursuant to it are public records, and violations of these provisions are subject to a fine of not more than $2,000.

Under New Jersey law, the representation fee for nonmembers covered by an agency shop provision cannot exceed "85% of the regular membership dues, fees and assessments." The law further establishes a "demand and receive" provision whereby any objecting nonmember can demand

> a return of any part of that fee paid by him or her which represents the employee's additional pro rata share of expenditures by the majority representative that is either in aid of activities or causes of a partisan political or ideological nature only incidentally related to the terms and conditions of employment or applied toward the cost of any other benefits available only to members of the majority representative. The pro rata share subject to refund shall not reflect however the costs of support of lobbying activities designed to foster policy goals in collective negotiations and contract administration or to secure for the employees represented advantages in wages, hours and other conditions of employment in addition to those secured through collective negotiations.

The demand and receive system provides that nonmember objectors may obtain review of the chargeable and nonchargeable amounts by a three-member review board whose members are appointed by the governor. The burden of proof falls on the union.

In Ohio, under §4117.09(c) of the public sector bargaining statute passed in 1983, all public sector labor organizations representing public sector employees *must* develop an internal procedure to determine the rebate which conforms to federal law and where a timely demand is made by the member. This section further provides that objecting nonmembers not satisfied with the determination may appeal it within thirty days to the State Employment Relations Board which will rule whether the determination was arbitrary or capricious.

California's Dills Act, Section 3515.8 protects the right of an objecting fair share payer to demand and receive any part of the fee "used for partisan politics or ideology incidentally related to terms or conditions of employment." Costs of lobbying to promote policy goals or to secure improvements in wages, hours, and working conditions, in addition to those which are negotiated, are not subject to refund, according to the law. In Delaware, Section 4019 of the Public School Employment Relations Act gives school districts authority to deduct fair share fees from noncertified personnel. It requires an "adequate explanation" of the basis for the fee, an opportunity to challenge the fee amount before an impartial decisionmaker, and further requires that an escrow account be used to deposit amounts in dispute.

Hawaii's law permits payroll deductions of nonmember fees only if the union has a procedure for determining the amount of rebate based on the pro rata share of expenditures of a political or ideological nature. The law provides a right to petition to object to the amount refunded.

Section 115 of the Illinois Education Labor Relations Act provides that fair share fees must exclude fees used for political purposes. When an employee objects, the fair share amount must be placed in an escrow account.

Finally, Massachusetts requires unions to establish a rebate procedure based on: (1) the pro rata share of expenditures on political contributions; (2) lobbying on legislation not directly related to the bargaining unit; (3) charitable, religious or ideological contributions; and (4) benefits not germane to governance or duties as the bargaining agent.

At least eight states have sought to codify to some extent the procedural safeguards set out in case law. Additionally, some states have explicitly identified what expenses are chargeable (Illinois, New Jersey, and California); some utilize more general guidelines, and others contain no guidelines at all. The development of procedural safeguards in state law appears to mirror developments in the case law, including notice requirements and development of internal union procedures. The development of state law and administrative regulations help unions bring their own internal procedures into line with case law. While it is difficult to predict the future, it is likely that several other states will follow suit, either through administrative rules or legislation.

Summary and Conclusions

Only eleven states have enacted new legislation governing public sector bargaining since 1987, and most laws have applied to only one or two sectors. Seven of these laws can be characterized as enhancing collective bargaining rights. Only one state (New Mexico) passed enabling legislation covering all public sector employees during this period. Education has received the most legislative attention: Six laws relate solely to education, and five focus on terminal resolution procedures for teachers. Currently 39 states have enabling legislation for at least one sector, and 23 states and the District of Columbia have laws covering all public employees. Education is most likely to have enabling legislation (36 jurisdictions), followed by police and fire (33), municipal (29), and finally state employees (24). Forecasting future legislative developments is always hazardous. *If* the pattern of activity over the last decade were to continue, we would see primarily marginal increases in coverage, expanding to previously uncovered sectors. Such expansion of coverage is likely to encounter obstacles, as in Nevada, where the governor vetoed enabling legislation for state workers, and in Indiana, where the governor issued an executive order providing less than full bargaining rights when he was unable to get enabling legislation adopted for state workers. Indeed, coverage is likely to continue to lag most for state workers as it is the sector in which the old obstacle of nondelegation of authority continues to exert the most influence.

There is no discernible trend in the legal treatment of strikes in the public sector. Indeed, since 1987 the right of public employees to strike has been enhanced in at least three states (legislatively in Alaska and judicially in Colorado and Louisiana) and prohibited in three (legislatively in New Mexico and Texas and judicially in West Virginia). The judicial activity is particularly intriguing in this area. Absent enabling legislation, the Colorado and Louisiana Supreme Courts have granted a very broad right to strike to public employees by extending laws previously thought to apply only to the private sector (the Industrial Relations Act in Colorado and the "Little Norris-LaGuardia Act" in Louisiana) to the public sector. Equally interesting is the absence of legislative initiatives in these states to reverse these decisions. In stark contrast, the West Virginia Supreme Court found no public employee right to strike, in the absence of enabling legislation, through the application of common law. It is particularly difficult to predict future trends in this area, given such widely opposing developments.

Twenty-one states and the District of Columbia now have mandatory arbitration for firefighters, and twenty have it for police. There is considerable diversity in the type and choice of terminal resolution procedures used. For example, choice of arbitration methods is a feature of the laws in Ohio and Pennsylvania, among others, and several states now permit the parties to include the fact-finder recommendations as one package of three from which the arbitrator may choose. There has been relatively little legislative action on interest arbitration.

The status of the finality of ratified collective bargaining agreements and arbitration awards appears to be one area with a great potential for change. While the contract clause of the U.S. Constitution appears to provide at least some protection against the abrogation of ratified and funded collective bargaining agreements, there appears to be little or no legal safety net for ratified contracts or even arbitration awards before they are funded through the appropriations process (the Iowa case being a notable exception). The right of the legislature to refuse to fund economic items in ratified contracts or "binding" arbitration awards is legislatively established in a number of states, including Alaska, Connecticut, Florida, and Rhode Island. But the Florida case which allows the legislature to unilaterally change economic items in ratified agreements which they underfund suggests even greater vulnerability for collective bargaining itself, should other state courts choose to adopt it as precedent. Binding interest arbitration may also come under increasing assault, both legislatively and judicially. Wisconsin's new law limits access of teachers to the arbitration process by effectively imposing a specified rate of increase (through its definition of a "qualified economic offer"). The law's confusing language has opened the doors to a legal challenge to interest arbitration for all nonteacher employees. Judicially, the New Jersey case, which requires a rigidly strict adherence to all arbitral criteria in the statute as well as the Local Government Cap Law, also provides a potential precedent which other state courts could adopt in order to limit the latitude and, thus, the fiscal impact of interest arbitration awards. A number of states have passed fiscal control measures which single out collective bargaining agreements. The Pennsylvania court upheld such a law which restricted both current and future collective bargaining agreements.

A number of federal and state court cases decided since *Lehnert* and *Hudson* have addressed a myriad of fact situations dealing with procedural and substantive issues involved in dues rebates for objecting fair share payers. A significant number of states have passed laws governing this process, and so far, these laws have been applied without significant legal challenge. It appears that litigation over rebate amounts and procedures will diminish as more states pass such laws.

Education has been the focus of legislative changes over the last seven years, presumably because the direct impact of educational spending on property taxes has generated the strongest fiscal pressures in that sector. The impact of impending federal budget cuts and the simultaneous devolution of responsibility for the administration of welfare-related programs to the states with less federal money will surely increase the fiscal pressures on states. Thus it is reasonable to predict that legislative attention will turn increasingly to the state sector. It is also likely that fiscal control measures focused on the local level which single out collective bargaining agreements (such as those in Pennsylvania and New Jersey) will become more common in the future.

Endnotes

[1] Virginia passed a law in 1993 which expressly prohibits public employee bargaining despite the law's redundancy with a 1977 Virginia Supreme Court decision that local governing bodies could not negotiate in the absence of express statutory authority (Partridge, in press). Since this law does not enable bargaining, it is not included in the above count of new statutes or their summary below.

[2] Minor restrictions include requiring a notice period before striking and the possibility of an injunction in cases of clear and present danger to public health and safety.

APPENDIX

Definitions for Appendix Table

Sector:

Police and firefighters	Primarily sworn and/or uniformed officers, excluding state police and nonsworn police and fire employees such as dispatchers.
State employees	All employees of the state, except employees of a higher education and/or community college system.
Primary and secondary school teaching and nonteaching personnel	Noted where nonteaching personnel are excluded from coverage.
Municipal employees	Employees of municipal and county government, excluding police and fire employees.
Duty to bargain:	This is an either/or proposition as to whether the law provides for a bargaining duty at least as extensive as that under Section 8(d) of the Labor-Management Act of 1947, as amended. Does the law impose the duty to meet and confer at reasonable times over wages, hours, and other conditions of employment and a good faith duty to bargain? If any of these elements are missing, this sector was listed as "no."

Terminal resolution
procedures[a]:

0 =	No provision explicitly mentioned.
1 =	Mediation.
2 =	Voluntary fact-finding.
3 =	Mandatory fact-finding.
4 =	Fact-finding with review/override by legislative body.
5 =	Final-offer interest arbitration—total package.
6 =	Final-offer interest arbitration—economic and non-economic packages.
7 =	Final-offer interest arbitration—issue by issue.
8 =	Interest arbitration—other format.
9 =	Interest arbitration—choice of procedures.
10 =	Parties determine terminal resolution procedure.
11 =	Final resolution by legislative body.
12 =	Other method.
13 =	Voluntary arbitration.

Strike penalties:

0 =	No provision explicitly mentioned.
1 =	Strikes allowed without restriction.
2 =	Strikes allowed following notice period.
3 =	Strikes allowed but with the possibility of injunctions where clear and present danger to public health and safety exists.
4 =	Strikes prohibited with no explicit penalties.
5 =	Strikes prohibited with injunctions specifically mentioned.
6 =	Strikes prohibited with employee fines.
7 =	Strikes prohibited with employee discipline.
8 =	Strikes prohibited with fines against union.
9 =	Strikes are possible unfair labor practices.
10 =	Union loses payroll deduction if illegal strike.
11 =	Bargaining duty suspended if union engages in illegal strike.
12 =	Union decertified if illegal strike.
13 =	Other.

[a] To the extent possible, this is the single code which best characterizes the present state of the law

APPENDIX TABLE

Summary of Current Features of State Public Sector Bargaining Laws, by Sector

State	Police & Firefighters			State Employees			P/S Education			Municipal		
	BD[a]	TRP[b]	SP[c]	BD[a]	TRP[b]	SP[c]	BD[a]	TRP[b]	SP[c]	BD[a]	TRP[b]	SP[c]
AL	No[1]	0	7	No	N/A	NA	No	N/A	N/A	No[1]	N/A	4
AK	Yes	8	5	Yes	13	1[2]	Yes	13	1[3]	Yes	13	1[2]
AZ	No	N/A	N/A	No	N/A	N/A	No	N/A	N/A	No	N/A	N/A
AR	No	N/A	N/A	No	N/A	N/A	No	N/A	N/A	No	N/A	N/A
CA	No[1]	0	4	No[1]	1	3[4]	Yes	2	3[4]	No[5]	1	3[4]
CO	No	N/A	1[6]	No	N/A	1[6]	No	N/A	1[6]	No	N/A	1[6]
CT	Yes	7	4	Yes	7[7]	4	Yes	7	5	Yes	7	4
DE	Yes	2	5,6,8	Yes	2	5,6,8	Yes	2	5,6,8	Yes	2	5,6,8
DC	Yes	5[8],7[9]	5,9	—	—	—	Yes	5[8],7[9]	5,9	Yes	5[8],7[9]	5,9
FL	Yes[10,11]	3,11	5,6,7,8,9,10,12	Yes[11]	3,11	5,6,7,8,9,10,12	Yes[11]	3,11	5,6,7,8,9,10,12	Yes[11]	3,11	5,6,7,8,9,10,12
GA	Yes[12]	12[13]	4	No	N/A	7[14]	No	N/A	N/A	No	N/A	N/A
HI	Yes	8	5	Yes	3,13	2,3	Yes	3,13	2,3	Yes	3,13	2,3
ID	Yes[12]	3	1[15]	No	N/A	N/A	Yes[16]	2	4[17]	No	N/A	N/A
IL	Yes	7	4	Yes	2	2,3	Yes	2,13	2,3	Yes	2	2,3
IN	No[18]	N/A	N/A	No[19]	0	7,12	Yes[20]	3	10	No[18]	N/A	N/A
IA	Yes	3,7	5,6,7,8,9,10,12	Yes	3,7	5,6,7,8,9,10,12	Yes	7	5,6,7,8,9,10,12	Yes	3,7	5,6,7,8,9,10,12

[a]BD = bargaining duty, [b]TRP = terminal resolution procedure, [c]SP = strike penalties

APPENDIX TABLE (Continued)

Summary of Current Features of State Public Sector Bargaining Laws, by Sector

State	Police & Firefighters			State Employees			P/S Education			Municipal		
	BD	TRP	SP	BD	TRP	SP	BD	TRP	SP	BD	TRP	SP
KS	No[1,21]	3,11	5,9	No[1]	3,11	5,9	Yes[22]	3,11	5,9	No[1,21]	3,11	5,9
KY	Yes[12]	2	4	No	N/A	N/A	No	N/A	N/A	No	N/A	N/A
LA	No	N/A	4	No	N/A	3[6]	No	N/A	3[6]	No	N/A	3[6]
ME	Yes	2,13[23]	9	Yes	2,13[23]	9	Yes	2,13[23]	9	Yes	2,13[23]	9
MD	No[12,24]	0	0	No	N/A	N/A	Yes	2	10,12	Yes[25]	3	10,12
MA	Yes	9	5	Yes	3,13	5	Yes	3,13	5	Yes	3,13	5
MI	Yes	7[8]	4	Yes	1	4	Yes	1	4	Yes	1	4
MN	Yes	9,13	9	Yes	9,13	2[26]	Yes	9,13	2[26]	Yes	9,13	2[26]
MS	No	N/A	N/A	No	N/A	N/A	No	N/A	N/A	No	N/A	N/A
MO	No	N/A	N/A	No[1]	N/A	4	No	N/A	4	No[1]	N/A	4
MT	Yes	8	0	Yes	3,13	0	Yes	3,13	0	Yes	3,13	0
NE	Yes	1,2[27]	4	Yes	1[27]	4	Yes	1,2[27]	4	Yes	1,2[27]	4
NV	Yes	8	6,7,8	No	N/A	N/A	Yes	8	6,7,8	Yes	3	6,7,8
NH	Yes	4	4,9	Yes	4	4,9	Yes	4	4,9	Yes	4	4,9
NJ	Yes	9,10	0	Yes	3	1	Yes	3	1	Yes	3	1
NM	Yes	3	5,12	Yes	4	5,12	Yes	4	5,12	Yes	4	5,12
NY	Yes	8	6,8,10	Yes	4	6,8,10	Yes	4	6,8,10	Yes[28]	4	6,8,10
NC	No	N/A	N/A	No	N/A	N/A	No	N/A	N/A	No	N/A	N/A
ND	No	N/A	N/A	No	N/A	N/A	Yes[29]	3	6	No	N/A	N/A

APPENDIX TABLE (*Continued*)

Summary of Current Features of State Public Sector Bargaining Laws, by Sector

State	Police & Firefighters			State Employees			P/S Education			Municipal		
	BD	TRP	SP	BD	TRP	SP	BD	TRP	SP	BD	TRP	SP
OH	Yes	7	5	Yes	3,10	2,3	Yes	3,10	2,3	Yes	3,10	2,3
OK	Yes	5[30]	6	No	N/A	N/A	Yes	3	6,11	No	N/A	N/A
OR	Yes	8	4	Yes	3,13	2,3	Yes	3,13	2,3	Yes	3,13	2,3
PA	Yes	8	0	Yes	3,13	3	Yes	9,10	3	Yes	3,13	3
RI	Yes	8	4	Yes	8[31]	4	Yes	8[31]	4	Yes	8[31]	4
SC	No	N/A	N/A	No	N/A	N/A	No	N/A	N/A	No	N/A	N/A
SD	Yes	1	5,6,8	No	1	5,6,8	Yes	1,11	5,6,8	Yes	1	5,6,8
TN	No	N/A	N/A	No	N/A	N/A	Yes[32]	3	5,9	No	N/A	N/A
TX	Yes[33]	8	6,8,10	No	N/A	N/A	No	N/A	N/A	No[34]	N/A	N/A
UT	No	N/A	N/A	No	N/A	N/A	Yes	3	0	Yes	N/A	N/A
VT	Yes	3,13	3,9	Yes	5	9	Yes	4	3	Yes	3,13	3,9
VA	No[35]	N/A	N/A	No[35]	N/A	N/A	No[35]	N/A	N/A	No[35]	N/A	N/A
WA	Yes	8	5,8	No[36]	4	4	Yes	3,13	0	Yes	3,4	4
WV	No	N/A	N/A	No	N/A	N/A	No	N/A	N/A	No	N/A	N/A
WI	Yes	9	5,6,8,10	Yes	3	6,9	Yes[37]	5	5,6,8,10	Yes	5	5,6,8,10
WY	Yes[12]	8	0	No	N/A	N/A	No	N/A	N/A	No	N/A	N/A

Notes:

[1] Right to present proposals/meet and confer.

[2] Excludes snow removal, public utility and sanitation workers, jail, prison and hospital employees.

[3] Requires majority vote plus submission to advisory arbitration before a strike.

[4] The laws are silent on the right to strike, but a 1985 Cal. Sup. Court decision ruled that public employee strikes (other than firefighters and law enforcement personnel) are not unlawful at common law unless or until a substantial and imminent threat to health and safety is clearly demonstrated. (*County Sanitation Dist. No. 2 v. L.A. County Employees Assoc.*, 1985).

[5] Although the Meyes-Milias-Brown Act states that Memoranda of Agreement (MOUs) are not binding, the Cal. Sup. Ct. ruled in 1975 that a city council's ratification of an MOU bound the city to grant the wage increases contained in the MOU (*City Employees Assoc. v. City of Glendale*, 1975). However, a 1991 AG opinion cites a 1978 Cal. Sup. Ct. case as stating that the meet and confer "process is not binding" (*L.A. County Civil Service Comm. v. Superior Court*, 1985).

[6] In 1992 the Colorado Supreme Court ruled, in *Martin v. Montezuma-Cortez*, that public employees have the right to strike. In 1990 the Louisiana Supreme Court ruled in *Davis v. Henry* that public employees have the right to strike.

[7] Connecticut State Employees Relations Act provides for interest arbitration awards, which can be rejected by the legislature if it finds insufficient funds. The parties then resume negotiations.

[8] Economic items.

[9] Noneconomic items.

[10] Police and firefighters may be determined by PERC to be managerial employees exempted from coverage.

[11] The right of public employees to bargain collectively is a constitutional as well as a statutory right.

[12] Firefighters only.

[13] Called mediation but like fact-finding.

[14] While there is no law conferring the right of state employees to bargain, there is a law which specifically prohibits state employees from striking.

[15] The Idaho Supreme Court ruled that, while strikes during the contract are specifically prohibited by law, firefighters have a "residual right" to strike after the expiration of a contract (*Firefighters v. City of Coeur d'Alene*, 100 LRRM 2079, Id. Sup. Ct., 1978).

[16] Covers certificated professional employees only.

[17] No mention in law regarding strikes, but a 1977 Idaho Supreme Court decision ruled that strikes are illegal under the law, though such illegality does not automatically require issuance of an injunction (*Oneida School Dist. v. Education Assn.*, 95 LRRM 3244, Id. Sup. Ct., 1977).

[18] Indiana's Public Employees Collective Bargaining Act was declared unconstitutional in 1977 because it prohibited judicial review of IERB's bargaining unit determinations. It was formally repealed in 1982.

[19] Governor Bayh issued an executive order on May 20, 1990 granting state employees the right to elect union representation.

[20] Only salary, wages, hours, and wage-related fringe benefits are mandatory subjects of bargaining. Other working conditions are permissive.

[21] Contains a "local option" provision. Political subdivisions (other than the state) must elect to be bound by the provisions of PERA.

[22] Though the law says "meet and confer," the state supreme court ruled the law requires negotiation and, that once a contract is ratified, the parties are bound by it (*NEA v. Shawnee Mission Board of Ed.*, 84 LRRM 2223, Kan. Sup. Ct. 1973).

[23] Arbitrator's award regarding economic issues is advisory; if majority of arbitrators on panel agree to the award on noneconomic issues, it is binding.

[24] Permits voluntary collective bargaining.

[25] Covers city of Baltimore only.

[26] Minnesota: Other conditions for lawful strikes include prior participation in mediation and neither party has requested interest arbitration. State employees may also strike if the legislature rejects or fails to ratify a negotiated agreement or arbitration decision.

[27] Nebraska: The Nebraska State Supreme Court has ruled that contractually based and statutory binding arbitration—both interest and rights types—under the State Uniform Arbitration Act, are an unconstitutional intrusion into the authority of the courts (see *AFSCME Local 61 infra.*).

[28] New York: New York City has its own ordinance which allows submittal of impasse items to final and binding arbitration.

[29] North Dakota: Applies to teachers only. A binding interest arbitration referendum was defeated in 1992.

[30] Oklahoma: If the city's final offer is not accepted by the factfinder, the city may submit its last best offer to the voters in a referendum.

[31] Rhode Island: All interest arbitration awards are advisory only on wages.

[32] Tennessee: Applies to certificated school employees only.

[33] Texas: Each municipality must first enact an ordinance authorizing police and firefighter bargaining. This ordinance may include final and binding interest arbitration.

[34] Utah: While there is no law authorizing municipal employee bargaining, Salt Lake City does have a local employee bargaining ordinance.

[35] Virginia: The law provides, "No state, county, municipal or like governmental officer, agent or governing body is vested with or possesses any authority to recognize any labor union or other employee association as a bargaining agent of any public officers or employees or to collectively bargain or enter into any collective bargaining contract with any such union or association or its agents with respect to any matter relating to them or their employment or service."

In 1993, a section was added to permit the formation of employee associations "for the purpose of promoting their interest before the employing agency." Teachers and public employees have a grievance procedure established by statute.

[36] Washington: State employees cannot negotiate wages. There is also a separate law for marine employees covering employees of the Washington State Ferry System which has its own Marine Employees Board which provides research, grievance administration and fact-finding assistance.

[37] Wisconsin: In 1993 the law was amended to cap the total economic package that could be accepted by an arbitrator at 3.8% per year (see Table 1).

References

Partridge, Dane M. Forthcoming. "Virginia's New Ban on Public Employee Bargaining: A Case Study of Unions, Business, and Political Competition." *Employee Responsibilities and Rights Journal.*

CHAPTER 2

Through Public Sector Eyes: Employee Attitudes toward Public Sector Labor Relations in the U.S.

RICHARD B. FREEMAN
Harvard University, NBER, and
London School of Economics

In 1993, eleven percent of workers in the private sector of the U.S. were organized into trade unions compared to nearly 40% of workers unionized in the public sector. From the 1970s through the early 1990s, private sector union density fell at nearly half a percentage point a year, while public sector density rose and then stabilized. Some forty years earlier in 1954, union density also differed greatly by sector, but in the opposite way: More than 40% of private sector workers were unionized compared to perhaps 5% of public sector workers (Burton and Thomason 1988; Freeman 1986).

Why has workplace organization developed so differently in the United States between the public and private sectors? How much, if at all, is the difference in density between the two sectors due to public sector and private sector employees having different attitudes toward workplace organization? How much, if at all, is the difference due to managements having different attitudes and responses to employee efforts to unionize in the two sectors? What underlies differing employee and management interactions in representation and participation at the workplace between the public and private sectors?

This chapter examines these questions "through the eyes" of public sector workers. It reports the results of a survey of a subset of American public sector workers undertaken in winter 1995 for the Secretary of Labor's Task Force on Excellence in State and Local Government through Labor-Management Cooperation. The survey, the Public Sector Worker Survey (PSWS), was conducted by Princeton Survey Research Associates under the direction of Joel Rogers and myself (Princeton Survey Research Associates 1996). It queried some one thousand public sector employees about labor-management relations in the public sector, their desires for participation or representation at the workplace, their views of management attitudes and behavior, and about the workplace organizations they might want. In this chapter I compare the responses of public sector workers to those of private sector workers reported in the Workplace Representation and Participation Survey (WRPS), also conducted in 1994–95 by Princeton Survey Research for Joel Rogers and myself (Freeman and Rogers 1994; PSRA 1994, 1995).

Due to its sampling design, the PSWS has a number of problems which make it more difficult to draw inferences about the public sector in general than would otherwise be the case. The sample is heavily weighted with unionized workers (drawn from a representative union employee population), which makes averages in the sample nonrepresentative of all public sector workers. In addition, most of the nonunion public sector workers come from a single southern state. The sampling procedures and problems in the PSWS are described in detail in the Appendix. These problems notwithstanding, the survey is the largest available survey of the attitudes of public sector employees in the U.S. toward workplace representation and participation issues and, thus, offers the potential of valuable insights into employee attitudes in that sector. By judicious comparisons, it is possible to draw inferences about union-nonunion differences within the public sector from the PSWS and to draw inferences about possible differences in attitudes between public sector workers and the private sector workers surveyed in the WRPS. These inferences, in turn, can contribute to our understanding of why public sector employees are more highly unionized than private sector employees.

The chapter begins with a summary of evidence on the phenomenon that motivates this study: the different rates of labor organization in the public and private sectors. It presents U.S. and cross-country evidence on unionization and collective bargaining coverage in the two sectors. It then contrasts the characteristics of workers and employers in the sectors and the labor laws governing them. With these "background facts" established, I turn to the main task: examining public sector employee views toward workplace representation and participation from the Task Force survey and comparing them to the views of private sector workers.

Public Sector vs. Private Sector Labor Organization

Table 1 shows that in 1993, approximately 11% of the nonagricultural private wage and salary workers were unionized and 12% were covered by a collective agreement. For all public sector workers, the corresponding rates were 39% and 46%, respectively. The union density and collective bargaining coverage rates were highest for local government employees, followed by federal and state government employees, and lowest for private employees. Because a sizeable number of nonunion public sector workers are covered by collective bargaining contracts, the private-public gap in the coverage rate is larger than is the gap in union membership.

TABLE 1

Percentages of Workers Unionized
and Covered by Collective Bargaining in the U.S., 1993

	Union	Coverage
Private sector	11.1	12.2
Public sector	38.6	46.0
Federal	31.2	39.2
State	32.3	37.1
Local	44.4	50.5

Source: NBER Extracts of Outgoing rotation groups of the Current Population Survey. The private sector sample has 166,578 observations; the public sector sample has 35,308 observations.

A higher rate of unionization in the public sector than in the private sector is not unique to the United States. To the contrary, as documented in Table 2, in every advanced country for which we have data, a much higher proportion of employees are unionized in the public sector than in the private sector. What distinguishes the U.S. is that the difference in unionization rates between the sectors is proportionately larger than in most other advanced countries.[1] The public sector unionization rate in the U.S. is 2.85 times the private sector rate; by contrast, taking unweighted averages, the public sector unionization rate is 1.6 times private sector unionization rate in the other advanced countries in Table 2. Only France and Switzerland have higher ratios of public to private sector unionization rates than does the U.S.[2]

Because Western European countries often extend collective contracts to nonunion workers in the private sector, whereas in the U.S. private sector only unionized workers are covered by contracts, the difference between the U.S. and other countries in the percent of workers covered by sector exceeds the difference in unionization rates by sector. This is shown in the right hand side of Table 2. In terms of the proportion of workers covered by a collective contract, the U.S. has the largest public sector/private sector gap in the industrialized world.[3]

TABLE 2

Percent Unionized and Covered by Collective Agreement
by Sector and Country, 1988-90

	Unionization [1988]			Collective Coverage [1990]		
	Public	Private	Ratio	Public	Private	Ratio
U.S.	37	13	2.85	43	13	3.31
Other Advanced	63	39	1.62	89	61	1.46
Canada	63	28	2.25	80	31	2.58
Japan	56	23	2.43		(25)	
Australia	68	32	2.13	98	72	1.36
New Zealand	80	42	1.90	94	55	1.71
Austria	57	41	1.39		(98)	
Denmark	70	72	.97		—	
Finland	86	65	1.32	100	66	1.52
France	26	8	3.25		(92)	
Germany	45	30	1.50	59	88	1.49
Italy	54	32	1.69		—	
Luxembourg	74	43	1.72		—	
Netherlands	49	20	2.45		(71)	
Norway	75	41	1.83	97	62	1.56
Sweden	81	81	1.00	100	72	1.39
Switzerland	71	22	3.23		(53)	
U.K.	55	38	1.45	78	40	1.95

Source: OECD, Employment Outlook, 1991, Table 4.6 and 1994, Table 5.2, chart 5.1.

Notes: Unionization data for 1988, except for Canada, Switzerland and Netherlands where they refer to 1985, the latest year for which the OECD gives data. New
Zealand public sector union density estimated by taking ratio of the numbers of
members to numbers covered reported in Table 4.6 and multiplying this by the percentage covered reported in the table. Figures in parentheses under collective agreement coverage are coverage rates for both the public and private sectors.

In short, there is a worldwide pattern of greater unionization in the
public sector than in the private sector, in which the U.S. fits. But the
magnitude of the difference in unionization and, even more, in collective
bargaining coverage between the public and private sectors is greater in
the U.S. than in other advanced countries.

Characteristics of Employees

A natural starting point for any explanation of the difference in unionization between public and private sector employees is in the demographic
and occupational composition of workers in the sectors. Perhaps the public sector employs relatively larger proportions of workers with characteristics associated with union membership than does the private sector.

Table 3 shows that this is not the case. To the contrary, public sector workers have characteristics that make them less likely to be union members than private sector workers. Specifically, relative to private sector workers, public sector workers are more likely to be women, nonwhite, older, more educated, white collar, or professional. Adjusting the public sector/private sector unionization gap for these characteristics would thus increase, not decrease, the difference in organization. Table 4 underscores this point in terms of occupation. It records rates of unionization and of collective bargaining coverage for selected occupations which have sizeable public sector and private sector employment. Occupation by occupation, unionization is higher among public sector workers. The greater

TABLE 3

Percentages of U.S. Public and Private Sector Workers
with Different Characteristics, 1993

	Private	Public	Federal	State	Local
Female	51	43	46	55	62
Nonwhite	16	19	25	19	18
College grad +	29	41	31	44	43
≥ 35 years	49	66	70	62	68
White collar	54	72	82	75	68
Prof/managerial	20	45	35	47	46
Observations	166,578	35,308	6,567	9,567	19,011

Source: NBER Extracts of Outgoing groups of the Current Population Survey.

TABLE 4

Percent Unionized and Covered by Collective Contracts,
for Selected Detailed Occupations, U.S. 1993

Occupation	Unionized		Covered	
	Public	Private	Public	Private
Teachers	63	08	72	12
College professors	23	08	28	12
Technicians	24	09	30	10
Nurses	33	13	38	15
Secretaries	28	03	35	04
Computer programmers	32	08	39	08
Craftworkers	44	29	49	29
Laborers	31	23	31	25

Source: Tabulated from NBER Extracts of Outgoing groups of Current Population Survey. Sample sizes varied by group. The smallest was laborers in the government, 110; the largest was secretaries in the private sector, 4353.

unionization of public sector workers is not due to the demographic or skill characteristics of those workers compared to private sector employees. It is due to something about the public sector per se.

Legal Framework

Might the difference in unionization be attributed to differences in the laws regulating the two sectors?

In the U.S., the main body of legislation covering worker rights—the Labor-Management Relations Act of 1936, as amended—is limited to private sector employees. Federal employees are governed by federal law. State and local employees are covered by state laws that vary across states and occupations. Until the 1960s, when many states began to enact collective bargaining statutes that roughly mimic the 1936 act, private sector law was more favorable toward unionization (Farber 1988). Private sector workers had clearly defined rights to collective bargaining and protections against unfair labor practices that public sector employees lacked (though many public sector workers were protected by civil service legislation). By the 1970s, however, the laws in most states were similar to the federal Labor-Management Relations Act; though in some, laws still did not allow collective bargaining for some workers. Thus while one might attribute the historically low unionization of the public sector to the previously unfavorable (to unions) laws governing collective bargaining, it is difficult to explain current higher public sector organization in terms of the public sector having a more favorable legal framework: It simply isn't so.[4] Any claim that differences in public and private sector unionization are due largely to the law must rest not on differences in the law governing unionization and collective bargaining between sectors but on different management responses to similar laws between the sectors.

Employee Desires for Influence on Workplace Decisions

Do public sector employees want greater participation and representation at their workplace? Do they desire participation and representation in the decisions that affect their working life more or less than do private sector workers?

A central finding of the WRPS was the existence of a large "representation/participation gap" in America's private sector workplaces—a shortfall between the level of representation or participation in workplace decisionmaking desired by employees and that which they actually had. The measure of this gap was the difference (for different areas of workplace decisionmaking) between the share of employees declaring it "very important" that they have influence in that area and the share declaring that in fact they have "a lot" of influence. The PSWS asked similar questions, permitting a similar measure of the "representation/participation gap" in the public sector. The results for these questions are reported in the upper panel of Table 5.

TABLE 5

Percentage of Employees Responding to Questions on
Desire for Influence in Employment Decisions,
Public vs. Private Sector Workers, by Union Status

Areas of Concern	Public Sector Nonmanagerial Workers					
	Very Important to have influence		Have a lot of Influence		Gap	
	Union	Non-Union	Union	Non-Union	Union	Non-Union
a. Deciding how to do job and organize work	79	74	63	61	16	13
b. Deciding on training	56	56	18	15	38	41
c. Deciding on raise in pay for people in work group	46	47	2	2	44	42
d. Setting goals for work group	66	57	29	15	38	32
e. Setting safety standards and practices	60	52	21	17	39	35
AVERAGE	61	57	26	22	35	35
	Private Sector Nonmanagerial Workers					
a. Deciding how to do job and organize work	66	76	38	55	28	21
b. Deciding on training	63	60	20	25	43	35
c. Deciding on raise in pay for people in work group	49	39	6	3	43	36
d. Setting goals for work group	40	50	14	28	26	22
e. Setting safety standards and practices	70	53	45	31	25	22
AVERAGE	58	56	24	28	33	28

Source: Public Sector tabulated from Public Sector Worker Survey conducted by Princeton Survey Research Associates. Private Sector, Freeman and Rogers (1994).

The data show a sizeable representation/participation gap among public sector workers in various areas of workplace concern taken individually and overall in terms of the average for these areas. The gap is lowest for "deciding how to do your job," but is high on "setting goals for your work group" or "setting safety standards and practices," and peaks with the compensation and training issues that most employees judge important to job satisfaction, autonomy, and career advancement, "deciding how much of a raise in pay the people in your work group should get" and "deciding what training is needed."

The average gap is similar in magnitude for public sector union workers and public sector nonunion workers (35 percentage points). But this apparent similarity masks an important difference in the magnitudes of desired and achieved influence by union status. A larger proportion of union workers (61%) than of nonunion workers (57%) say it is very important for them to have influence on decisions that affect their jobs; and a larger proportion of union workers (26%), compared to nonunion workers (22%), also report that they have a lot of influence. The reason for this is the presence of a large number of teachers in the union sample. When teachers (who show exceptionally high demand for and achievement of influence) are removed from the union portion of the sample, the proportions of union employees desiring and claiming lots of influence falls slightly below the proportion of nonunion employees (perhaps because of differences in occupation in this smaller sample).

The bottom panel of Table 5 gives comparable responses for private sector workers. Here, the representation/participation gap is larger for unionized workers than for nonunion workers. Proportionately more union workers say it is very important to have influence than do nonunion workers, and proportionately fewer union workers than nonunion workers report having a lot of influence. The lowest proportion of workers saying they have a lot of influence is in the nonunion public sector (22%); the highest is in the nonunion private sector (28%). By contrast, a slightly higher proportion of public sector unionized workers report having a lot of influence (26%) than do private sector unionized workers (24%), the result of the large number of teachers in the public sector group. Finally, comparing responses across sectors, Table 5 shows that unionized and nonunion public sector workers have larger participation/representation gaps (35 points each) than their counterparts in the private sector.

Having asked about satisfaction with influence over specific sorts of workplace decisions, the PSWS went on to ask respondents, "Overall, how satisfied are you with the influence you have in company decisions that affect your job or work life?" The results (not given in the table) showed that only 17% of respondents reported themselves "very satisfied"; a larger 26% reported themselves "not too satisfied" or "not satisfied at all"—while 56% described themselves as "somewhat satisfied." Again, within the public sector, the biggest differences were not attributable to union status but occupation. Unionized teachers led in satisfaction with 20% describing themselves as "very satisfied"; unionized public safety workers registered the lowest "very satisfied" share at 10%. For comparison, 19% to 22% of private sector nonmanagerial workers reported themselves as very satisfied with their influence on decisions (Freeman and Rogers 1994); here too, nonunion workers were modestly more likely to be very satisfied than union workers.[5]

In sum, the evidence suggests that there are, at most, small sectoral differences in the representation/participation gap and in satisfaction with employee influence on management decisions that affect their job or work life. While these differences might lead public sector workers to be more favorably inclined toward unionization (although unionization does not reduce the reported gap in either sector), they are hardly large enough to be a significant factor differentiating the two groups of workers. The bottom-line message is that workers in both sectors, union as well as nonunion, want more say about their working lives.

Employee Satisfaction

How satisfied are public sector workers with their working life overall, and how do they view the state of labor-management relations at their workplace?

The PSWS asked the following job satisfaction question: "On an average day, what best describes your feelings about going to work?"—with respondent options of "look forward to it," "wish I didn't have to go," and "don't care one way or the other." Panel 1 in Table 6 records the results by union status and by whether the employee was salaried or hourly. The majority of public employees report that they looked forward to going to work. Some 74% of unionized workers and 69% of nonunion ones, and 79% of salaried workers and 68% of those paid hourly, gave this positive response. But between a quarter and a third of employees responded affirmatively to "wish [they] didn't have to go to work" or were indifferent. Some 31% of nonunion workers and 33% of hourly workers, for example, fell into this latter class.[6] The final four columns in panel 1 show that both salaried and hourly employees in the public sector are more likely to "look forward" to work than comparable private sector employees.

In terms of union status, the rank order in terms of positive feelings toward their job was thus: (1) unionized public sector, (2) nonunion public sector, (3) nonunion private sector, and (4) unionized private

TABLE 6

Percentage of Employees Responding to Questions about Job Satisfaction
and Labor-Management Relations, by Sector and Union Status

1. On an average day, which best describes your feelings about going to work?

	Public Sector		Private Sector		Salaried		Hourly	
	Union	Non-Union	Union	Non-Union	Public Sector	Private Sector	Public Sector	Private Sector
a. Look forward to it	74	69	60	65	79	74	68	61
b. Wish didn't have to go	17	23	29	26	13	20	22	28
c. Don't care one way or the other	8	8	11	8	8	6	11	10

2. How would you rate relations between employees and management at your company?

	Public Sector		Private Sector		Salaried		Hourly	
	Union	Non-Union	Union	Non-Union	Public Sector	Private Sector	Public Sector	Private Sector
Excellent	16	17	8	19	18	22	12	16
Good	49	51	51	48	49	51	49	49
Only fair	26	24	24	23	26	21	28	23
Poor	8	8	17	10	7	7	10	12

TABLE 6 (*Continued*)

Percentage of Employees Responding to Questions about Job Satisfaction and Labor-Management Relations, by Sector and Union Status

3. How would you rate the performance of management on a scale similar to school grades?

| | All Respondents | | | | | | | | Difference for All (A-D/F) | | Difference for Union Workers (A-D/F) | |
| | Public Sector | | | | Private Sector | | | | | | | |
	A	B	C	D/F	A	B	C	D/F	Public Sector	Private Sector	Public Sector	Private Sector
a. Understanding and knowledge of business	34	40	19	7	46	32	14	6	27	40	27	30
b. Overall company leadership	18	41	29	12	20	43	23	14	6	6	3	-7
c. Concern for employees	21	38	25	16	23	33	27	17	5	6	2	-15
d. Giving fair pay increases and benefits	12	30	28	23	18	32	28	21	-11	-3	-10	-1
e. Willingness to share power and authority	15	34	31	19	13	31	31	24	-4	-11	-9	-20

Source: Public Sector tabulated from Public Sector Worker Survey conducted by Princeton Survey Research Associates. Private Sector, Freeman and Rogers (1994).

employees. In terms of mode of payment, it was: (1) public sector salaried, (2) private sector salaried, (3) public sector hourly, and (4) private sector hourly. Multivariate regressions show that the markedly different relation between union status and satisfaction toward work between the sectors cannot be fully explained by demographics or occupational status, though the differences are not statistically significant at the usual levels.[7] The markedly different public and private sector differences between salaried and hourly employees also cannot be explained by demographics or occupational status but are statistically stronger.

Item 2 of Table 6 turns from individual satisfaction with one's job to employees' assessment of labor-management relations at their workplace. The question about labor-management relations asked respondents to rate those relations on an "excellent/good/only fair/poor" scale. In the public sector, both union and nonunion respondents had roughly similar views of employee-management relations. Twice as many respondents (32% to 34%) rated relations "only fair" or "poor" as rated them "excellent" (16% to 17%). There was only limited variation in these responses by pay arrangements (last four columns in Table 6, item 2), or by education, or race (not reported in the table). This contrasts with the markedly worse labor relations reported by union workers than reported by nonunion workers in the private sector.[8]

Finally, the PSWS asked respondents to "grade" management performance on a variety of dimensions—understanding and knowledge of their business, leadership, concern for employees, fairness in compensation, and willingness to share power—on a conventional A to F school grade scale. Item 3 in Table 6 gives the full grade distributions for all public sector and private sector workers (union as well as nonunion) and then summarizes the grades in a single statistic—the difference between the proportion giving management an A and the proportion giving management a D or F. The tabulations show that employees make fairly sharp distinctions about management performance among areas. Overall, public sector employees give public sector managers relatively high marks for general competence, less good ones for leadership and concern, and poor ones for fairness and willingness to share power. Compared to private sector workers, public sector workers grade their management lower on knowledge of the business and in giving fair pay/benefit increases. But they grade their management higher (though poorly) in willingness to share power and authority. Because of the difference in unionization rates between the Task Force Survey and the WRPS, I also report the grades given by union workers in both samples: Here public sector workers report more favorably on their managers than do private sector workers on all issues except increases in pay. The sizeable difference in the perceived willingness of management to share power and authority between sectors is consistent with an explanation of the higher unionization in the public sector in terms of the greater willingness of management to accept a dilution of management authority. This in turn may reflect the nature of work activities in the two sectors. Public sector managers may in fact be more willing to share power, particularly in education, because they are dealing with white-collar and professional workers whose work involves greater autonomy than does the work of blue-collar employees who predominate in the private sector.

Unionism and Managerial Responses to Unionism through "Public Sector Eyes"

How do public sector employees in fact view unions and the potential management responses to union activity?

The PSWS asked nonunion workers whether or not they would vote for a union if an election were held today. Given traditional antiunion sentiment in the South, I expected the PSWS sample of public sector nonunion workers, largely from the southern state sampling frame, to show less willingness to vote union than the WRPS's nationally representative sample of private sector workers. But item 1 in Table 7 shows the opposite pattern: The public sector respondents expressed a greater desire for unionization than did their private sector counterparts. One interpretation of this result is that there is indeed a greater preference for unionization in the public sector, which presumably contributes to its higher degree of unionization, but that the higher unionization in the public sector is not sufficient to reduce the desire for organization to the same levels among nonorganized as in the private sector. The difference in preferences could reflect also, however, employee perceptions of likely management reactions to union drives. Private sector employees may be less likely to vote for a union because they feel their employers are more likely to resist unionization and to react negatively to collective bargaining. Why support a union if it will produce management hostility?

The PSWS asked current union members in the public sector to describe their personal experience with the union and whether or not they wanted to keep the organization. Item 2 of Table 7 shows that an overwhelming majority of workers in the public sector would prefer to keep their union, as in the private sector, but that this pro-union sentiment was modestly lower among members in the public sector than in the private sector.

TABLE 7

Percentage of Workers with Varying Experiences with Unions and
Views of Management Behavior, by Sector and Union Status

1. (Based on nonunion members) If an election were held today to decide whether employees like you should be represented by a union, would you vote for the union or against it?

	Public Sector	Private Sector
For the union	39	32
Against it	48	55

2. (Based on current union members) If a new election were held today to decide whether to keep the union, would you vote to keep it or get rid of it?

	Public Sector	Private Sector
Keep the union	83	90
Get rid of the union	13	8

3. How would you describe your personal experience with the union or employee organization at your workplace?

	Public Sector	Private Sector
Very good	24	26
Good	40	45
Bad	6	5
Very bad	2	2
Neither good nor bad	26	22

4. How might your management respond to a union drive?

	Public Sector	Private Sector		
	All°	Nonunion	Union	Had an organizing drive
Welcome union	17	3	12	5
Oppose through information	33	51	34	43
Threatening or harassing union supporters	17	15	28	23
Do nothing	20	19	14	24

Source: Public Sector tabulated from Public Sector Worker Survey conducted by Princeton Survey Research Associates; Private Sector, Freeman and Rogers (1994).

Note: ° There was virtually no difference in union and nonunion, so I report them as "all."

Consistent with this, item 3 in Table 7 shows that while most workers in the public sector reported having very good or good experiences with the union, proportionately fewer public sector workers reported very good or good experiences than did private sector workers. One interpretation of the seemingly greater commitment of private unionized workers to their organization is the Table 6 finding that they give management exceptionally low grades in sharing authority. Presumably, these workers see a greater need for their union to balance management power.

Though not shown in the tables, employees who prefer to have the help of fellow employees in resolving a workplace problem are more likely to desire a union or other employee organization than employees who prefer to solve a workplace problem on their own. The PSWS asked workers about their preferences in this regard, and the results can be compared to those from the WRPS. Among the unionized employees, 50% of respondents in the public sector, compared to 54% in the private sector, said they preferred having help from fellow employees in dealing with a workplace problem. Among nonunion employees, 43% in the public sector, compared to 40% in the private sector, said they preferred having help from fellow employees. Thus, on this dimension, there is little evidence that public sector employees have greater desire for group or collective action. A sizeable proportion of public sector workers, as well as of private sector workers, prefer dealing with problems as a group; and a sizeable proportion prefer dealing with them by themselves.

The key question regarding employee perceptions of management attitudes toward union organization is, "How might your company or organization respond to a union drive?" The responses for union and nonunion employees in the public sector were almost identical, so I report them together in the first column of item 4 of Table 7. Most employees expect management to oppose the union, in some cases with (illegal) threats or harassment. But a sizeable minority—17%—believe that management would welcome a union, and many felt management would do nothing. In contrast, in the private sector only a small minority believed that management would welcome a union, and they were largely in unionized firms. Only minuscule numbers of workers who had experienced an actual organizing drive or of nonunion workers expected their employer to welcome the union. And, while 12% of union workers in the private sector expected management to welcome a union, 28% of them expected threats or harassments, the highest proportion in the table. The bottom line is that public sector employees view their managements as less opposed to unionization than do private sector employees.

Modern Human Resource Practices

One of the major findings of the private sector WRPS was the prevalence of advanced human resources practices, including the employee involvement programs of various kinds that the U.S. Commission on the

Future of Worker-Management Relations heralded in its 1994 *Fact-Finding Report* on the private sector. Are these practices also found in the public sector? Do employees see them as effective?

Surprisingly, in view of the widespread belief that public sector management is less innovative than private sector management, modern modes of communication between management and groups of employees are somewhat more prevalent in the public sector. In the public sector, 52% of employees reported their firm having regular "town meetings," called by management to discuss workplace concerns (the private sector figure was 47%); 70% reported an "open door" policy for groups of employees to raise concerns to upper management (vs. 63% in the private sector); 60% reported having a "committee of employees that discusses problems with management on a regular basis" (vs. 37% in the private sector). The high proportion of public sector employees reporting committees reflects the high rate of unionization, but even among the nonunion employees, 43% report having a committee that discusses problems with management. By comparison, just 34% of nonunion private sector workers reported having such a committee.

In addition, a sizeable proportion of public sector workers have civil service regulations, which provide due process and protection for public workers who may otherwise be subject to pressures from politicians at their workplace. In the Task Force survey, 40% of employees reported being covered by civil service. Of those, 71% viewed the system as making it more likely employees would be fairly treated, and 61% thought it improved the quality of service provided by their department or agency. Since unionization drives are often sparked by employers treating workers in ways that the employees view as unfair, the longstanding presence of civil service protections ought to have reduced the desire for unionization among public sector employees. Similarly, the prevalence of modern modes of management ought to do the same. Thus the greater extent of these practices in the public sector does not help explain the greater level of unionization.

The most innovative activity in labor relations is the development of employee involvement (EI) programs. Here, too, the PSWS Task Force survey has a surprising result: EI programs are, if anything, more prevalent in the public sector. Sixty percent of unionized public sector employees on the PSWS Task Force survey report the existence of an EI program at their workplace, and 37% report personal involvement in that program (lines 1 and 2 of Table 8). These percentages are modestly above those for all private sector workers reported in the right hand panel (55% and 49% for union and nonunion workers, respectively). This pattern of a greater prevalence and greater involvement in EI in the public sector, prevails for both union and nonunion employees. But lines 3 and 4 of Table 8 show that public sector unionized employees have a very different assessment of the effectiveness of their EI programs and of the dedication of management to them than do private sector unionized employees. A much smaller proportion of unionized public sector workers than of unionized private sector workers report that their EI program is very effective. And a much smaller proportion of unionized public sector employees than of unionized private sector employees believe that upper management is completely dedicated to these programs. Among nonunion workers, there is a similar though less pronounced difference, with the public sector workers again rating EI programs as less effective and management as less dedicated to these programs.[9] Finally, as in the private sector, the vast majority of public sector employees believe that if employees, as a group, had more say in how these programs were run, the programs would be more effective (line 5 of Table 8). This suggests that public sector workers, like their private sector peers, are prepared to make efforts to make their organizations work better, if management finds ways to devolve authority to them.

TABLE 8
Percentage of Employees with Varying Assessments of Employee Involvement (EI) Programs, by Sector and Union Status

	Public Sector		Private Sector	
	Union	Nonunion	Union	Nonunion
1. EI program at workplace	60	54	55	49
2. Participate in EI	37	31	33	28
3. Effectiveness				
Very	18	27	32	32
Somewhat	59	51	56	55
Not too / not at all	20	18	12	13
4. How dedicated is upper management to these kinds of programs?				
Completely	28	43	47	44
Mostly	56	37	43	47
Not too / not at all	16	16	10	8
5. If employees, as a group, had more say in these programs, would they be . . .				
More effective	86	88	91	82
Less effective	5	6	5	10
No change	9	4	2	5

Source: Public Sector tabulated from Public Sector Worker Survey conducted by Princeton Survey Research Associates; Private Sector, Freeman and Rogers (1994).

Ideal Workplace Organization

Determining the "ideal" policy, program, or institution that workers favor to resolve any gaps between their desired participation/representation and current workplace operations is difficult. It is difficult because it requires respondents to assess potential new workplace arrangements which they have not directly experienced. Also, assessments may depend on employee perception of management cooperation, or lack thereof, to new arrangements and of what they perceive other workers may or may not want. Moreover, the wide diversity in employees and workplaces implies that the same nominal program or policy will have different connotations to different employees. The PSWS tried to get some notion of the attributes of the organizations or programs that employees would like by asking the following question: "Thinking now of all different kinds of employee organizations, including unions and committees, how would YOU like them to work? If it was your decision alone to make, and everyone else went along with it, would you prefer . . . ?"

Table 9 presents the responses of public sector employees to this question and compares them to those of private sector workers on the WRPS. Item 1 shows that the vast majority of both groups of workers prefer a workplace organization to be "run jointly" by employees and management to one run by "employees" and that the majority of both public and private sector workers favor election of employee representatives. In both sectors, unionized employees are more favorable to this mode of selection. At the same time, public sector workers want an employee workplace organization that has greater independence and authority than do private sector workers. In cases of conflict, unionized workers in both sectors overwhelmingly favor arbitration to resolve conflicts. But among nonunion workers a much larger proportion in the public sector favor arbitration to resolve conflicts than in the public sector. The biggest difference between the sectors is in financing a workplace organization. Public sector workers are more likely to favor an organization that relies on its own budget and staff as opposed to one that draws on company budget and staff than are private sector workers. In fact, public sector nonunion workers are more favorably inclined to this option (though the majority favored the alternative of having the organization draw on company budget or staff) than union private sector employees. The implication is that, consistent with a higher rate of unionization, public sector workers favor an employee organization that is more independent of management than do private sector workers.

TABLE 9
Percentage of Employees Assessing Employee Organizations, by Sector and Union Status

1. Desirable characteristics of employee organizations:

	Public		Private	
	Union	Nonunion	Union	Nonunion
"Run jointly" by employees and management	82	85	83	85
"Employees" alone	17	11	14	9
Employee representatives are elected	71	60	76	56
Employee reps are volunteers	23	26	16	26
Management select employee reps	4	8	6	11
Conflicts settled by outside arbitrator	89	67	86	55
Management makes final decision	7	26	10	37
Draws on company budget and staff	32	49	48	54
Relies on own budget and staff	60	42	37	32

2. Which one of these employee organizations would you prefer?
   "One that management cooperated with in discussing issues, but had no power to make decisions"
   "One that had more power, but management opposed"

	Public		Private	
	Union	Nonunion	Union	Nonunion
Management cooperate, no power	50	43	65	63
More power, management opposes	40	42	23	22

3. Do you think employee organizations can be effective even if management does not cooperate with them, or do you think they can only be effective if management cooperates?

	Public		Private	
	Union	Nonunion	Union	Nonunion
Can only be effective if cooperate	60	65	75	73
Can be effective without cooperation	37	30	17	17

4. Would prefer organization with

	Public	
	Union	Nonunion
More power than management	12	11
Less power than management	12	23
Same power	73	60

Source: Public Sector tabulated from Public Sector Worker Survey conducted by Princeton Survey Research Associates; Private Sector, Freeman and Rogers (1994).

This inference is supported by the remaining items in Table 9. One of the most striking and controversial findings of the WRPS was that the vast majority of private sector employees, including unionized workers, favored an employee organization that had "no power" but which enjoyed management cooperation to an organization that had some power but that management opposed. The reason was that employees believed that an employee organization could not be effective if management was noncooperative. Items 2 and 3 show that public sector workers have a very different response to the same question. Public sector union members were almost twice as likely (40% vs. 23%) as private sector union members to prefer an organization with power that management opposed and considerably less certain (60% vs. 75%) that management cooperation was the *sine qua non* of effective employee organization. Nonunion public sector workers were also nearly twice as favorable to an organization with more power (42%) as were nonunion private sector workers (22%) and were also more likely than their private sector counterparts to believe that an organization could be effective even without management cooperation, though the difference here is smaller than among unionized employees in the two sectors. Indeed, it is private sector union members who show the highest sensitivity (65%) to the need for management cooperation, followed by nonunion private sector workers (63%), unionized public sector workers (50%), and nonunion public sector workers (43%). Finally, item 4 shows that the vast majority of public sector workers would like an organization that had similar power to management.[10] In short, public sector workers in general—unionized and not—seem more confident of their independence and power vis-à-vis management than do private sector workers.

Why might this be the case? One plausible explanation, consonant with the way in which the two sectors operate, rests on the fact that public sector employees have greater power outside of collective bargaining to affect management decisions than do private sector employees. They have this power through the political process: They are voters and, through unions, a force in electing public sector leaders; whereas in the private sector, workers rarely are shareholders who can vote and appoint management. Related to this are two other differences between the sectors. In many situations, there is greater confluence of interest between public sector managers and employees than between private sector managers and employees. In the public sector, both sides benefit when the budget for their agency—be it the school board, fire department, or police department—is increased. Some public sector managements welcome unions as an ally in lobbying legislatures or convincing voters to support public sector budgets (Courant, Gramlich, and Rubinfeld 1979). This enhances the power of employees outside of the collective bargaining arena. Second, public sector management is more constrained in its opposition to unions than is private sector management. It is constrained by civil service regulations and by the likely greater citizen uproar if it breaks the law in fighting unions than is private sector management, or if it spends taxpayers dollars on antiunion consultants, as is common in the private sector. Public sector management is also constrained by the difficulty in moving government activities to other locales or in closing plants, although privatization may be increasing its ability to do this. Moreover, in the private sector, decades of severe antiunion campaigns have arguably created a situation in which management has a much greater impact on the viability of an employee organization than in the public sector. In short, I interpret the differences in Table 9 between public sector employees and private sector employees as reflecting reasonably realistic perceptions of the differing economic environments in which they live.

Conclusion

What are the implications of the Public Sector Worker Survey for the question of why public sector employees are so much more highly unionized in the U.S. than private sector employees?

The analysis in this chapter decisively rejects two possible explanations for the difference in unionization. It rejects the hypothesis that the greater unionization results from a special demographic or skill composition of public sector employees. And it rejects the hypothesis that greater unionization results from more favorable labor laws.

This puts the onus of an explanation on the needs and attitudes of workers and of employers and their interaction under roughly similar labor laws. There is some evidence that workers in the public sector have preferences that favor employee organizations compared to private sector employees: Public sector workers report modestly greater desires for more influence or voice on the job (Table 5) and believe that management is less committed to employee involvement programs (Table 8). These factors could lead public sector workers to seek influence through an organization. There is stronger evidence that management behavior is critical in affecting employee attitudes. Public sector employees give their management higher grades in willingness to share authority (Table 6) and believe management is more likely to welcome a union (Table 7). These factors should make independent organizations more successful. There is also evidence that public sector workers believe that an organization has a greater chance of succeeding without management cooperation (Table 9) than do private sector workers. Without gainsaying a role for differences in attitudes toward collective action between public sector and private sector workers due solely to differences in their work, I place greater weight on differences in labor-management interactions between the sectors that make management less resistant to unionization in the public sector. An explanation that stresses the incentives and activity of management is, at the minimum, consistent with the differences in responses on the Public Sector Worker Survey and on the equivalent WRPS for private sector workers. But more analysis is needed, particularly of management attitudes and behavior directly to "prove" that this is the major reason why unionization is higher in the public sector.

Data Appendix

The survey of public sector workers on which this chapter relies, the "Public Sector Work Force Survey" or "PSWS," was commissioned by the Secretary of Labor's Task Force on Excellence in State and Local Government through Labor-Management Cooperation. The survey was supervised by Joel Rogers and Richard Freeman and conducted by Princeton Survey Research Associates. Field interviewing was conducted November 29–December 18, 1995. It covered 1,002 workers in state, county, and municipal government departments and agencies and public schools with 25 or more employees. The PSWS is not a nationally representative poll of public sector workers. The expense in identifying the 16% of American workers who are employed in the public sector by standard telephone polling forced us to adopt another polling strategy. The PSWS randomly surveyed public sector workers in departments, agencies, and schools with 25 or more employees from lists of union members provided by six major public sector unions and from a list of public sector workers from one southern state, exclusive of schools. It used conventional techniques of randomized dialing CATI (Computer Assisted Telephone Interviewing) to do the actual interviewing.

The lists of public sector workers from unions were in three areas: education (National Education Association, American Federation of Teachers); protective services (International Association of Firefighters, International Union of Police Associations); and general public sector work (Service Workers International and the Association of Federal, State, County, and Municipal Employees). Quotas for interviewing were set so that the number of interviews represented the size of a given group in the public sector and the size of a given union among unionized workers in that sector. As NEA and AFSCME are the two largest unions in the public sector (and among the largest in the country as a whole) and the Service Workers have also organized many public sector workers, the union sample is broadly representative of unionized public sector workers, though it does not include unionized workers in other unions and in occupations not covered by the unions whose members were surveyed. Roughly half of the sample consists of employees in education, primarily teachers, and over a quarter are public safety workers (police, fire, corrections). The remainder are scattered among skilled tradespersons, clerical or office workers, service workers, and laborers. A small proportion of the nonmanagerial employees from the union lists (7%) were not members of the union or reported that there was no union at their workplace, despite being on the union list.[11] The southern state sample excluded teachers, so that it contains proportionately fewer professionals and more clerical and public safety workers than the sample from union lists. Because most of the public sector workers in the southern state are nonunion (just 12 of the non-managerial workers were union members), three-quarters of the nonunion employees on the PSWS Task Force survey are from the southern sample. As a result, the nonunion responses may not be representative of nonunion public sector workers generally. Of the total sample of 1,002 workers, 803 of the interviews were completed from the list of union members and 199 interviews were completed with the southern state workers, most of whom were nonunion. Reflecting the lists on which it is based, the sample is heavily skewed toward unionized workers; they made up 80% of the nonmanagerial employees surveyed or about twice the level of actual unionization among this group nationally.

The sampling design has obvious drawbacks for assessing the attitudes of public sector workers in the U.S. and for comparing their attitudes with those of private sector workers. Formally, the responses are representative solely of the relevant union and a single southern state populations. The fact that the southern state sample excludes teachers, who may have different attitudes than other public employees, moreover, further complicates within sample comparisons of union and nonunion employees. It is thus not possible to distinguish differences within the PSWS deriving from union status, occupational mix of employees, and geographic locale of workers, save by assumption that one or the other difference is the dominant one in a given comparison. Comparison of PSWS public sector workers with WRPS private sector workers is complicated by another factor. Public safety workers—police, fire, corrections officers—have relatively unique workplace environments with only limited private sector counterparts. And teachers have too few private sector analogues to provide much occupation-controlled comparison. Thus while one can use the PSWS to compare the "typical" public sector unionized worker to the "typical" private sector unionized worker, it is not possible to differentiate any observed differences between public and private employees to the "public sector" per se as opposed to the particular kind of work performed there.

In some calculations I dealt with these problems by eliminating the teachers from the union sample or by examining whether or not results depended on including teachers. In other calculations, I use regressions to narrow comparisons. The regressions hold fixed the broad one-digit occupation of employees, as well as other characteristics, to identify better the independent effect of unionism on attitudes within the sector. In most tables, I have reported responses separately for union and nonunion public sector respondents to differentiate between the roughly representative group of union employees and the largely southern state-based nonunion employees.

Endnotes

[1] For many years in the post-World War II era, the U.S. had higher unionization in the private sector than in the public sector. Thus the question for labor historians is why it took so long to organize the U.S. public sector worker rather than why public sector workers are more unionized than private sector workers.

[2] Because the unionization rates in the U.S. are so low, the greater percentage or ratio difference between unionization in the public and private sectors does not translate into a bigger *absolute* difference in unionization rates between the public and private sectors. The absolute difference in public and private sector unionization rates in the U.S. at 0.24 (i.e., 0.37–0.13) is the same as in the other advanced countries (i.e., 0.63–0.39 based on unweighted averages).

[3] The countries that do not report separate collective bargaining coverage rates for the public and private sectors tend to have high overall coverage rates (indicated in parentheses). Given the proportion of employees in the public sector, this implies that they have high coverage rates in both the private and public sectors which would yield a low ratio of public and private sector coverage.

[4] Some states have compulsory arbitration laws to resolve labor disputes that might make unionism more attractive to some workers than the right to strike that prevails in the private sector. Most of those laws tended to follow rather than lead the growth of public sector unionism, though they may have contributed to ensuing union growth (Ichniowski 1988).

[5] The PSWS asked the question about overall satisfaction *after* respondents were questioned about their influence in particular areas, so I have compared responses to the responses from the private sector WRPS question that was also asked after employees considered specific decisions. In the private sector survey, more workers reported themselves very satisfied with their influence when the question on influence came before they were asked about specific areas of concern than when the question came after.

[6] Consistent with other polls on employee satisfaction, satisfaction also varied significantly by race and education. Whereas only 16% of white workers reported not wanting to go to work (with 9% indifferent), for example, 29% of black workers felt that way (with only 4% indifferent). By education, 22% of college graduates reported open dissatisfaction or indifference, but 32% of those with no college experience and 31% of those with some college experience short of a four-year degree were dissatisfied or indifferent.

[7] Specifically, for both the public and private sectors, a 0–1 dummy dependent variable for whether or not a worker looked forward to going to work was regressed on age and dummy variables for sex, race, one-digit occupation, and union status. The coefficient on unionization in the private sector was -.03 (.03) compared to .03 (.05) in the public sector, where the numbers in parentheses are standard errors.

[8] In this case, the differences are highly significant in multivariate regressions, as well. Specifically, for each of the public and private sectors, a 0–1 dummy dependent variable for whether or not a worker reported the employee-management relations were excellent was regressed on age and dummy variables for sex, race, dummy variables for one-digit occupation, and union status. The coefficient on unionization in the private sector was -.10 (.02) compared to -.02 (.03) in the public sector, where the numbers in parentheses are standard errors.

[9] It is possible that the perceived lower effectiveness of EI programs and of management commitment to these programs in the public sector may reflect an underlying difficulty in the sector in devolving authority to workers that could, arguably, produce

greater demands for unionization. If employees find that programs designed to give them greater involvement are not all that effective and think management is not fully committed to them, they might see greater need for unionism than otherwise. Because the programs are recent, however, this argument postulates that the responses reflect a longstanding management problem. It also runs counter to the finding in Table 6 that public sector employees saw their management as more willing to share power and authority than private sector management.

[10] There is no comparable private sector question.

[11] There are three possible reasons for this. They could have changed jobs. There could be some miscoding or misreporting. They could have dropped membership while remaining in the bargaining unit.

References

Burton, John, and Terry Thomason. 1988. "The Extent of Collective Bargaining in the Public Sector." In Benjamin Aaron, et al., eds., *Public Sector Bargaining*, 2d ed. Washington, DC: Bureau of National Affairs.

Courant, Paul, Edward Gramlich, and Daniel Rubinfeld. 1979. "Public Employee Market Power and the Level of Government Spending." *American Economic Review*, Vol. 69 (December), pp. 806–17.

Farber, Henry. 1988. "The Evolution of Public Sector Bargaining Laws." In R. Freeman and C. Ichniowski, eds., *When Public Sector Workers Unionize*. Chicago: University of Chicago Press.

Freeman, Richard. 1986. "Unionism Comes to the Public Sector." *Journal of Economic Literature*, Vol. 24 (March), pp. 41–86.

Freeman, Richard, and Joel Rogers. 1994. "Worker Representation and Participation Survey: First Report of Findings." Mimeo, NBER (December 5).

Ichniowski, Casey. 1988. "Public Sector Union Growth and Bargaining Laws: A Proportional Hazards Approach with Time-Varying Treatments." In R. Freeman and C. Ichniowksi, eds., *When Public Sector Workers Unionize*. Chicago: University of Chicago Press.

OECD. 1989. *Employment Outlook*. Paris: OECD.
_____. 1991. *Employment Outlook*. Paris: OECD.
_____. 1994. *Employment Outlook*. Paris: OECD.

Princeton Survey Research Associates (PSRA). 1994a. *Worker Representation and Participation Survey: Wave One, Detailed Tabulations*, volumes 1 and 2. Princeton, NJ (October).
_____. 1994b. *Worker Representation and Participation Survey: Report on the Findings*. Princeton, NJ: PSRA (October).
_____. 1995a. *Worker Representation and Participation Survey: U.S. Public Sector Workers, Final Top-Line Results*. Princeton, NJ (December).
_____. 1995b. *Worker Representation and Participation Survey: Wave Two, Detailed Tabulations*. Princeton, NJ (January).
_____.1996. *Worker Representation and Participation Survey: Public Sector Workers, Final Detailed Tabulations*. Princeton, NJ (January).

U.S. Commission on the Future of Worker-Management Relations. 1994. *Fact-Finding Report*. Washington, DC: U.S. Department of Labor and U.S. Department of Commerce (May).

Chapter 3

Public Sector Dispute Resolution in Transition

Robert Hebdon
Cornell University

Most public sector dispute resolution mechanisms were designed over twenty years ago to avoid strikes. The belief was that essential public employees simply could not be allowed to walk off their jobs because of the irreparable harm that might be done to the public and because "excessive" union bargaining power would result in excessive wage gains in negotiations. This provided the rationale for extensive intrusions into the collective bargaining process in the public sector, in contrast to the voluntarism of private sector dispute resolution. The result was the current North American legislative patchwork of compulsory mediation, fact-finding, and arbitration.

In recent years public sector strikes have declined, and new issues of concern have emerged, associated with such factors as wage freezes, layoffs, restructuring, contingent workers, privatization, and employee benefits. Restructuring may be defined as permanent change in the way services are delivered. It appears in such forms as shifts to private-for-profit and not-for-profit providers, competitive bidding, transfers of services to other levels of government, and contracting in of formally privatized services. In this new environment, it is not surprising that policymakers are reassessing the necessity of these intrusive procedures that focus on avoiding the strike *outcomes* and not the *process* for dealing with these new issues. It is entirely possible that both fact-finding and arbitration will come under even more scrutiny as their costs and benefits are re-evaluated.

In what may be described as a period of heightened aggression against public sector collective bargaining, the 1990s represent the fourth generation of public sector collective bargaining. The first generation represented the growth phase of employment and unions of the 1960s, the second was characterized by the taxpayer revolts of the 1970s, and the third generation in the 1980s involved greater emphasis on the performance and productivity of public services (Lewin, Feuille,

Kochan, and Delaney 1988:1). In the current fourth generation of collective bargaining, public employees are increasingly under attack on the related fronts of job security and compensation through privatization and challenges to collective bargaining rights. Public sector dispute resolution procedures are at the center of the assault on public sector bargaining. An important issue, for example, is the extent to which interest arbitration[1] (a dispute resolution procedure adopted when the focus was on prohibiting strikes) is appropriate to the current environment, when the focus is on retrenchment and restructuring.

Dispute resolution in the public sector is adapting to meet the more extreme economic, political, and financial environment of the 1990s. Intensifying fiscal pressures and more conservative political forces have combined to create the apparent need for major cost reductions and/or layoffs in many jurisdictions. Paradoxically, this crisis atmosphere has created a unique opportunity for labor and management to experiment with cooperative approaches to dispute resolution. Experiments in interest-based bargaining abound at federal, state, and local levels of government covering a wide range of occupations from blue-collar municipal employees in Wisconsin to clerical and administrative employees in the federal Department of Labor. In Wisconsin, for example, the Wisconsin Employment Relations Commission (WERC) now offers training to the parties in "consensus bargaining," a problem-solving approach to negotiations and dispute resolution. The WERC (1992) reported that it trained 25 sets of municipal negotiators (over 525 persons) in this new approach. Interest-based and problem-solving bargaining has also been employed in bargaining at the federal level. The Labor Department and the American Federation of Government Employees (AFGE) recently negotiated two "major agreements" using a win/win approach (McKee 1993:506; Federal Labor Relations Authority 1995:5). Probably the most pervasive changes in collective bargaining are occurring as a result of reform of the nation's educational system. As teachers become increasingly involved in educational policymaking, more cooperative approaches to bargaining are beginning to appear, although this has not spelled the end of adversarial bargaining (Bacharach, Schedd, and Conley 1988).

While the number of strikes has remained low after the steep decline of the early '80s, other forms of conflict such as grievance arbitrations and unfair labor practices have steadily increased in some jurisdictions. To meet this new challenge, public sector agencies have institutionalized new forms of mediation—particularly grievance mediation.[2]

The courts continue to play an inconsistent but important role in shaping dispute resolution procedures as indicated in Maranto and Lund (this volume). The right to strike has recently been extended by decisions of state supreme courts to all public employees in Louisiana (1990) and Colorado (1992) but denied in common law to public employees in West Virginia (1990).[3] Additionally, interest arbitration awards have been reviewed in the supreme courts of Iowa (1992) and New Jersey (1993), and a recent binding interest arbitration law was found to be unconstitutional by Nebraska's Supreme Court (1991).

The antigovernment mood has placed public sector collective bargaining under severe scrutiny. What appeared just a few years ago as acceptable dispute resolution methods are increasingly under assault from taxpayers, employers, and politicians. For example, the utility of interest arbitration is being questioned in Wisconsin, Iowa, New Jersey, and New York. For both fact-finding and interest arbitration, the debate focuses on the appropriate weight to be attached to the criteria of taxpayer concerns and ability to pay.

This reassessment of dispute resolution procedures comes after two or three decades of experience in many states. To shed light on the continued viability of these procedures, it may be helpful to fully evaluate their strengths and weaknesses based on the current literature. We begin with an examination of some data on industrial conflict in the public and private sectors.

Strikes and Other Forms of Conflict

General Trends

Since the early 1980s, only major strikes (involving over 1,000 employees) have been recorded by the Bureau of Labor Statistics (BLS). Nevertheless, this relatively small BLS sample is useful given the obvious importance of large strikes and the fact that they tend to be representative of all strikes. This is illustrated in Figure 1 which compares the BLS sample of large strikes with a much larger sample of all strikes reported to the Federal Mediation and Conciliation Service (FMCS). (For our purposes, the FMCS data cannot be used because it does not break out the public sector.) Clearly, both series display similar patterns, particularly the precipitous fall in strikes starting about 1980.[4]

The only available breakdown of the BLS major strike series between public and private sectors is for the period 1983–94. Table 1 shows a decline in major private sector strikes from 306 in the earlier

FIGURE 1

U.S. Strikes 1960-1994

(Number of Strikes)

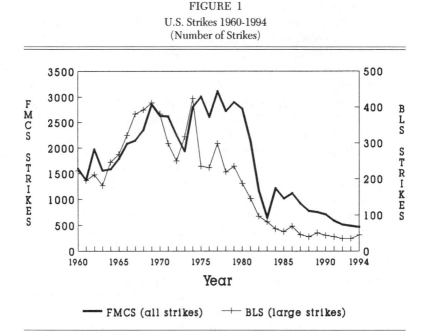

— FMCS (all strikes)   —+— BLS (large strikes)

Sources: Bureau of Labor Statistics (over 1000 employees) and The Federal Mediation and Conciliation Service (all reported strikes)

(1983–88) period, to 208 in the later (1989–94) period. Over the same period, public sector strikes also declined but only slightly (from 46 to 42 between the first and the second half of the period). Thus public sector strikes accounted for a larger proportion of total strikes in the second half of the period (16.8%) than the first half (13.1%). However, in terms of strike rates, these proportions are still well below the public/private union membership ratio in the U.S. population. In 1994, for example, the public sector accounted for 42.5% of all union members, but only 17.8% of major strikes, 12% of days lost, and just 3.8% of days idle. Thus strike rates continue to remain lower in the public sector, reflecting, in part, the laws banning public sector strikes.

While public sector strikes accounted for a slightly larger share of major strikes over the 1983–94 period, they accounted for a declining share of both workers involved (from 14.3% to 11.4%) and days idle (from 6.0% to 3.7%) from the first to the second half of the period (Table 1). This is due to greater public sector declines in the 1989–94 period in

TABLE 1
Major (Over 1000) U.S. Strikes—1983-1994

	Major Strikes				Workers Involved (000)				Days Idle (000)			
	Tot	Pub	Priv	Public Share (%)	Tot	Pub	Priv	Public Share (%)	Tot	Pub	Priv	Public Share (%)
1983	81	13	68	16.0	909	76.6	832.4	8.4	17461	990.6	16470.4	5.7
1984	62	5	57	8.1	376	54.2	321.8	14.4	8499	486.0	8013.0	5.7
1985	54	7	47	13.0	324	55.8	268.2	17.2	7079	217.2	6861.8	3.1
1986	69	6	63	8.7	533	32.6	500.4	6.1	11861	382.8	11478.2	3.2
1987	46	10	36	21.7	174	113.6	60.4	65.3	4481	964.4	3516.6	21.5
1988	40	5	35	12.5	118	15.3	102.7	13.0	4381	158.0	4223	3.6
Subtotal	352	46	306	13.1	2434	348.1	2085.9	14.3	53762	3199.0	50563	6.0
1989	51	7	44	13.7	452	40.7	411.3	9.0	16996	305.2	16690.8	1.8
1990	44	8	36	18.2	185	64.6	120.4	34.9	5926	375.9	5550.1	6.3
1991	40	7	33	17.5	392	33.3	358.7	8.5	4584	239.6	4344.4	5.2
1992	35	6	29	17.1	364	17.7	346.3	4.9	3989	288.3	3700.7	7.2
1993	35	6	29	17.1	182	20.5	161.5	11.3	3981	112.1	3868.9	2.8
1994	45	8	37	17.8	322	38.7	283.3	12.0	5020	192.6	4827.4	3.8
Subtotal	250	42	208	16.8	1897	215.5	1681.5	11.4	40496	1513.7	38982.3	3.7
Total	602	88	514	14.6	4331	563.6	3767.4	13.0	94258	4712.7	89545.3	5.0

Source: Bureau of Labor Statistics, Work Stoppage Survey

both the size (from 348,100 to 215,500 employees) and duration (from 3,199,000 to 1,513,700 days) than in the private sector. The proportion of days idle in public sector strikes remains very small (5.0%). This is consistent with previous research of public sector strikes that revealed their relatively short duration (Kochan 1979:158).[5]

Table 2 illustrates that school board strikes account for two-thirds of the 78 major public sector strikes, increasing to over 75% when universities are added. Teachers account for over 70% of all major public sector strikes. In part, this reflects the fact that bargaining units in the education sector tend to be larger and, hence, included in the data set of major public sector strikes of over 1,000 employees.

TABLE 2

Major (over 1000) Public Sector Strikes
by Employer and Occupation, 1983-94

	Number	Percent
All Employers	78	100.0
Board of Education	52	66.7
University	7	9.0
Utility	6	7.7
County	4	5.1
State	4	5.1
City	3	3.8
Transit	1	1.3
Welfare	1	1.3
All Occupations	78	100.0
Teacher	55	70.5
Blue collar	14	17.9
State/comprehensive	3	3.8
Hospital/comprehensive	2	2.6
Nurse	1	1.3
Police and fire	1	1.3
Social work	1	1.3
Unknown	1	1.3

Source: Bureau of Labor Statistics, Current Wage Developments (Monthly), 1983-94. The analysis was possible for 78 of the 88 strikes identified in the annual data provided by the BLS (shown in Table 1)

Table 3 shows modestly higher mean strike rates (7.7% of the unionized public sector workforce) in states where public sector workers have the right to strike compared to states where strikes are banned (5.3%). It also reveals that 43% of the major public sector strikes were illegal. As expected, these illegal strikes were shorter (8.8 days) than the legal strikes

TABLE 3
Major Public Sector Strikes, 1983-94
by Legal/Illegal Status[a]

Strike Property	Legal	Illegal	Overall
Number of strikes	44	34	78
Avg. duration (days)	14.7	8.8	11.7
Total employees (000)	258.0	218.5	476.5
Total days idle (000)	2938.5	1693.2	4631.7
Mean strike rate	7.7	5.3	6.4

Source: Analysis of Bureau of Labor Statistics Current Wage Developments Data

[a] It was assumed that the legal status of the strike depended only on the legal right to strike before the start of the strike, this assumption could be invalid in the case of longer strikes or ones deemed to threaten the health and safety of the public.

(14.7 days) and accounted for fewer days idle. Table 4 illustrates the distribution of these major public sector strikes by state. Five states (California, Illinois, Michigan, Ohio, and Pennsylvania) accounted for over 60% of the strikes. Interestingly, another five states that have no collective bargaining laws for public employees (Arkansas, Colorado, Louisiana, Missouri, and West Virginia) experienced major strikes. The highest strike rates[6] were recorded in Hawaii and Illinois, both states where public sector workers have the right to strike, but high rates were also recorded in states that ban strikes, including Michigan, Oklahoma, Washington, and West Virginia.

Strikes and Conflict—Some State Data

Figure 2 reveals a sharp decline in public sector strikes in New York State starting in 1980. This parallels the steep drop shown in the combined public and private data shown above in Figure 1. The dramatic fall in strikes may be explained by such changes in the collective bargaining environment as the fiscal crisis, taxpayer revolts,[7] economic restructuring, the recession, the PATCO strike (1981), and in New York, the passage of the Triborough Amendment (1982). The latter provided a freeze of existing conditions during negotiations but allowed conditions to change if a strike took place.[8] In today's bargaining climate of rollbacks and concessions, this freeze provision of the New York Taylor law (and others like it in other states) has enhanced the ability of unions to resist these changes in negotiations.

Public sector strikes in California also experienced a similar decline but commenced their fall a few years earlier than New York due, no

TABLE 4

Major Public Sector Strikes by State, 1983-94

State	# Strikes	%	Type of Law[a]	Right to Strike[b]	# Employees	Strike Rate
Alaska	1	1.3	C	Y	2,900	5.71
Arkansas	1	1.3	N	N	1,750	1.21
California	11	14.1	C	Y	70,300	4.11
Colorado[c]	1	1.3	N	Y	3,000	1.30
Connecticut	1	1.3	C	N	2,400	.68
Hawaii	1	1.3	C	Y	15,250	20.38
Illinois	12	15.4	C	Y	162,210	23.57
Indiana	1	1.3	S	N	2,000	.58
Louisiana[c]	1	1.3	N	Y	6,000	2.17
Massachusetts	2	2.6	C	N	10,700	3.35
Michigan	10	12.8	C	N	46,900	8.10
Missouri	1	1.3	N	N	1,300	.45
Montana	1	1.3	C	Y	4,500	6.56
New Jersey	2	2.6	C	N	5,500	1.17
New York	6	7.7	C	N	19,600	1.53
Ohio	7	9.0	C	Y	16,300	2.52
Oklahoma	1	1.3	S	N	18,000	8.36
Oregon	2	2.6	C	Y	6,500	3.36
Pennsylvania	7	9.0	C	Y	41,000	7.27
Rhode Island	3	3.8	C	N	3,400	6.38
Washington	5	6.4	S	N	39,700	12.75
West Virginia	1	1.3	N	N	20,000	19.45
Totals	78	100.0			Mean	6.41

Source: Bureau of Labor Statistics, Current Wage Developments

[a] C = comprehensive, S = some workers covered, N = no law
[b] Y = yes, N = no
[c] Colorado and Louisiana became right-to-strike states through court decisions in 1992 and 1990, respectively.

doubt, to the impact of Proposition 13 in 1978 (Johnston 1994:7–8). Based on the California experience, Johnston argues that the shorter duration of strikes in the public sector (10 days) compared to the private sector (25 days), reflects a greater intensity of conflict in the private sector. Some unions in the public sector, given the nature of public sector labor markets, seem to prefer political action (forming coalitions and lobbying) over industrial action and strikes. This preference should not be surprising, given that the political activities of police and firefighters' unions have been shown to be more important than collective bargaining in pay determination (O'Brien 1994).

FIGURE 2

Public Sector Strikes
New York State, 1968-1994

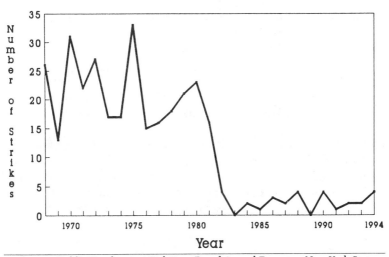

Source: Public Employment Relations Board Annual Reports—New York State—1968-1994.

Strikes and Public Policy

Strike avoidance continues to be the primary motivating force behind public policy with respect to public sector collective bargaining in most states. As indicated above, comprehensive strike data have been unavailable after 1980; nevertheless, a number of conclusions are possible from earlier research and the little strike information that has been obtained from BLS and FMCS sources as presented previously. First, it seems clear that statutory bans on the right to strike cannot eliminate strikes (Kearney 1992:287). As indicated in Table 3, 44% of all major public sector strikes over the period 1983–94 were illegal. Second, most studies have found that right-to-strike laws have no significant effect on strike incidence.[9] On the other hand, there is evidence that poorly enforced penalties in such states as Ohio and permissive strike laws in Pennsylvania increased strikes in those states.[10] In addition, Partridge (1988:257) finds that moderate strike penalties for teachers are more effective in reducing strikes than either permissive or extreme sanctions. Third, most studies have found that the presence of compulsory interest arbitration reduces strike activity.[11] Finally, laws that provide finality in the form of mediation or fact-finding were found to be insignificantly related to strike activity (Partridge 1990). It should be remembered that the findings of the U.S. studies listed in this section are limited by the lack of data on public sector strikes after 1980 (except for the over 1,000 BLS sample discussed above). Thus some fifteen years of experience after 1980 under these laws are necessarily omitted from much of the analysis.[12]

Other Conflict Forms

The precipitous fall in strikes in the public sector may mask a corresponding rise in other conflict forms. Just as unionized private sector workers are turning away from strikes to other forms of conflict expression such as slowdowns, work-to-rule, and overtime bans (Katz and Kochan 1992:225), conflict may be taking some new directions in the public sector.[13]

Figure 3 illustrates that this appears to be occurring, as evidenced by the increase in individual expressions of conflict (grievance arbitrations)

FIGURE 3
Conflict in New York and Wisconsin
Grievance Arbs. and Unfair Practices

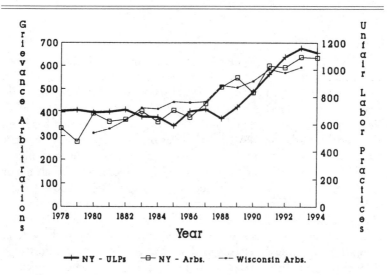

Sources: Public Employment Relations Board, New York, Annual Reports, 1978-1994, and Employment Relations Commission, Wisconsin, Biennial Reports, 1980-1993.

in Wisconsin and New York as well as through collective expressions of conflict (unfair labor practices) in New York[14] after 1980—the year when strike activity began to plummet. Unfair labor practices almost doubled in New York from 686 cases in 1980 to 1,126 in 1994. Grievance arbitrations also almost doubled in New York from 396 in 1980 to 635 in 1994 and in Wisconsin from 312 in 1980 to 594 in 1993.[15]

At the federal level there is also evidence of increasing levels of conflict, but this is not a redirection away from strikes since unions have not used the strike in bargaining (except in the postal service in 1970). The Federal Labor Relations Authority reported 9,047 unfair labor practices (ULPs) in 1993. This represents the seventh year in a row of increased ULP filings and a 42% increase since 1989 (FLRA Annual Report 1993; McKee 1993). Some 96% of the filings were by unions and involved such major issues as interference, restraint, or coercion (24.1% of the total), failure to bargain—unilateral change (23.6%), and bad faith bargaining (9.1%) (FLRA Annual Report 1992:58). The preliminary ULP total for the fiscal year 1994–95 indicates a significant drop in filings to 6,839. The reasons for this decline require more research, but a plausible cause is the increase in interest-based and cooperative forms of bargaining recently implemented in the federal government.[16]

In Ontario an "exponential increase" in the percentage of grievances going to arbitration (from 28% in 1989–90 to 45% in the first four months of 1990–91) was cited by the government as one of the reasons for reforming the collective bargaining process (Management Board Secretariat 1992). Such reform ultimately led to legislation providing the right to strike for Ontario provincial employees (Hebdon 1995). Increases in conflict expressions (other than strikes) were also found in jurisdictions with the right to strike. In Pennsylvania, for example, unfair labor practices under the Public Employment Relations Act increased from 347 in 1988 to 477 in 1992 but decreased to 447 in 1993 (PLRB Reports 1992–93). As an indicator of bargaining intensity in the 1990s, the most common reason for filing an ULP against an employer in Pennsylvania was a failure to bargain in good faith (PLRB 1990–92:10).

In summary, while public sector disputes in the form of strikes have decreased since the 1980s, such other conflict expressions as grievance arbitrations and unfair labor practices have increased at least in a number of prominent jurisdictions.[17] Thus a decline or absence of public sector strikes does not imply a lack of conflict. Public sector employees and their unions appear more willing and able to use both collective (ULPs) and individual (grievances) expressions of conflict to express their dissatisfaction with conditions of employment. To meet these increases in caseloads, public sector agencies are implementing such innovative collective bargaining techniques as interest-based bargaining and such third-party procedures as grievance and ULP mediation. This latter change will be discussed next as part of an overview of the public sector mediation process.

Mediation

Advances in Mediation Theory

The most common form of mediation is a voluntary, accommodative, nonbinding, third-party dispute resolution procedure. As such, it is less intrusive than either fact-finding or arbitration.[18] There are two approaches to the study of mediation (Dilts, Karim, and Rassuli 1990). The institutionalists, who focus on the activities of mediators and the parties, see mediation as an extension of the negotiation process. The empiricists are almost exclusively concerned with mediation outcomes. Mediation success is determined by four sets of factors: source of impasse, situational aspects of the impasse, mediator characteristics, and mediator strategies (Kochan and Jick 1978). Mediator characteristics and strategies (and perhaps their interaction) help determine the parties' attitudes toward mediation (Dilts et al. 1990). As information is acquired by the parties about the mediator, they are more able to weigh the costs and benefits of mediator strategies. Thus mediator activities and characteristics may act as intervening variables affecting mediation outcomes only through the parties' attitudes.

Two studies have concluded that the parties and the issues rather than the mediator were the main determinants of success at mediation (Kochan and Jick 1978; Hiltrop 1985). But mediators can increase the probability of their success by adopting more aggressive strategies (Kochan and Jick 1978; Dilts, Rassuli, and Karim 1992). A study of police and firefighters in New York State discovered a negative relationship between success at mediation and the employer's inability to pay (Kochan and Jick 1978). A more recent study, however, of mediation in Iowa of disputes between teachers and school boards found an insignificant association between state funding and mediator success (Dilts, Rassuli, and Karim 1992). Dilts et al. (1992) account for this apparent inconsistency by observing that the requirement to bargain in good faith in Iowa (and most collective bargaining states) forces the employer to prove a claim of inability to pay. This, in turn, means that the ability to pay issue is rarely confronted directly by the parties but rather is deflected through some other mechanism such as lack of management's authority to bargain. In this way, ability to pay becomes an indirect constraint on settlement as perceived by the union. These studies suggest that as inability of employers to pay intensifies as a constraint in the 1990s, a decrease in mediator effectiveness might be expected. Some state evidence of this is examined next.

State Evidence on Mediation

Voluntary mediation may play a significant role in assisting the parties through these troubled times for public employers, unions, and employees. Table 5 illustrates that in New York the proportion of settlements mediated by mediators increased from 27% in 1983 to 60% by 1994.[19] The Massachusetts' public sector probably enjoys the highest success at mediation with success rates of 82% in 1987, 97% in 1988, 97% in 1989, and 98% in 1990 (Board of Conciliation 1987–90). In the Wisconsin municipal sector, mediators were successful in 66% of cases in 1991–92 and 72% in 1992-93 (WERC 1991–93).

This sketchy evidence of success at mediation in the face of heightening financial pressures is difficult to reconcile with the literature that tends to support a negative relationship between employer inability to pay and the probability of success. The fiscal crises generate the kinds of hard tradeoffs between, for example, job security and layoffs on the one hand and wage and benefits concessions on the other. Union perceptions at the bargaining table are shaped by the potential loss of job security and the increasing likelihood of layoffs. Faced with heightening financial pressures, more hostile political environments, and imminent threats of layoffs, it is possible that public employees' expectations on economic issues have steadily declined over the latter 1980s and early 1990s. Also, the issue of the public employer's inability to pay may have assumed greater credibility with unions throughout the period. This more competitive economic environment may have increased the cost to both parties at mediation, and this may have increased the pressure on unions and employees to settle. Thus increased economic and financial pressures into the 1990s may be creating a sense of urgency for the parties and positively contributing to success at mediation. This hypothesis would be consistent with the growing trend toward increased cooperation between the parties, the use of problem-solving and interest-based bargaining techniques, and a decline in the effectiveness of strikes.

TABLE 5

Mediation and Fact-Finding in New York State, 1983-94

(Percent)

	No. of disputes resolved	Mediated by mediator	Mediated by fact-finder	Settled on fact-finder report	Accepted fact-finder report	Concili-ated after fact-finding	Arbi-trated	Other	Total
1983	684	26.5	35.5	13.3	12.7	7.3	3.5	1.2	100.0
1984	656	29.7	35.1	15.4	9.5	6.8	3.5		100.0
1985	615	30.9	29.8	11.2	9.8	6.1	3.3	8.9	100.0
1986	534	32.8	28.1	11.0	10.5	4.1	2.8	10.7	100.0
1987	547	38.0	29.8	10.2	5.3	4.6	4.4	7.7	100.0
1988	476	32.1	35.5	8.0	8.4	4.0	2.5	9.5	100.0
1989	493	30.8	32.3	8.3	8.7	5.7	4.7	9.5	100.0
1990	486	37.6	28.2	13.0	6.6	3.7	4.5	6.4	100.0
1991	480	45.0	18.5	11.7	5.0	5.4	4.6	9.8	100.0
1992	578	57.6	10.0	11.3	4.3	5.2	3.6	8.0	100.0
1993	612	55.7	7.4	13.8	4.4	4.6	5.1	9.0	100.0
1994	555	59.6	8.1	9.4	2.9	6.1	3.8	10.1	100.0

Source: Annual Reports, Public Employment Relations Board (PERB), New York State 1983-1994.

It is important to remember that mediation must be evaluated in the context of the legislative scheme available. For example, mediation appears more effective if followed immediately by conventional or final offer selection (FOS) arbitration (Kochan 1979). In Ohio the mandatory nature of mediation (compulsory 45 days before settlement) offers both advantages and disadvantages (Herman and Leftwich 1985). Advantages include assistance for inexperienced negotiators, a narrowing of issues going to fact-finding, and the provision of a face-saving mechanism for making bargaining concessions. Disadvantages include time-limit rigidities, greater expense than voluntary mediation (due to its use in cases with little or no probability of success), misuse as a delay tactic, creation of dependency if used too early, and ineffectiveness when followed by other dispute resolution processes (Herman and Leftwich 1985:316; Kearney 1992:328).

Who Make the Best Mediators?

Mediators who are more proactive in packaging issues, offering solutions, and applying pressure are more likely to achieve success than those who merely passively identify the issues and intervene only if asked to do so (Kochan and Jick 1978; Dilts and Karim 1990; Downie 1992). Thus, in the Ontario education sector, an attempt has been made to recruit and train these "high-intensity" mediators (Downie 1992). In Iowa ad hoc mediators are less effective than either FMCS or PERB mediators (Dilts and Haber 1989). The success of the professional mediator is attributed to their greater experience combined with a wider array of mediation techniques.

In summary, the best mediators are experienced professionals who have an assortment of various strategies and are able to act aggressively to exploit settlement opportunities at critical junctures in negotiations. Mediators are more successful when the parties are under some pressure from the possibility of a strike, the uncertainty of arbitrations, or some environmental factor such as a financial crisis.

Special Mediation: Grievance and Problem-solving Procedures

Given that this chapter has emphasized that it is important to broaden the scope of dispute resolution to include grievance arbitrations and unfair labor practices, it is appropriate that advances in grievance mediation and problem solving or preventative mediation be explored.[20] Public employers have led the way in the use of mediation for both grievances and unfair labor practices (Labor-Management

Committee 1992). With success rates ranging from 50% to 90%, grievance mediation has become institutionalized in the public sector in such states as California, Massachusetts, Michigan, Pennsylvania, Wisconsin, New York, Minnesota, Oregon, and Washington (Labor-Management Committee 1992). In Massachusetts, for example, 80% of grievances referred to arbitration over a four-year period were successfully resolved at mediation. This process uses the same techniques as collective bargaining mediation but with at least one difference—the grievant as party to the dispute is present at all meetings. Grievance mediation has also found its way into federal collective bargaining; for example, the Department of Health and Human Services has negotiated grievance mediation procedures in agreements with various unions (McKee 1993).

The public sector is also using preventative mediation[21] procedures to improve the relationship of the parties often away from the collective bargaining table. For example, California has institutionalized preventative or advisory mediation as a means of providing "information or counsel" to prevent pending or existing disputes. California reports 115 cases of preventative mediation in the fiscal year 1990–91, up from 55 in 1987–88 and 83 in 1989–90 (Dept. of IRMCS 1987–91). The uncertain economic times may provide rare opportunities for more accommodative approaches in the search for creative solutions. In the education sector in Ontario, for example, some thirty cases of preventative mediation (called Relationship by Objectives or RBO) have been undertaken since 1981 (Hebdon and Mazerolle 1995). RBO applies joint problem-solving mediation techniques to bargaining units with abnormally high-conflict relationships. RBO was found to reduce the time in subsequent negotiations, decrease grievances over language (i.e., noneconomic) issues, and reduce industrial conflict in the short run (three years and less), but it generally failed to contain conflict over the long run (more than three years) (Hebdon and Mazerolle 1995). This apparent half-life of RBO may be due to the eventual resurfacing of underlying economic factors that are not linked to the relationship of the parties or may be due to the failure of RBO to institutionalize the relationship changes.

Fact-Finding

Although there are numerous exceptions, public sector fact-finding is a dispute resolution procedure in which the fact-finder makes a written nonbinding report with public recommendations on all outstanding matters in dispute after a formal hearing. In theory the process was designed to impose reasonableness on the parties through public pressure.

Fact-finding may be compulsory (required if at impasse), voluntary (if requested by one or both parties), or at the discretion of the public administrative agency (Valletta and Freeman 1988:399).

Each fact-finding procedure must be evaluated within the total dispute resolution context. For example, fact-finding in Iowa has effectively evolved into advisory arbitration. There, fact-finding is followed by a tri-offer, final-offer arbitration system in which the arbitrator must select either of the employer's last offer, the union's last offer, or the fact-finder's recommendation. In practice, the fact-finder's report has been selected so often that it has become a de facto arbitration award (Gallagher and Veglahn 1990). The law in Ohio also turns fact-finding into a quasi-arbitration procedure but for different reasons. In Ohio the parties must vote on the fact-finder's report. Reports routinely become agreements because the only circumstance for the report not to be binding is when at least three-fifths of the union members or the legislative body vote to reject it within seven days (Herman and Leftwich 1988). The more common fact-finding model (e.g., teachers in New York) arises when there are no further sanctions possible under the law after fact-finding.

Fact-finding has been in existence in the public sector for more than twenty years in many jurisdictions. It exists in one form or another in no less than 34 states (Nelson 1992:159). Its increased usage has occurred in spite of a trend away from fact-finding in the '70s as several jurisdictions eliminated fact-finding in favor of arbitration to provide finality to the dispute resolution process.[22] Kochan (1979) and others have identified this early trend away from fact-finding as evidence of a "half-life" effect. The focus of this part will be on the somewhat conflicting evidence for and against its performance. In evaluating fact-finding, it will be important to take into account the often unique legal and institutional context of the jurisdiction under analysis.

Who Makes the Best Fact-Finder?

In Iowa it is assumed that the same criteria for arbitrator selection will apply to fact-finders (Dilts, Haber, and Elsea 1990).[23] Dilts et al. (1990) test two hypotheses concerning the parties' preferences. The interchangeability proposition of Farber (1980) and Ashenfelter (1987) suggests that arbitrators are close substitutes. The parties preference for predictability means that they will choose the one whose awards come closest to the mean of all arbitrators. The other proposition, advanced by Bloom and Cavanaugh (1986), postulates selection based on the parties preferences for certain demographic characteristics of arbitrators, with management preferring economists and unions favoring lawyers, and both preferring experience. Regression results support the interchange-ability hypothesis, but only for the successful fact-finders. For the unsuc-cessful ones (less used), they were less likely to be selected if they had more experience and were an attorney. Suggested explanations for these unexpected latter results are the necessity of a fact-finder's track record (hence more experience) before the parties can make an assessment and an over-legalistic approach by attorneys (Dilts et al. 1990).[24]

Evaluations of Fact-Finding

There are four criteria for evaluating fact-finding: (1) the success rate in resolving disputes, (2) the views of the parties, (3) frequency of utilization and impact on collective bargaining, and (4) ability to reduce conflict and prevent strikes (Stern 1966:11).[25]

Success rates. In Iowa, where the fact-finder's recommendation may be chosen by an arbitrator as part of the tri-offer system of arbitration, research indicates a reduced usage of arbitration and an increased reliance by the parties on the fact-finder's recommendations (Gallagher and Veglahn 1990). Since arbitrators consistently choose the fact-find-er's position over those of the parties, fact-finding has developed into a form of advisory arbitration. However, its success in gaining the accep-tance of the parties is apparently due more to its arbitration properties than its fact-finding properties.

In Ontario about 47% of Ontario teacher disputes were settled at fact-finding and recommendations were accepted in 60% of cases and partly accepted in another 28% (Jackson 1989). This high acceptance rate may be due in part to the high costs of the final step in Ontario—the strike.

There is evidence in support of the fact-finding atrophy hypothesis in New York State (Karper 1994). The previous Table 5 shows a general decline in both the use of the fact-finder report in the settlement of dis-putes and, more importantly, in the acceptance of reports by the parties. In 1983, fact-finder reports representing 12.7% of all disputes that year were accepted by the parties, but by 1994 acceptance had dropped to only 2.9% of disputes.

Views of the parties. Where the parties to collective bargaining have been asked their views of fact-finding, the results have been at best mixed. School superintendents and teacher association presidents in

Kansas, Iowa, and Wisconsin were "universally dissatisfied with their lack of control over the decision-making process" and were opposed to the excessive delays in these dispute processes (Giacobbe 1988:295). Moreover, school superintendents rejected "in principle" both fact-finding and issue arbitration; association presidents, on the other hand, universally accepted third-party procedures (Giacobbe 1988). In Florida, where the fact-finder is called a "special master," hearings were viewed as objective, but the parties disagreed over the weight that should be given to comparability (Helsby, Jennings, Morre, Paulson, and Williamson 1988; Magnuson and Renovitch 1989). Helsby et al. (1988) also found general agreement that the fact-finder reports were not adequately taken into account by the legislative body—the final step in the dispute resolution process. In a survey of Ontario school boards and teacher associations, 46% of the parties believed that the fact-finder's report assisted them in reaching a settlement, but 50% indicated that the report did not cause them to change their position (Downie 1992:237).

Impact on collective bargaining. Fact-finding can have a positive impact on collective bargaining by assisting the parties with intraorganizational problems (Karper 1994:291). For example, the fact-finding process may be used to adjust the expectations of union or management team members. There is evidence of a positive effect in Ohio particularly in difficult economic times as fact-finders act as "scapegoats" for the bad news (Marmo 1995). In general, there is little evidence in support of a "chilling" or half-life effect (see Downie 1992:239).

Impact on conflict. Partridge (1990) finds that state laws with mediation and/or fact-finding as the final stage in the bargaining process had insignificant effects on work stoppages in the U.S. from 1974–80. As discussed previously, moderate strike penalties were more successful in deterring strikes. But as shown in Figure 3, the 1980s saw increases in such alternative conflict expressions as grievance arbitrations and unfair labor practices in some key jurisdictions.

Summary on Fact-Finding

Fact-finding appears to have found a permanent place as a public sector dispute resolution procedure. It seems to work best where it is followed by the threat of a legal sanction (strike or lockout), arbitration, or legislative determination. Thus for such occupations as teachers in New York State, where fact-finding is the final dispute procedure, its utility in resolving disputes would appear to be declining over time. In spite of its growth in the public sector as a dispute resolution mechanism, there is some evidence that the parties are becoming dissatisfied with its performance. The rather negative endorsements of fact-finding by the parties can be matters of concern for policymakers but should not be surprising given the judgmental nature of the process and the stresses of bargaining in the '90s.

Firm conclusions about its performance are difficult because much of the research on fact-finding lacks methodological rigor in two important areas. First, there is a lack of interjurisdictional comparisons that take into account contextual differences in fact-finding. For example, factors affecting the performance of fact-finding might be classified into two categories: environmental factors over which the participants exercise little or no control (e.g., economic, political, and financial) and internal factors subject to some control (e.g., timing of intervention, voluntary/mandatory nature, choice of procedures, joint administration, and training of neutrals). Isolating the effects of this latter category of internal factors is important for policymakers because they are more likely within the control of the administrative agency. Second, little attention is given to a key policy question concerning fact-finding—namely, the consequences of replacing it with mediation. Mediation is cheaper, faster, and less intrusive than fact-finding; also, mediators may have more experience in dispute resolution in terms of the range of occupations covered and array of techniques available. Therefore, a question that needs to be addressed is, Could mediation more effectively achieve the same or better results than fact-finding?

Interest Arbitration

What Is Arbitration?

Conventional arbitration (CA), the most common form of interest arbitration, is the final and binding determination by a single arbitrator or tripartite board of arbitration on all outstanding matters in dispute. Arbitration may be voluntary[26] or compulsory and may be available in conventional (CA) or final offer (FOS) forms. The latter constrains an arbitrator to select either the union or management last offer. In the case of tri-offer, the arbitrator may also select the fact-finder's recommendation (described above for Iowa). FOS may be based on the total package, or it may be broken down by each issue in dispute. The package or issues may be divided into economic and noneconomic matters.[27]

Developments in Arbitration Theory[28]

The considerable attention given by researchers to the development of theoretical models of interest arbitration may be attributed, in part, to the burgeoning use of alternative dispute resolution (ADR) procedures outside of labor-management relations. As cheaper and faster alternatives to the courts, mediation and arbitration are now well-established mechanisms for disputes in such diverse fields as workers' compensation, family law, the courts, tax, commerce, employment, and international relations.[29] For example, one national data bank reports no less than 1,100 ADR programs under state court jurisdiction (Trevelin 1992; Olson 1994). Thus there is wide interest in questions about the appropriate arbitration mechanism—conventional, final offer, or tri-offer. Experience with public sector dispute resolution procedures provides fertile ground for research.

The role of offers and facts at arbitration. Arbitration research has concentrated on the role that offers and the facts of the case play in models of arbitrator behavior—a critical issue if arbitrators split the difference between union and management offers. Ashenfelter and Bloom (1984) were able to make inferences about the weight given to the parties' offers by arbitrators by utilizing a unique property of the New Jersey arbitration system for police (i.e., if the parties cannot agree to CA, they must use FOS). An alternative method was to ask experienced arbitrators to render decisions in 25 scenarios and then construct a simulation that avoids observability and simultaneity problems (Bazerman and Farber 1985).[30] A major weakness of these experimental studies is the artificial creation of offers that are independent of the facts of the case—a property unlikely to hold at arbitration where the offers, for example, may already take into account settlement patterns that are a component of the facts of the case.

The consensus that appears to emerge from both field and experimental studies is that arbitrators give weight to both the facts of the case and the offers. Experimental research would give greater weight to the facts of the case (Bazerman and Farber 1985), but field studies generally give greater weight to the offers (Bloom 1986). The extent of the methodological problems associated with field and experimental studies has been tested (Olson, Dell'Omo, and Jarley 1992). By comparing arbitrator decisions from the field with experiments using the same arbitrators, arbitrator decision models were found to be the same in each, but only where wages were the only issue (i.e., in 85 out of 208 arbitrations).

A different decision process was found in the more complex multi-issue field cases vis-à-vis the single-issue experimental ones (Olson et al. 1992).

Impact of arbitration on negotiated settlements. An early model of arbitration theorizes that differences between negotiated and arbitrated outcomes arise because of uncertainty about the arbitrator's behavior and differences in the relative bargaining power and risk preferences of the parties (Farber and Katz 1979). An important consequence of this model is that negotiated settlements are a function of the arbitration context and not vice versa (see Farber 1980; Ashenfelter and Bloom 1984). However, recent empirical work casts some doubt on this property. A study of interest arbitration for teachers in Wisconsin found that arbitrators place considerable weight on recent comparable settlements in their awards (Olson and Jarley 1991). A similar finding was obtained under FOS in major league baseball where significant differences between negotiated settlements and arbitration outcomes were discovered (Burgess and Marburger 1993). Arbitration models are also limited by their uniform focus on wages, and they may be inappropriate for package FOS arbitration where the arbitrator's preferred position on a given issue may not match his/her result (Olson 1992). They may also understate nonwage issues since arbitrators often give equal weight to wage and nonwage issues.

Evaluating Interest Arbitration

Arbitration impact on dispute rates. A central issue about arbitration as a strike substitute is its ability to produce freely negotiated settlements. This may occur because of the lack of bargaining pressure (without the potential of a strike), the fear that a concession made in negotiations would negatively affect the arbitration outcome (e.g., if an arbitrator splits the difference between the parties last offers), or simply because the parties prefer to avoid tough compromises. If conventional arbitration chills negotiations[31] because arbitrators tend to split the difference between the parties' offers at arbitration, then FOS ought to avoid this effect by simply preventing this "negative" arbitrator behavior. But forcing an arbitrator to choose between what may be unreasonable positions could create a win/lose outcome adversely affecting the loser's commitment to the award settlement. A tri-offer system could overcome this criticism by permitting an arbitrator to select the fact-finder's recommendation, thus avoiding the negative consequences of an extreme outcome.

In theory, therefore, FOS might be expected to induce more settlements than conventional arbitration (CA). However, to the extent that the FOS constraint on arbitrator behavior is relaxed, issue-by-issue FOS and tri-offer FOS may also be expected to have a chilling effect on bargaining.

An experimental study that controls for arbitrator "fair" awards and objective uncertainty faced by arbitrators compared the effect on dispute rates of three alternative arbitration systems—CA, FOS, and tri-offer (Ashenfelter, Currie, Farber, and Spiegel 1992). In general, dispute rates were inversely related to both the monetary and uncertainty costs of disputes, indicating that bargainers are influenced by costs and exhibit risk averse behavior.[32] As expected, this research shows a significantly lower settlement rate (i.e., a chilling effect) for all three arbitration procedures when compared to the simulated right-to-strike bargaining group.[33] Also, following from our discussion above, there were no significant differences between CA and tri-offer settlement rates. The most surprising result was a significantly lower settlement rate for FOS. The suggested reason for this finding was the ability of the parties under FOS to lower their risk by positioning their final offers—a feature not available under CA.

The tri-offer system may be more difficult to simulate than Ashenfelter et al. (1992) indicate. Because some settlements under tri-offer are based on the acquired knowledge that fact-finder recommendations will be "rubber stamped" by the tri-offer arbitrator, it may be difficult to distinguish between freely negotiated settlements and those as a result of this coercive aspect of the tri-offer system. This may, in effect, be a hidden chilling effect.

Table 6 summarizes settlement rates taken from 17 studies of 38 North American jurisdictions covering a wide range of time periods (from two to twenty-three years), occupations, and dispute resolution mechanisms (strike, CA, FOS—by issue and package, and tri-offer). The results of a number of these studies are discussed next.

In a comprehensive study, Lester (1984) compared settlement rates in eight states.[34] Rates ranged from a low of 71% for firefighters and police in Pennsylvania to a high of 94% for the same occupations in Minnesota.[35] Lester identifies five facilitating conditions contributing to voluntary settlements: (1) joint participation in the development and administration of the law; (2) choice of and participation in the procedures; (3) permitting the arbitrator to mediate; (4) a limited right to strike; and (5) the professionalism of the mediators, fact-finders, and arbitrators.

TABLE 6

Comparison of Settlement Rates

Study	Settlement Rates		Arb. Type	Years	Occupations	Jurisdiction
	Strike (%)	Arb. (%)				
Hines (1972)		81	C	1966-70	Hospital	Ontario
Stern et al. (1975)		79	C	1969-74	Fire, Police	Pennsylvania
		84	FOS-I	1970-73	Fire, Police	Michigan
Dunham (1976)	91			1970	Public Sector	Pennsylvania
	99			1973	Public Sector	Oregon
	98			1973	Public Sector	Montana
Lipsky & Barocci (1977)		78	C	1974-76	Fire, Police	New York
		86	FOS-P	1975-77	Fire, Police	Massachusetts
Anderson (1977)	93			1976-77	Municipal	Canada
Olson (1978)		86	FOS-P	1972-77	Fire, Police	Wisconsin
Gallagher & Pregnetter (1979)		96	TRI	1975-77	State	Iowa
Ponak and Wheeler (1980)	88		C	1967-79	Federal	Canada
Thompson (1981)		65	C	1960-80	Teachers	B.C.
Mitchell (1982)		82	C	1969-82	Federal	Canada
Blouin (1982)		73	C	1973-81	Fire, Police	Quebec
Lester (1984)		81	TRI	1975-77	Local Option	Iowa
		84	FOS-P	1974-79	Fire, Police	Massachusetts
		84	FOS-I	1972-75	Fire, Police	Michigan
		93	FOS-I	1976-82	Fire, Police	Michigan
		94	C/FOS-I	1975-83	Fire, Police, Guards	Minnesota

TABLE 6 (*Continued*)
Comparison of Settlement Rates

Study	Settlement Rates		Arb. Type	Years	Occupations	Jurisdiction
	Strike (%)	Arb. (%)				
Lester (1984) *cont.*		85	C/FOS-P	1978-83	Fire, Police	New Jersey
		86	C	1974-83	Fire, Police	New York
		71	C	1968-76	Fire, Police	Pennsylvania
		90	FOS-P	1975-83	Fire, Police	Wisconsin
		93	FOS-P	1978-82	Local	Wisconsin
Ashenfelter (1985)		62	FOS-P	1978-80	Police	New Jersey
Swimmer & McDonald (1985)	93			1979-82	Teacher, Hydro Municipal	Ontario
		70	C	1979-82	Fire, Police, Hospital, Crown	Ontario
Loewenberg and Kleintop (1992)		88	FOS-P	1978-87	Fire, Police	Pennsylvania
Mazerolle	95			1983-93	Labor Act	Ontario
Hebdon &	97			1983-93	Teacher	Ontario
Hyatt (1995)	96			1983-93	Construction	Ontario
		58	C	1983-93	Hospital	Ontario
		73	C	1983-93	Crown	Ontario
		84	C	1983-93	Police	Ontario
		78	C	1983-93	Fire	Ontario
Gunderson, Hebdon & Hyatt (1996)	90	69	C	1964-87	Municipal, Provincial	Canada

Sources: Ponak and Falkenberg (1989); Lester (1984).

The second decade of interest arbitration for fire and police in Pennsylvania (1978–87) revealed some evidence of a narcotic effect,[36] but evidence of a reduced chilling effect since settlement rates increased from 71% in the first decade to 88% in the second (Loewenberg and Kleintop 1992).

Another study compared settlement rates for four sectors using interest arbitration (health, crown, firefighters, and police) and two with the right to strike (teachers and all other public and private sectors) in Ontario from 1984 to 1993 (Mazerolle, Hebdon, and Hyatt 1995). The substantially higher impasse rates under Ontario's interest arbitration laws provides stark evidence of the chilling effect of arbitration and the failure of the parties to craft their own solutions to mutual problems.[37] Incredibly, the health care sector (hospitals and nursing homes) had a settlement rate of only 58% indicating a reliance on interest arbitration in 42% of all negotiations over the ten-year period. In contrast, the teachers and school boards who have the right to strike and lockout respectively, were able to freely negotiate settlements 97.4% of the time. It is worth pointing out that not all jurisdictions have experienced low settlement rates under arbitration. In New York, for example, fire and police arbitrations have remained relatively constant from 3.5% of all disputes in 1983 to 3.8% in 1994 (Table 5).[38]

As a rough measure, Table 7 compares average settlement rates of those summarized in Table 6 for the right-to-strike category and various arbitration types. As expected, the settlement rates are highest under the right to strike and lowest under conventional arbitration (i.e., between 94.7% and 75.7%). The range of rates of the mechanisms in between these extremes (final offer by package and by issue, a category combining years under both FOS and conventional, and tri-offer) are not in the expected order. For example, it was anticipated that it would be more difficult for arbitrators to use a split-the-difference approach under final offer by package than under final offer by issue. Nonetheless, a number of tentative conclusions are possible.[39] First, settlement rates are significantly lower under conventional arbitration indicating a chilling effect on negotiations. Second, this chilling effect appears to be somewhat mitigated by various forms of final offer selection arbitration. Third, the size of this moderating effect on the settlement rate does not appear to be significantly affected by the choice of alternative nonconventional procedure.

Arbitration impact on outcomes. It has been hypothesized that interest arbitration will have a leveling effect on wages because over time the comparability criterion will dominate local factors. This proposed effect

TABLE 7

Mean Settlement Rates by Dispute Settlement Mechanism

Type of Dispute Resolution	Settlement Rate	Number of Jurisdictions
Strike	94.7	9
Final offer—by package	84.1	7
Final offer—by issue	87.0	3
Combined FOS and conventional arbitration	89.5	2
Tri-offer	89.5	2
Conventional arbitration	75.7	15

is expected to assist small units with little bargaining power and is independent of arbitration usage. Some support was found for a reduced salary dispersion for Wisconsin teachers within their own conference of school districts (Jarley 1992). However, on a statewide basis, observed salary dispersion increased after the implementation of interest arbitration. Also, for police officers the research does not support this leveling effect of interest arbitration (Bloom 1981; Feuille, Delaney, and Hendricks 1985).

The evidence of the impact of the availability of arbitration on wages continue to be mixed but generally support a positive but small relationship.[40] Some recent studies illustrate divergent results. Using a unique set of Canadian public sector data from 1964 to 1987, Currie and McConnell (1991:713) find that negotiated wage rates are about 2% higher under interest arbitration than where there is a right to strike. They attribute this difference to the greater weight under arbitration of three factors: (1) wage settlements previously agreed to by bargaining units in the same occupation (i.e., comparability), (2) "catch-up" defined as compensation for prior real wage loss, and (3) less attention to employer ability to pay. On the other hand, Bluestone (1989) finds that interest arbitration had an insignificant effect on higher teacher salaries in Connecticut compared to those in New York, Massachusetts, and New Jersey. The higher teacher salaries in Connecticut were due to additional funding pumped into the system in 1986–87 under the Educational Enhancement Act (Bluestone 1989:16). Another study that compared fact-finding outcomes for teachers in New Jersey with those under compulsory arbitration in Connecticut shows higher salaries and benefits under fact-finding (Ries 1992). While this latter study has several weaknesses, including its failure to control for differences between unions and managements in New Jersey and Connecticut, it does suggest that previous studies may have failed to adequately take into account the impact of teacher and union political action on the outcomes of collective bargaining (see also O'Brien 1994). Finally, there is some support for better nonwage provisions under arbitration (for example, see Feuille et al. 1985).

Most studies demonstrate that interest arbitration reduces strikes (Olson 1986; Currie and McConnell 1991; Partridge 1992; Rose 1994; Gunderson, Hebdon, and Hyatt 1996), although enforcement of strike penalties tends to be more important. While interest arbitration laws may reduce strikes, they may also have the unintended effect of increasing conflict in such other expressions as grievance arbitrations (Hebdon 1992; Rose 1994).

Arbitration—Special Topics

Challenges to arbitration. Historically, compulsory binding arbitration has been contested as an illegal delegation of authority. For example, the courts in at least four states (Colorado, Maryland, South Dakota, and Utah) have found it either unconstitutional or illegal (Kearney 1992:340; DiLauro 1989). While several other states have upheld arbitration laws, these laws continue to be challenged, particularly as fiscal pressures intensified through the 1990s. In Iowa, for example, the state government refused to implement an arbitrator's award on the ground that arbitration awards were subordinate to the appropriation process. The state supreme court ruled in March of 1992 that the state was bound by the terms of the arbitration award (GERR 1992). Wisconsin may be moving toward repealing its interest arbitration law for all occupations except police.[41] Cost-cutting goals are being implemented by means of legislated restrictions on collective bargaining rights including arbitration and/or direct wage freezes.[42]

At the local level, the New Jersey State Appeals Court ruled in 1993 that arbitrators in police and firefighter cases must consider all of the criteria identified in the law and give written reasons for their decisions. The employer representatives alleged that arbitrators had failed to take into account the financial impact on taxpayers and that firefighter and police pay increases in New Jersey exceeded national averages. Arbitration for fire and police came under similar criticism by municipalities in the state of New York in 1995. While the arbitration legislation was renewed for two more years on July 1, 1995, an employer municipal organization actively sought to have it repealed due to a perceived failure by arbitrators to give sufficient weight to taxpayers' inability to pay and alleged higher-than-average pay awards. Finally, in 1991 the Nebraska Supreme Court found an act providing interest arbitration for all public employees to be unconstitutional because it removes jurisdiction from the courts.[43] Thus in several states, as these examples show, arbitration is once again under critical examination by state legislatures, public employers, and their organizations. In some extreme cases it may be failing the test as a viable dispute resolution technique.

Arbitration criteria. Much of the current wave of criticism of interest arbitration can be attributed to its perceived failure to handle economic issues. The debate would appear to be over the appropriate relative weights to be given to the three major wage determination criteria: comparability, ability to pay, and cost of living (see Samavati, Haber, and Dilts 1991; Dilts 1994). On the pivotal criterion of ability to pay, there are critical differences in approach between public and private sectors (Pfeffenberger, Laudeman, Haber, and Dilts 1992:264). For example, a private sector employer claim of inability to pay must be supported by "credible evidence" or it may be judged to be bargaining in bad faith by the National Labor Relations Board. But in the public sector, since there is no precise method of accounting for tax revenues, ability to pay is inevitably a more obscure concept. Some have suggested that there will be more public sector disputes over ability to pay (in negotiations and at arbitration) because unions are given accounting data showing the results of budget allocations but not how or why those decisions were made (Pfeffenberger et al. 1992).

For a sample of 22 experienced arbitrators in Wisconsin, an experimental study revealed that much greater emphasis was placed on comparability (75%) than ability to pay (18%) (Dell'Omo 1989). Part of the difficulty faced by public employers in making the case for ability to pay was the failure by arbitrators to articulate standards to judge the issue. Arbitrators' reluctance to accept the concept of ability to pay would appear to be rooted in their belief that major changes in the relationship should only be effected by the parties in direct negotiations. Thus comparability (either internal or external) could be used to apply an ability-to-pay argument only if the comparables have freely negotiated restraint settlements.

Summary on Interest Arbitration

Interest arbitration is coming under increasing scrutiny as financial pressures mount on governments at all levels. The criticism is coming from public employers and governments, in part, because of a perceived failure by arbitrators to adequately take into account employers' "inability" to pay. Evidence from the field provides inconclusive support for the proposition that interest arbitration has a positive impact on wages. There are signs, however, that arbitrators are having difficulty effecting the kind of tough trade-offs necessary in today's harsh political and economic environment. Thus arbitration may be ill-equipped to fashion such major changes to collective bargaining agreements as wage freezes, layoffs, and rollbacks of medical benefits—these fundamental alterations to the collective bargaining relationship are better left to the parties to work out.

The evidence does show that impasse rates are significantly higher under conventional interest arbitration than if a limited right to strike exists. While FOS may moderate the chilling effect, it may have the negative side effect of a loser's lack of commitment to the imposed solution. More research is needed to test this proposition.

There appears to be ample evidence supporting a widely held belief among practitioners that CA arbitrators more or less split the difference between the offers of the parties. To the outside observer this behavior might be attributed to the arbitrators' desire for acceptability. But this view is too cynical; a more generous view would suggest that arbitrators are engaging in more than just a mathematical exercise. In attempting to replicate the free collective bargaining compromise, arbitrators utilize information from both the offers and the facts of each case to form an implicit moral judgment about what is a fair settlement. At the same time, the parties' offers may already take into account their best guess at the arbitrator's notion of a fair settlement (Farber 1981). Viewed in this light, splitting the difference is a deliberate and often complex strategy designed to accommodate the conflicting interests of management and labor.

The real question, however, is whether this strategy is appropriate or even possible in today's restructuring climate. It may be asking too much of arbitrators to fashion compromise solutions, for example, on trade-offs between layoffs and wage rollbacks. It may be more important than ever before that fundamental decisions affecting the bargaining relationship (such as wage freezes, rollbacks, and layoffs) be left to the parties to work out for themselves.

On the positive side, arbitration does reduce strikes (but may increase other expressions of conflict), and it gives finality to a public sector bargaining process that, in the absence of meaningful strike pressure, can drag on endlessly. This latter point is important because several jurisdictions in the U.S. lack finality in the form of either a strike or arbitration. The frustration of the parties engendered by delays in bargaining can increase conflict and cause lasting damage to the relationship of the parties (see Ries 1992).

Conclusion

U.S. public sector bargaining is conducted under a multitude of collective bargaining schemes at the federal, state, and local levels of government.[44] This decentralized patchwork of more than one hundred laws, executive orders, and local ordinances has profound consequences for public sector bargaining. Unlike many of its European counterparts, U.S. national initiatives and policies of public sector restraint and restructuring have lacked coherence in implementation since they must be filtered through a maze of state and local political systems. This fragmentation has had the unintended consequence of creating a durability for public sector unionism and collective bargaining since any threat is necessarily piecemeal.[45] This diversity of laws and policies also posed unique challenges for a study of trends in public sector bargaining. One result was the necessity of a selective approach—developments in some jurisdictions were ignored in favor of more representative changes in key sectors.

The decline of public sector strikes has been accompanied by the widespread emergence of such new issues of concern as wage freezes, layoffs, restructuring, contingent workers, privatization, and employee benefits. As indicated above, it is not surprising that policymakers are reassessing the necessity of the intrusive public sector procedures of fact-finding and arbitration that focus on avoiding the strike *outcomes* and not the *process* for dealing with these new issues. It is entirely possible that these dispute resolution procedures will come under even more scrutiny as their costs and benefits are reevaluated.

At the same time, a transition is taking place to new forms of mediation (grievance, unfair labor practice, and preventative) as shifts occur away from strikes to new forms of conflict expression in the public sector. Finally, the extensive experiments with cooperative forms of bargaining may have profound effects on dispute resolution procedures depending on the durability of these new approaches.

There is insufficient evidence to determine whether there has been a permanent transformation of the current adversarial public sector collective bargaining process. It does seem certain, however, that there will continue to be a substantial evolution of dispute resolution techniques as the nature of conflict evolves in the public sector and as bargaining continues to focus on restructuring issues.

Acknowledgments

The author acknowledges the contribution of the two prior IRRA chapters on public sector dispute resolution by Kochan (1979) and Olson (1988).

Endnotes

[1] Interest or "contract" arbitration involves the establishment of agreement provisions by a third party; grievance or "rights" arbitration deals with matters of contract interpretation during the life of the agreement.

[2] Unfair labor practices refer to complaints to a labor relations administrative agency (such as the NLRB) either by a union or employer over such matters as bargaining in bad faith or interference and/or coercion in the organizing process. Grievance mediation represents the application of voluntary mediation techniques to grievance disputes as an intermediate step before formal binding arbitration.

[3] These decisions are summarized by Cheryl Maranto and John Lund, "Public Sector Labor Law: An Update," in this volume.

[4] The BLS and FMCS series have a correlation coefficient of .83 (p<.001) after 1960.

[5] Similar strike patterns have been observed in Canada. A decline in public sector strikes in the early '80s was followed by a leveling off and modest increase in the late '80s and early '90s. Since private sector strikes steadily declined over this period, the public sector increased its share of total days lost due to strikes (Gunderson and Reid 1995; Ponak and Thompson 1995; and Gunderson and Hyatt in this volume).

[6] Strike rates were calculated by dividing the number of employees by the estimated number of state unionized public employees. The source for the number of state unionized public sector employees was the AFL-CIO (1993).

[7] Partridge (1990) found the percentage of personal income paid to state and local taxes negatively related to public sector strike activity, indicating that the same factors that cause taxpayer revolts may reduce strikes.

[8] This freeze condition of the New York Taylor law is not found in private sector law but has counterparts in several other state public sector bargaining laws.

[9] See, for example, Currie and McConnell (1991:693); Gunderson, Hebdon, and Hyatt (1996); Olson (1986:539); Partridge (1992). Alternatively, Partridge (1990) found a limited right to strike was positively related to strike incidence.

[10] See Olson (1986). In Pennsylvania multiple or rotating teacher strikes have been restricted by the passage of Bill 88 in 1992 that, among other restrictions, removes the right to strike automatically if the 180-day instructional period is threatened. As a result of Bill 88, teacher strikes have fallen from 36 in 1991–92 to 17 in 1992–93 and 14 in 1993–94 (Stoltenberg 1995).

[11] See Currie and McConnell (1991, 693); Gunderson, Hebdon, and Hyatt (1996); Olson (1986, 539); Partridge (1992). But note that Olson (1986) found a weak relationship and Partridge (1990) found a statistically insignificant relationship between interest arbitration and strike incidence.

[12] The problem of the applicability of studies utilizing pre–1980 strike data may be more serious than presented here if the relationship between no-strike laws and strike outcomes has structurally changed in recent years. Likewise, interest arbitration may be a less satisfactory substitute for a strike if the courts and legislatures continue to undermine the binding nature of arbitration awards.

[13] For evidence of higher grievance arbitration rates when strikes are banned, see Hebdon (1992).

[14] Unfair labor practices are referred to as "improper practices" under New York State's Taylor law.

[15] See the New York State PERB Annual Reports 1978–94 and Wisconsin Employment Relations Commission, Biennial Reports, 1980–93.

[16] Interest-based techniques have not been limited to negotiations. The FLRA (1995) reports a successful resolution of 53 unfair labor practices using an interest-based, problem-solving approach.

[17] Walsh (1990) finds no evidence of an increase in unfair labor practices as potential indicators of a "deteriorating bargaining atmosphere" for Indiana teachers, although his data only go to 1982.

[18] As the name implies, fact-finding is a process that normally involves a formal hearing with briefs and evidence in support of the parties' positions, followed by a written public report in which the fact-finder makes a nonbinding recommendation on each issue in dispute. Interest arbitration differs mainly in the private and binding nature of the arbitrator's (or board's) award.

[19] Table 5 also reveals a steady decline over the period in the use of fact-finders who employ mediation techniques from 36% in 1983 to 8% by 1994. However, caution must be taken in interpreting this since part of the drop in mediated settlements by fact-finders after 1991 was due to a change in PERB's policy of combining the mediator/fact-finder roles. After 1991, fact-finders were discouraged from mediating, but this policy change does not explain the steady decline prior to 1991. In New York State, at least, it would appear that mediation is increasingly more effective if performed by a trained mediator rather than a fact-finder.

[20] For a discussion of grievance mediation see Skratek (1993) and Butt (1988).

[21] Preventive mediation is a process that uses problem-solving techniques to improve relationships and/or reduce conflict by anticipating its occurrence.

[22] For example, fact-finding for teachers in Wisconsin and for police and firefighters in New York was eliminated in the '70s.

[23] This is a reasonable assumption given the unique statutory framework in Iowa where fact-finders have evolved into "quasi" arbitrators.

[24] This result is the opposite of that by Bloom and Cavanaugh in New Jersey where the parties preferred experience and attorneys.

[25] For recent surveys of this literature see Hill, Zuelke, Landry, and Halver (1990); Kearney (1992); and Downie (1992:233–49).

[26] For example, teacher associations and school boards in Pennsylvania may mutually agree to arbitration in lieu of using the strike or lockout (see Stoltenberg 1995).

[27] New Jersey's collective bargaining law for police and fire employees offers a complete menu of these arbitration choices to the parties (see Lester 1984).

[28] For a critical review of research on arbitration, see Lavan (1990).

[29] For evaluations of ADR in court and family disputes, see Rosenberg and Folberg (1994) and Whiting (1994), respectively.

[30] The observability problem simply refers to the difficulty of obtaining the last offers of the parties prior to conventional arbitration. The simultaneity problem arises because the parties' offers are not independent of the facts of the case. See also Farber and Bazerman (1986).

[31] The chilling effect of arbitration may be defined as the lack of bargaining flexibility caused by the fear of the parties that a concession made in negotiations will reduce the arbitration outcome. This effect is caused, in part, by arbitrators that split the difference between the parties last offers. Its impact, in theory, should be reduced if the arbitrator is constrained to select one of the parties last offers (FOS arbitration). The narcotic or dependency effect occurs because high rates of arbitration usage may cause the parties to lose the ability to negotiate without third-party assistance. For a discussion of these negative effects of arbitration, see Olson (1994:169–73).

[32] In a simulation test of an economic model of negotiations, Farber, Neale, and Bazerman (1990) also find that the direct costs of arbitration (delays, arbitrator fees, etc.) lead to higher rates of agreement but found weak evidence that risk aversion is related to the probability of agreement.

[33] A control group simulated bargaining under the right to strike (i.e., without arbitration) by having a zero payoff if no settlement was reached. As expected, FOS, CA, and tri-offer arbitration each had lower settlement rates than the control group.

[34] For a literature survey of settlement rates, see Ponak and Falkenberg (1989: 280–84).

[35] This study was summarized in Olson (1988).

[36] The parties were more likely to arbitrate if they had an award more than two years earlier. Some evidence of a dependency on arbitration was also found for Ohio's safety employees (firefighters, police, and sheriffs) (Graham and Perry 1993). For example, since 1984, 52.7% of all final best-offer (issue by issue) interest arbitrations involved only 34 employers (Graham and Perry 1993).

[37] Regression results reveal significant differences between impasse rates in the Ontario jurisdictions with interest arbitration and those with the right to strike, controlling for such differences as occupation, bargaining unit size, union, and industry (Table 6).

[38] These percentages cannot be compared to settlement rates because the New York State PERB does not break out police and firefighter negotiations from all other public sector negotiations.

[39] These results must be tentative because economic, financial, political, and occupational factors have not been taken into account in the comparisons.

[40] For discussions of this literature, see Finch and Nagel (1984:1641), Mitchell (1988:157), Kearney (1992:341–42), and Ries (1992:48).

[41] There is also proposed legislation to remove the right to strike for teachers (Pennsylvania State Education Association 1995).

[41] In Wisconsin collective bargaining has effectively been suspended by means of a legislated 3.2% cap on total compensation.

[43] *Nebraska V. AFSCME Local 61*, 239 Neb. 653 (1991), summarized in Maranto and Lund in this volume.

[44] See Maranto and Lund in this volume.

[45] Contrast, for example, the decline in public sector union density in the U.K. from 80% in 1984 to 72% by 1990 under conservative governments (Millward 1992) with the increase in U.S. density from 36.7% in 1983 to 37.7% in 1993 (BLS 1994).

References

AFL-CIO, Public Employee Department. 1993. "Public Employees Bargain for Excellence." Washington: AFL-CIO.

Anderson, J. C., and Thomas Kochan. 1977. "Impasse Procedures in the Canadian Federal Service: Effects on the Bargaining Process." *Industrial and Labor Relations Review*, Vol. 30, pp. 283–301.

Ashenfelter, Orley. 1985. "Evidence on U.S. Experiences with Dispute Resolution Systems." In D. W. Conklin, T. J. Courchene, and W. A. Jones, eds., *Public Sector Compensation*. Toronto: Economic Council, pp. 13–35.

_____. 1987. "Arbitrator Behavior." *American Economic Review, Papers and Proceedings*, Vol. 77, pp. 342–46.

Ashenfelter, Orley, and David E. Bloom. 1984. "Models of Arbitrator Behavior: Theory and Evidence." *American Economic Review*, Vol. 74, pp. 578–86.

Ashenfelter, Orley, Janet Currie, Henry S. Farber, and Mathew Spiegel. 1992. "An Experimental Comparison of Dispute Rates in Alternative Arbitration Systems." *Econometrica*, Vol. 60, no. 6, pp. 1407–31.

Bacharach, Samuel B., Joseph B. Shedd, and Sharon C. Conley. 1988. "School Management and Teacher Unions: The Capacity for Cooperation in an Age of Reform." *Proceedings of the 41st Annual Meeting of the Industrial Relations Research Association*. Madison, WI: IRRA, pp. 60–69.

Bazerman, Max H., and Henry S. Farber. 1985. "Arbitrator Decision Making: When Are Final Offers Important?" *Industrial and Labor Relations Review*, Vol. 79, no. 1 (October), pp. 76–89.

Bloom, David E. 1981. "Collective Bargaining, Compulsory Arbitration, and Salary Settlements in the Public Sector: The Case of New Jersey's Municipal Police Officers." *Journal of Labor Research*, Vol. 2, no. 3, pp. 369–84.

_____. 1986. "Empirical Models of Arbitrator Behavior under Conventional Arbitration." *Review of Economics and Statistics*, Vol. 68 (November), pp. 578–86.

Bloom, David, and C. L. Cavanaugh. 1986. "An Analysis of the Selection of Arbitrators." *American Economic Review*, Vol. 76, pp. 408–22.

Blouin, R. 1982. "Arbitration of Bargaining Disputes in Quebec." *Proceedings of the 19th Annual Meeting of the Canadian Industrial Relations Association*. Ottawa: University of Ottawa, pp. 209–38.

Bluestone, Barry. 1989. "The Impact of Binding Arbitration on the Salaries of Public School Teachers in Connecticut." Mimeo, University of Massachusetts at Boston, pp. 1–27.

Board of Conciliation and Arbitration of the Commonwealth of Massachusetts, Annual Reports 101–104, 1987–90.

Bureau of Labor Statistics. 1983–94. *Major Work Stoppages*. Washington: U.S. Government.

_____. 1983–94. *Current Wage Developments*. Washington: U.S. Government.

Burgess, Paul L., and Daniel R. Marburger. 1993. "Do Negotiated and Arbitrated Salaries Differ under Final-Offer Arbitration?" *Industrial and Labor Relations Review*, Vol. 46, no. 3, pp. 548–59.

Butt, Elizabeth Rae. 1988. "Grievance Mediation: The Ontario Experience. Research Essay Series No. 14." Kingston, Ont.: Queen's University.

Currie, Janet, and Sheena McConnell. 1991. "Collective Bargaining in the Public Sector: The Effect of Legal Structure on Dispute Costs and Wages." *American Economic Review*, Vol. 81, no. 4 (September), pp. 693–718.

Delaney, J. T. 1983. "Strikes, Arbitration, and Teacher Salaries: A Behavioral Analysis." *Industrial and Labor Relations Review*, Vol. 36 (April), pp. 431–46.

Dell'Omo, Gregory G. 1989. "Wage Disputes in Interest Arbitration: Arbitrators Weigh the Criteria." *Arbitration Journal*, Vol. 44, no. 2 (June), pp. 4–13.

Department of Industrial Relations Mediation/Conciliation Service. Report of Activities, State of California, Fiscal Years 1987–88, 1989–90, 1990–91.

DiLauro, Thomas J. 1989. "Interest Arbitration: The Best Alternative for Resolving Public-Sector Impasses." *Employee Relations*, Vol. 14, no. 4 (Spring), p. 568.

Dilts, David A. 1994. "The Consumer Price Index as a Standard in Negotiations and Arbitration." *Journal of Collective Negotiations in the Public Sector*, Vol. 23, no. 4, pp. 279–86.

Dilts, David A., and Lawrence J. Haber. 1989. "The Mediation of Contract Disputes in the Iowa Public Sector." *Journal of Collective Negotiations in the Public Sector*, Vol. 18, no. 2, pp. 145–51.

Dilts, David A., and Stanley W. Elsea. 1990. "Selection of Factfinders in Iowa Public Sector Labor Disputes: Characteristics of Acceptable and Unacceptable Neutrals." *Journal of Collective Negotiations in the Public Sector*, Vol. 19, no. 3, pp. 207–16.

Dilts, David A., Lawrence J. Haber, and A. Karim. 1990. "The Effect of Mediators' Qualities and Strategies on Mediation Outcomes." *Relations Industrielles/Industrial Relations*, Vol. 45, pp. 22–33.

Dilts, David A., Ahmad R. Karim, and Ali Rassuli. 1990. "Mediation in the Public Sector: Toward a Paradigm of Negotiations and Dispute Resolution." *Journal of Collective Negotiations in the Public Sector*, Vol. 19, no. 1, pp. 49–60.

Dilts, David A., Ali Rassuli, and Ahmad R. Karim. 1992. "Mediation and the Path Toward Settlement: An Analysis of Union Negotiators Behavior." *Journal of Collective Negotiations in the Public Sector*, Vol. 21, no. 2, pp. 171–82.

Downie, Bryan M. 1992. *Strikes, Disputes and Policymaking: Resolving Disputes in Ontario Education*. Kingston, Ont: IRC Press, pp. 233–49.

Dunham, R. 1976. "Interest Arbitration in Non-Federal Public Employment." *Arbitration Journal*, Vol. 31, pp. 45–57.

Farber, Henry S. 1980. "An Analysis of Final-Offer Arbitration." *Journal of Conflict Resolution*, Vol. 24, no. 4 (December), pp. 683–705.

_____. 1981. "Splitting-the-Difference in Interest Arbitration." *Industrial and Labor Relations Review*, Vol. 35 (October).

Farber, Henry S., and Harry Katz. 1979. "Interest Arbitration, Outcomes, and the Incentive to Bargain." *Industrial and Labor Relations Review*, Vol. 33, no. 1 (October), pp. 55–63.

Farber, Henry S., and Max S. Bazerman. 1986. "The General Basis of Arbitrator Behavior: An Empirical Analysis of Conventional and Final-Offer Arbitration." *Econometrica*, Vol. 54, no. 6 (November), pp. 1503–28.

Farber, Henry S., Margaret A. Neale, and Max H. Bazerman. 1990. "The Role of Arbitration Costs and Risk Aversion in Dispute Outcomes." *Industrial Relations*, Vol. 29, no. 3 (Fall), pp. 361–84.

Federal Labor Relations Authority. 1992, 1993. Annual Reports.

_____. 1995. Quarterly Summary, Vol. 4, no. 2 (second quarter).

Federal Mediation and Conciliation Service. 1960–94. All reported strikes.

Feuille, P., J. T. Delaney, and W. Hendricks. 1985. "The Impact of Interest Arbitration on Police Contracts." *Industrial Relations*, Vol. 24, no. 2, pp. 161–81.

Finch, Michael, and Trevor W. Nagel. 1984. "Collective Bargaining in the Public Schools: Reassessing Labor Policy in an Era of Reform." *Wisconsin Law Review*, pp. 1573–1670.

Gallagher, Daniel G., and R. Pregnetter. 1979. "Impasse Resolution under the Iowa Multistep Procedure." *Industrial and Labor Relations Review*, Vol. 32, pp. 327–38.

Gallagher, Daniel G., and Peter A. Veglahn. 1990. "Changes in Bargaining Behavior as a Result of Experience under a Statutory Impasse Scheme: Theory and Evidence." *Journal of Collective Negotiations in the Public Sector*, Vol. 19, no. 3, pp. 175–88.

Giacobbe, Jane. 1988. "Factfinding and Arbitration: Procedural Justice for All?" *Journal of Collective Negotiations in the Public Sector*, Vol. 17, no. 4, pp. 295–308.

Government Employment Relations Report. 1992. Vol. 30, April 27, 615.

Graham, Harry, and Jeffrey Perry. 1993. "Interest Arbitration in Ohio, the Narcotic Effect Revisited." *Journal of Collective Negotiations in the Public Sector*, Vol. 22, no. 4, pp. 323–26.

Gunderson, Morley, and Douglas Hyatt. 1996. "Canadian Public Sector Employment Relations in Transition," in this volume.

Gunderson, Morley, and Frank Reid. 1995. "Public Sector Strikes in Canada." In G. Swimmer and M. Thompson, eds., *Public Sector Collective Bargaining in Canada*. Kingston, Ont.: IRC Press.

Gunderson, Morley, Robert Hebdon, and Douglas Hyatt. 1996. "Collective Bargaining in the Public Sector: Comment." *American Economic Review*, Vol. 86, no. 1, pp. 315-26.

Hebdon, Robert. 1992. "Ontario's No-Strike Laws: A Test of the Safety-Valve Hypothesis." *Proceedings of the 28th Conference of the Canadian Industrial Relations Association*, pp. 347-57.

_____. 1995. "The Freezing Effect of Public Sector Bargaining: The Case of Ontario Crown Employees." *Journal of Collective Negotiation*, Vol. 24, no. 3, pp. 233-54.

Hebdon, Robert, and Maurice Mazerolle. 1995. "Mending Fences, Building Bridges: The Effect of RBO on Conflict." *Relations Industrielles/Industrial Relations*, Vol. 50, no. 1 (Winter), pp. 164-85.

Helsby, Robert, Kenneth Jennings, David Moore, Steven Paulson, and Steven Williamson. 1988. "Union-Management Negotiators' Views of Factfinding in Florida." *Journal of Collective Negotiations in the Public Sector*, Vol. 17, no. 1, pp. 63-73.

Herman, Edward E., and Howard M. Leftwich. 1985. "Mediation and Fact-Finding under the 1983 Ohio Public Employee Collective Bargaining Act." *Proceedings of the 38th Annual Meeting of the Industrial Relations Research Association*. Madison, WI: IRRA, pp. 316-23.

_____. 1988. "Fact-Finding in Ohio Public Sector Bargaining Revisited." *Labor Law Journal* (August), pp. 513-19.

Hill, Richard L., Dennis C. Zuelke, Richard G. Landry, and David J. Halver. 1990. "Fact-finding as a Bargaining Impasse Resolution Procedure: A North Dakota Study and Related Literature Review." *Journal of Collective Negotiations in the Public Sector*, Vol. 19, no. 3, pp. 217-42.

Hiltrop, Jean M. 1985. "Dispute Settlement and Mediation: Data from Britain." *Industrial Relations*, Vol. 24, no. 1 (Winter), pp. 139-46.

Hines, R. J. 1972. "Mandatory Contract Arbitration—Is It a Viable Process?" *Industrial and Labor Relations Review*, Vol. 25, no. 4 (July), pp. 533-44.

Jackson, R. 1989. *Fact Finding under the School Boards and Teachers Collective Bargaining Act of Ontario*. Toronto: Ontario Education Relations Commission.

Jarley, Paul. 1992. "The Effect of Interest Arbitration on Salary Dispersion among Employers." *Industrial Relations*, Vol. 31, no. 2, pp. 292-308.

Johnston, Paul. 1994. *Success While Others Fail*. Ithaca, NY: ILR Press.

Karper, Mark D. 1994. "Fact Finding in Public Employment: Promise or Illusion, Revisited." *Journal of Collective Negotiations in the Public Sector*, Vol. 23, no. 4, pp. 287-97.

Katz, Harry C., and Thomas A. Kochan. 1992. *An Introduction to Collective Bargaining and Industrial Relations*. New York: McGraw-Hill.

Kearney, Richard C. 1992. *Labor Relations in the Public Sector*. New York: Marcel Dekker.

Kochan, Thomas A. 1979. "Dynamics of Dispute Resolution in the Public Sector." In B. Aaron, J. R. Grodin, and J. L. Stern, eds., *Public-Sector Bargaining*. Washington, DC: Bureau of National Affairs.

Kochan, Thomas A., and Todd Jick. 1978. "The Public Sector Mediation Process: A Theory and Empirical Examination." *Journal of Conflict Resolution*, Vol. 22, no. 2 (June), pp. 209-40.

Labor-Management Committee of the State and Local Government. 1992. "Grievance Mediation in State and Local Government." Washington, DC: Labor-Management Committee.

Lavan, Helen. 1990. "Arbitration in the Public Sector: A Current Perspective." *Journal of Collective Negotiations in the Public Sector*, Vol. 19, no. 2, pp. 153–63.

Lester, Richard A. 1984. *Labor Arbitration in State and Local Government: An Examination of Experiences in Eight States and New York City*. Princeton, NJ: Princeton.

Lewin, David, Peter Feuille, Thomas A. Kochan, and John Thomas Delaney. 1988. *Public Sector Labor Relations: Analysis and Readings*. Lexington, MA: Lexington Books.

Lipsky, D. B., and T. A. Barocci. 1977. *The Impact of Final Offer Arbitration in Massachusetts: An Analysis of Police and Firefighter Collective Bargaining*. Cambridge, MA: M.I.T.

Loewenberg, J. Joseph, and William A. Kleintop. 1992. "The Second Decade of Interest Arbitration in Pennsylvania." *Journal of Collective Negotiations in the Public Sector*, Vol. 21, no. 4, pp. 353–67.

Magnusen, Karl O., and Patricia A. Renovitch. 1989. "Dispute Resolution in Florida's Public Sector: Insight into Impasse." *Journal of Collective Negotiations in the Public Sector*, Vol. 18, no. 3, pp. 214–52.

Management Board Secretariat. 1992. "Employer Report on the Reform of the Crown Employees Collective Bargaining Act." Toronto: Queen's Printer.

Maranto, Cheryl, and John Lund. 1996. "Public Sector Labor Law: An Update," in this volume.

Marmo, Michael. 1995. "The Role of Fact Finding and Interest Arbitration in 'Selling' a Settlement." *Journal of Collective Negotiations in the Public Sector*, Vol. 24, no. 1, pp. 77–96.

Mazerolle, Maurice, Robert Hebdon, and Douglas Hyatt. 1995. "Dispute Resolution in Ontario 1984–93." Working Paper, New York State School of Industrial and Labor Relations, Cornell University.

McKee, Jean. 1993. "Beyond Litigation: New Approaches to Federal Labor Relations—Let's Give Change a Chance." *Proceedings of the Spring Meeting* (Seattle, WA, April 29-May 1). Madison, WI: IRRA, p. 506.

Millward, Neil. 1992. *Workplace Industrial Relations in Transition*. Aldershot: Dartmouth.

Mitchell, Daniel J.B. 1988. "Collective Bargaining and Compensation in the Public Sector." In B. Aaron, J. M. Najita, and J. L. Stern, eds., *Public-Sector Bargaining*. Washington, DC: Bureau of National Affairs, pp. 124–59.

Mitchell, L. 1982. "Interest Arbitration in the Federal Public Service." *Proceedings of the 19th Annual Meeting of the Canadian Industrial Relations Association*. Ottawa: University of Ottawa, pp. 239–58.

Nelson, Nels E. 1992. "How Factfinders View the Criteria in Factfinding." *Journal of Collective Negotiations in the Public Sector*, Vol. 21, no. 2, pp. 159–70.

O'Brien, Kevin M. 1994. "The Impact of Union Political Activities on Public-Sector Pay, Employment, and Budgets." *Industrial Relations*, Vol. 33, no. 3 (July), pp. 322–45.

Olson, Craig. 1978. "Final Offer Arbitration in Wisconsin after Five Years." *Proceedings of the 31st Annual Meeting of the Industrial Relations Research Association*. Madison, WI: IRRA, pp. 111–19.

_____. 1980. "The Impact of Arbitration on the Wage of Firefighters." *Industrial and Labor Relations Review*, Vol. 39 (Fall), pp. 325–39.

_____. 1986. "Strikes, Strike Penalties, and Arbitration in Six States." *Industrial and Labor Relations Review*, Vol. 39, no. 4 (July), pp. 539–51.

_____. 1988. "Dispute Resolution in the Public Sector." In B. Aaron, J. M. Najita, and J. L. Stern, eds., *Public-Sector Bargaining*. Washington, DC: Bureau of National Affairs, pp. 160–88.

_____. 1992. "Arbitrator Decision Making in Multi-Issue Disputes." *Proceedings of the 44th Annual Meeting of the Industrial Relations Research Association*. Madison, WI: IRRA.

_____. 1994. "Final Offer Versus Conventional Arbitration Revisited: Preliminary Results from the Lab." Paper presented at the 4th Bargaining Group Conference. Toronto: Center for Industrial Relations (October).

Olson, Craig, and Paul Jarley. 1991. "Arbitrator Decisions in Wisconsin Teacher Wage Disputes." *Industrial and Labor Relations Review*, Vol. 44, no. 3 (April), pp. 536–47.

Olson, Craig, Gregory G. Dell'Omo, and Paul Jarley. 1992. "A Comparison of Interest Arbitration Decision-Making in Experimental and Field Settings." *Industrial and Labor Relations Review*, Vol. 45, no. 4 (July), pp. 711–23.

Ontario Ministry of Labor, Settlement Stage Dataset, 1994.

Partridge, Dane M. 1988. "A Reexamination of the Effectiveness of No-Strike Laws for Public School Teachers." *Journal of Collective Negotiations in the Public Sector*, Vol. 17, no. 4, pp. 257–66.

_____. 1990. "The Effect of Public Policy on Strike Activity in the Public Sector." *Journal of Collective Negotiations in the Public Sector*, Vol. 19, no. 2, pp. 87–96.

_____. 1992. "A Cross-Sectional Analysis of Teacher Strike Activity." *Journal of Collective Negotiations in the Public Sector*, Vol. 21, no. 1, pp. 27–43.

Pennsylvania State Education Association. 1995. "The Voice" (April), p. 4.

Pennsylvania Labor Relations Board. 1988–1993. Annual Reports.

Pfeffenberger, Dyne, Max Laudeman, Lawrence J. Haber, and David A. Dilts. 1992. "The Ability to Pay: Accounting and Collective Bargaining in the Public Sector." *Journal of Collective Negotiations in the Public Sector*, Vol. 21, no. 3, pp. 263–69.

Ponak, Allen M., and H. N. Wheeler. 1980. "Choice of Procedures in Canada and the United States." *Industrial Relations*, Vol. 19, pp. 292–308.

Ponak, Allen M., and Loren Falkenberg. 1989. "Resolution of Interest Disputes." In Amarjit S. Sethi, ed., *Collective Bargaining in Canada*. Scarborough, Ont.: Nelson Canada.

Ponak, Allen M., and Mark Thompson. 1995. "Public Sector Collective Bargaining." In M. Gunderson and A. Ponak, eds., *Union-Management Relations in Canada*. 3d. Don Mills, Ont.: Addison-Wesley.

Public Employment Relations Board. 1978–94. Annual Reports Edition, New York State.

Ries, Edith Dunfries. 1992. "The Effects of Fact-Finding and Final-Offer Issue-by-Issue Compulsory Interest Arbitration on Teachers' Wages, Fringe Benefits, and Language Provisions: A Comparative Analysis of New Jersey and Connecticut 1980–86." *Journal of Collective Negotiations in the Public Sector*, Vol. 21, no. 1, pp. 45–67.

Rose, Joseph B. 1994. "The Complaining Game: How Effective is Compulsory Interest Arbitration?" *Journal of Collective Negotiations in the Public Sector*, Vol. 23, no. 3, pp. 187–202.

Rosenberg, Joshua D., and H. Jay Folberg. 1994. "Alternative Dispute Resolution: An Empirical Analysis." *Stanford Law Review*, Vol. 46, pp. 1487–551.

Samavati, Hedayeh, Lawrence J. Haber, and David A. Dilts. 1991. "Comparability and the Interest Arbitration of Economic Disputes in the Public Sector." *Journal of Collective Negotiations in the Public Sector*, Vol. 20, no. 2, pp. 159–66.

Skratek, Sylvia. 1993. "Grievance Mediation: How to Make the Process Work for You." *Proceedings of the Spring Meeting, Industrial Relations Research Association*. Madison, WI: IRRA, p. 507.

Stern, James. 1966. *Fact Finding under Wisconsin Law*. Madison, WI: Univ. of Wisconsin Press.

Stern, J. L., C. M. Rehmus, J. J. Loewenberg, H. Kasper, and B. D. Dennis. 1975. *Final-Offer Arbitration: The Effects on Public Safety Employee Bargaining*. Toronto: D.C. Heath & Co.

Stoltenberg, Eric C. 1995. "Act 88: The Changing Face of Impasse Resolution for Pennsylvania's Teachers." *Journal of Collective Negotiations in the Public Sector*, Vol. 24, no. 1, pp. 63–75.

Swimmer, G., and A. MacDonald. 1985. "Dispute Resolution in the Ontario Public Sector: What's So Wrong with the Right to Strike?" In D. W. Conklin, T. J. Courchene, and W. A. Jones, eds., *Public Sector Compensation*. Toronto: Economic Council, pp. 154–78.

Thompson, M. 1981. "Evaluation of Interest Arbitration: The Case of British Columbia Teachers." In J. M. P. Weiler, ed., *Interest Arbitration*. Toronto: Carswell, pp. 79–97.

Trevelin, David I. 1992. "The Future of Alternative Dispute Resolution." *Forum*. National Institute For Dispute Resolution (Winter).

Valletta, and Richard B. Freeman. 1988. "The NBER Public Sector Collective Bargaining Law Data Set." *When Public Sector Workers Unionize*. Appendix B. Chicago: Univ. of Chicago Press.

Walsh, William. 1990. "Did the Indiana Teacher Collective Bargaining Act Foster Labor Peace?" *Journal of Collective Negotiations in the Public Sector*, Vol. 19, no. 4, pp. 305–17.

Whiting, Raymond. 1994. "Family Disputes, Nonfamily Disputes, and Mediation Success." *Mediation Quarterly*, Vol. 11, no. 3 (Spring), pp. 247–60.

Wisconsin Employment Relations Commission (WERC). 1980–93. Biennial Reports, State of Wisconsin.

CHAPTER 4

The Structure of Compensation in the Public Sector

DALE BELMAN AND JOHN S. HEYWOOD
University of Wisconsin–Milwaukee

The level of public sector compensation helps determine both the competence and efficiency of government services. Too high a level wastes the resources of governments, depriving them of the opportunity to address other costly objectives or to reduce burdens to taxpayers. Too low a level makes it impossible for governments to attract workers of the quality needed to provide the services that citizens demand. Determining compensation in the public sector is unavoidably influenced by administrative and political processes. At issue is how well these processes work. Comparability stands as the generally, but not uniformly, accepted standard by which researchers make such judgments. Both equity and efficiency have been thought to require that public sector compensation be comparable to that of similar workers performing similar tasks in the private sector. Equity requires that workers should not be paid differently for identical work simply because their employer is the government. Efficiency requires that the compensation be just adequate to attract the appropriate supply and quality of workers.

The next section of this chapter reviews the criterion of comparability and briefly compares it to alternative standards. An effort is made to identify the settings in which the standard has taken hold and those in which it has not. While the focus is primarily on the United States, other countries are discussed in passing. The possible components of comparability are discussed, and issues of measurement are considered. Information is provided on public and private sector differences in earnings and on pension coverage.

The third section of the chapter reviews the literature on the estimation of comparability. This literature includes studies of earnings that compare positions and studies that compare people. The latter is grounded firmly in the human capital tradition and often results in sharply different estimates than the first. This has given rise to studies which are hybrids of the two approaches. At issue is how to include potentially important components of comparability that go beyond the standard measures of human capital and how to account for the sector selection choices of individuals. A less extensive literature studies the comparability of benefit provision.

The fourth section presents our current empirical contribution to this issue of longstanding interest. We estimate human-capital-based earnings differentials over a period 1973 to 1993. These estimates incorporate an increasingly complete set of controls which mirror those used in the "positions and people" hybrid estimation. Of interest is the pattern over time and the pattern as the list of controls expands. In addition, we estimate the government earnings differential within broad occupational groups and demonstrate that even though aggregate measures may indicate comparability, there is no evidence of comparability within subgroups. The final section of this review draws several conclusions and highlights potentially fruitful lines for future research.

The Standard of Comparability

Understanding Comparability and Its Alternatives

The principle of comparability has shown notable persistence in the promulgated standards of the U.S. government. Smith (1987:177) traces this principle as far back as an 1862 law requiring that wages of U.S. government blue-collar workers "conform with those of private establishments in the immediate vicinity." Although this early version of "locality pay" has been supplanted, the principle of comparability already had a long history when President Kennedy called for legislative action to implement the "Comparability Doctrine." The consequence of the Federal Salary Reform Act of 1962 was to tie the earnings of the majority of federal workers to private sector earnings. The current statutory basis for most federal civilian pay is the Federal Pay Comparability Act of 1970.

Federal government workers are typically part of the General Schedule (GS) for white-collar workers, the Federal Wage Schedule (FWS) for blue-collar workers, or the Postal Service Schedule. Each schedule explicitly incorporates comparability with the private sector, but implementation is substantially different. The Postal Service Schedule is the outcome of collective bargaining and the interest arbitration process in which comparability is the only explicit criteria.[1] The setting of earnings for FWS workers reflects prevailing wages—the going rates in particular localities as determined by local wage boards

(Nesbit 1976). The setting of earnings for the GS workers follows the survey of private establishment wages by the Bureau of Labor Statistics (BLS). Employing this survey of professional, administrative, technical, and clerical jobs, recommended increases are made for each grade in the general schedule.[2] The recommendations are typically modified by the President, who is allowed to submit an alternative proposal to Congress.[3] The frequent use of this presidential option has been interpreted as an attempt to maintain comparability in the face of a flawed survey or, alternatively, as the de facto adoption of a standard other than comparability. We will return to this debate both when we consider standards other than comparability and when we discuss implementing an appropriate empirical test for comparability.

Even the military is subject to comparability. The Pay Comparability Act of 1967 requires that military wages be indexed to those of federal civilian workers which are, in turn, tied to private sector earnings. Although military comparisons are particularly complex (Phillips and Wise 1987), comparability remains an implicit guideline.

While wage comparability has long been accepted by the federal government, comparability for fringe benefits has only recently and tenuously been accepted. Matching of fringe benefits to those of the private sector was discussed as early as 1976 but has not been pursued systematically.[4] While the traditional BLS survey does not collect information on fringe benefits, and while military pensions have not been structured with private sector comparability in mind (Leonard 1987), the postal statute mentions both earnings and benefits (Venti 1987:150, fn. 3). In 1979 President Carter proposed, in the Federal Employees Compensation Reform Act, to broaden the scope of the comparability surveys and to expand the principle of compensation comparability to include fringe benefits. The act would have provided the President with authority to adjust all benefits, except retirement. The private sector yardstick was to be a data intensive "standardized cost approach" (Hobt and Weissenborn 1980). Although benefits are an obvious and substantial portion of total compensation, the lack of a consistent policy of comparability in fringe benefits, combined with the paucity of cost data, has limited most research on federal compensation to earnings comparisons.

Although determining compensation for state and local employees depends on specific legislation, many states incorporate comparability standards either in dispute resolution processes (Hill and DeLacenserie 1991) or as a central principle in the legislation of compensation. Many states have established surveys in the last two decades to support legislated comparability (Belman, Franklin, and Heywood 1994). While most limit the surveys to earnings, some explicitly consider "total compensation," including fringe benefits. For instance, the Bureau of Personnel of South Dakota surveys the earnings and the fringe benefits of private employers and neighboring state governments. Participants are required to cost out the value of fringe benefits, and these are compared with those in the public sector.

While the use of comparability to determine public compensation is widespread, the objectives sought from comparability are more ambiguous. The Reform Act of 1962 establishes three purposes for comparability. First, federal employees should have equity with equivalent employees throughout the nation. Second, the federal government should compete "fairly" with private firms for qualified workers. Third, there should exist a "logical and factual basis" for determining federal earnings. While the third objective suggests that some standard is better than no standard, the other two seem to take equity as their major concern.[5]

These objectives differ in emphasis from those which most economists might highlight. Stated briefly, the government sector lacks market forces to guide pay setting. The public sector should then follow private sector compensation not simply to attract the appropriate number of workers away from the private sector, but because it involves replicating wages that reflect the correct marginal evaluations of utility-maximizing workers and profit-maximizing firms. Yet, even government wages which accurately reflect those in the private sector will be weighted averages of wages that reflect discrimination, monopsony power, unionization, product market power, and other noncompetitive factors. This weighted average has few claims to reflecting a competitive norm equating the nondistorted marginal costs and benefits of hiring additional labor. Thus it would seem that comparability has, at most, an appeal to equity between workers, equity between employers, and to that restricted notion of efficiency which says that a comparable wage should allow the government to attract the needed workers at a wage that doesn't include large rents *relative* to those elsewhere in the economy.

The economists' notion of efficiency, which cannot be achieved by simple comparability, raises the issue of whether there might be a superior standard for government pay setting. Specifically, the appropriate government wage might be the competitive wage, even if that wage is not always observed in the private sector. Under such a standard, the government would not duplicate private sector wages that are inflated by market power or deflated by discrimination. Obviously, such factors could push the government wage above or below the "comparable" private wage.

These concerns routinely enter the discussions of researchers in a somewhat disguised form. For example, typical human-capital-based estimates suggest that the earnings of federal workers are much higher than private sector workers for women but only very modestly higher for men.[6] Federal women workers do not receive *comparable* wages which may reflect discrimination in the private sector, but they may nonetheless receive the *appropriate* wage if the public sector premium is taken as offsetting discrimination. Similarly, the government might lower earnings for workers whose private sector counterparts have elevated wages reflecting less than competitive markets.

The suggestion that the government should set an example with its compensation practices raises the idea of the "model employer." Historically, governments have seen this model as being one of advocating and demonstrating employment policies, such as due process, merit systems, pensions, and anti-discrimination measures.[7] Yet, the substance of a government as model employer criteria can vary greatly with the values and objectives of the government. The Conservative governments of the United Kingdom viewed public sector pay awards as a key element in a broader national wage and income policies. The hope was that low public pay awards would serve as "a standard" for bargainers in the private sector and as an informal incomes policy (Elliot, Murphy, and Blackaby 1994). Obviously, there may be little consensus on the objectives of a model employer.

Another standard for public wage setting which frequently supplements comparability is the "ability to pay." The logic for this standard is that, as with employees of private firms, the pay of public employees should reflect the economic health of their employer. Interest arbitrators are often required to consider the ability to pay of the local community in establishing an economic settlement (Hill and Delacenserie 1991). Brown and Medoff (1988) find that the average wealth in governmental jurisdictions—a proxy for ability to pay—helps explain the earnings differences across jurisdictions.

Ability to pay frequently enters as justification for the presidential prerogative to modify the BLS wage recommendations. For example, President Reagan recommended cutting federal wages 5% in January 1986 to help reduce the budget deficit. For similar reasons, the Netherlands consciously abandoned an explicit comparability standard in 1982 and allowed public sector earnings to lag behind those in the private sector (van Ophem 1993). In 1982 a British government-sponsored inquiry virtually repudiated comparability in favor of ability to pay, arguing that comparability was just one standard among many and was not even the most important one, given the problems facing the economy (Gregory 1990).

Applying ability-to-pay standards involves the difficult task of measuring that ability and distinguishing inability from reluctance. Although communities can face financial stringency, arguments for wage relief may reflect an unwillingness to tax adequately or discretionary decisions in other areas of expenditure. For example, the United States has a large budget deficit but, by international standards, low tax rates. Does this argue that federal earnings should be restrained or expanded? Surely, ability to pay in the public sector is a concept that goes to the heart of political differences on the role of government and is a subject about which economists can offer only very few words of wisdom. First, there is an inherent ambiguity in such a standard. Second, the standard of comparability, when applied in the context of fiscal federalism, necessarily means that some localities will have larger proportional tax burdens to hire the same quantity and quality of public sector workers. Such inequities are not unique to this issue but permeate everything from public school finance to local economic development. Third, if true comparability has been achieved, the issue of ability to pay may be moot. If a local jurisdiction reduces wages below both the level in the private sector and in other public jurisdictions, it will not be able to attract needed workers and might be compelled to re-adopt comparability.[8]

Complications in Applying Comparability

Comparability retains favor as an easily understood benchmark which attracts broad support. The details of what should be compared between sectors generates substantial disagreement even among those committed to the general principle. Given comparable earnings, should fringe benefit levels be made comparable and if so, how? One of the defining characteristics of compensation in the 1980s was the decline in the share of the private sector prime-age male workforce that receive pensions (Bloom and Freeman 1992). Strict comparability would require that fewer public sector workers receive pensions. This is an unlikely and potentially illegal response, but the value of the pensions could be reduced to reflect the average value of private sector pensions—presumably declining in value as fewer private workers are covered. Yet, this might be viewed as the public sector employer reneging on an (implicit) contract with its workers. Following the notion of "total compensation," the value of public fringe benefits might be reduced in some element other than pensions, so that the decline in private sector coverage could be reflected in total compensation without changing retirement arrangements with existing workers. Obviously, similar challenges surround health insurance, a benefit not provided by many smaller private sector firms. Should public sector health benefits or other elements of compensation be reduced to reflect incomplete private sector coverage? The issue would be complicated by the fact that the federal government provides health insurance at costs per employee that are below those typical of the private sector (Levitan and Nodel 1983).

More generally, it is unwieldy and inappropriate to require comparable compensation to match the average in the private sector *element by element*. The resulting package would make little sense to workers, be costly to provide, and might render the government uncompetitive in the labor market. Rather than matching element by element, an alternative standard might simply be comparable dollars spent on the complete fringe benefit package. The difficulty with such a standard is that it serves only one of the original equity objectives of comparability. Focusing on matching the costs of fringe benefits may ensure that private sector employers do not face "unfair" competition from the public sector, but it need not guarantee equity for workers between sectors. A scheme requiring equal costs implies that workers will actually receive higher total compensation in the sector that can provide benefits in the cheapest fashion. Similarly, while an identical benefit package may ensure that workers are treated equally in each sector, it may create inequality between employers since one sector may provide them for less cost. Thus the fact that dollars of cost spent on fringe benefits are not translated one to one into dollars of benefits received by workers leaves even those committed to comparability unsure how to implement the standard. Economists would favor an equality of fringe benefit compensation, thereby encouraging employers to provide benefits in the least costly fashion, or better, equality of total compensation, which would additionally allow the trade-off of wages and fringe benefits according to their costs and benefits.

Nonpecuniary aspects of work may also differ between sectors. It is not clear what guidance comparability provides for working conditions such as employment stability or risk of injury. Comparability might imply that the government should strive to replicate nonpecuniary aspects of private sector employment. Yet this may be impossible or undesirable. Even those favoring comparability may want the government to behave as a model employer by providing an environment that is safer and more secure than that of the private sector. Furthermore, accomplishing the objectives of the government may require different employment characteristics than found in the private sector. Thus, even if it is costless or necessary for the government to provide more stable employment, workers will be better off because of the reduced risk. Again, comparability of costs need not translate into comparability of benefits (in this case reduced risk). Nonetheless, a strict version of comparability in worker benefits would seem to require a reduction in some other dimension of compensation in order to offset the reduced risk.

Once this view of comparability in benefits is accepted, there seems no end to compensating wage adjustments that might be made. How many characteristics of the job would be included in making earnings adjustments? What would they be? How much would each adjustment be worth in earnings? Even if credible private sector earnings equations could reveal the value at the margin of certain characteristics, the changes being contemplated are not marginal and could even be outside the values of the characteristics upon which the estimate was derived. Moreover, the process of using these earnings equations in public sector pay determination is daunting. Finally, it should not be taken for granted that credible and stable private sector compensating wage estimates could be easily obtained.

All of this returns us to presidential decisions to ignore the BLS survey in recommending earnings increases. Some researchers suggest that this decision can be understood as a response to biases in the survey (Smith 1977; Venti 1987). These researchers note that among other biases, the BLS survey has had a high minimum employer size and consequently oversampled large, high-wage employers. Thus the survey results indicating federal earnings were below comparability results from an unrepresentative private sector sample. Johnson and Libecap (1994) have suggested that lacking economic bargaining rights, federal unions have focused on influencing the process that determines wage comparability (including the nature of the BLS survey). Others argue that the size limitation can be viewed as a refinement on comparability (Belman and Heywood 1990). The federal government (a large employer) should be concerned with comparability with similar also large private sector employers. Indeed, the issue of whether private and public sector earnings are comparable hinges in good measure on judgements of just this sort.

Descriptive Statistics on the Private and Public Sectors

As Table 1 indicates, average wages are highest at the federal level, next highest at the state and then local level, and lowest in the private sector. Moreover, pension coverage is almost twice as high (76% to 80%) in the public sector, compared to the 46% coverage in the private sector.

TABLE 1

Descriptive Statistics: Private, Federal, State, and Local Employees for 1993

	Private	Federal	State	Local
Compensation				
Wage	$11.26	$16.08	$13.40	$12.92
Pension	45.9%	80.0%	76.4%	78.6%
Demographics				
Age	37.2	42.5	40.2	41.8
Female	47.5%	44.2%	54.5%	62.0%
Black	8.5%	15.1%	11.9%	11.8%
Hispanic	7.3%	5.1%	3.6%	5.2%
Education/Experience				
Less than HS	14.4	2.8	3.8	6.1
High school	37.9	8.1	23.0	26.1
Some college	20.7	24.7	21.5	16.0
Associate arts	7.8	9.6	6.9	7.2
College degree	14.8	22.2	22.4	24.5
Graduate degree	5.4	15.8	22.4	20.1
Job Characteristics				
Weekly hours	38.4	40.7	38.1	38.0
Annual weeks	43.9	45.8	42.4	41.2
Pay by hour	63.3%	53.3%	41.1%	42.4%
Tenure (years)	6.5	11.8	8.9	9.8
Collective bargaining	12.2%	27.8%	38.4%	51.1%
Positions				
Managers	12.3	22.5	15.6	9.0
Professional	9.6	21.6	31.6	39.4
Technical	3.9	7.9	5.7	1.8
Sales	12.9	0.3	0.8	0.6
Clerical	16.6	23.1	21.5	18.7
Service	13.0	4.8	10.0	10.3
Protective	0.1	2.8	6.7	10.2
Craft	11.2	9.6	3.0	4.0
Operative	8.4	1.6	2.2	0.6
Transportation	4.5	1.6	2.4	4.3

Source: April 1993 Benefits Supplement to the CPS.

Weekly hours tend to be highest at the federal level, while at the state and local level they are similar to the private sector. Weeks worked are also highest at the federal level. Pay by the hour is more prominent in the private sector, with salaried pay being more common in the public sector, especially at the state and local levels. Relative to the 12% of employees covered by collective bargaining coverage in the private sector, such coverage is twice as high in the federal sector, three times as high in the state sector, and four times as high in local government.

Public sector workers tend to be slightly older and have considerably longer tenure than do private sector workers. The public sector tends to have higher proportions of females (at the state and especially local levels) and blacks, albeit not Hispanic workers.

The public sector also has a much higher proportion of its workforce having higher levels of education. As well, it has a higher proportion in white-collar occupations (managers, professional, technical, sales, and clerical) and especially in the higher paying managerial, professional, and technical jobs.

Clearly, wages and pension benefit coverage are higher in the public sector than in the private sector. The extent to which this simply compensates for the higher age and tenure, as well as education and occupational attainment, cannot be determined by such gross comparisons. The next section outlines the methodologies that have been used to control for the impact of these different wage determining factors so as to isolate a pure public-private sector compensation differential.

Methodologies to Isolate the Public Sector Wage Differential

Two main approaches have been used to isolate an appropriate public-private sector wage differential and thereby test for comparability. The first involves comparisons between similar "positions"; the second involves comparison between similar "people." More recently, hybrid and alternative approaches which attempt to combine the "best" elements of the dominant methodologies have appeared.

The Position Approach

The earliest methodology for testing the comparability of public sector earnings involved comparing similar "positions" within narrow and specific occupations. Accountants are compared with accountants, computer operators with computer operators (Fogel and Lewin 1974). These earnings differences can be aggregated across occupations to construct a measure of central tendency.

The limitations of this methodology are numerous. First, many occupations are unique to one or the other sector. Of the 509 three-digit occupations in the 1991 Current Population Survey (CPS) Outgoing Rotation file (ORG), approximately 150 are unique to the private or federal sector (Belman and Heywood 1995a), accounting for 29% of the federal workforce. As occupational surveys only compare positions common to both sectors, aggregate comparisons of earnings are derived from an unrepresentative sample of the sectors and should only apply to that part of the federal workforce with well-defined private sector counterparts. This problem can be even more extreme at the local level. The comparability studies based on the Wisconsin State Wage Survey result in 128 occupations that appear in the private sector and either state or local government. These account for only one-fifth of all private sector occupations and only 43% of all private sector workers (Belman, Franklin, and Heywood 1994). Thus, depending on the exact occupational categories being used, less than half a given sector might be employed in the comparability exercise. This contrasts with the more inclusive "people" methodology discussed later.

Second, judgment is required in matching positions that appear comparable but may not on close examination be identical. For instance, it is unclear whether public school teachers should be compared with teachers in the private sector. Many of the latter are in religious institutions or are teaching only a narrow cross-section of potential students. The objectives of the schools, the level of training, and workplace conditions may differ substantially by sector. Similar questions of judgment arise in comparing nurses or in comparison of executive officers of corporations to high-ranking elected officials. Restricting the analysis to identical occupations would make the earnings comparisons more accurate, but at the cost of further reducing the already limited sample of occupations covered by the surveys. In general, the position-based approach can only be accurate when the work is very similar between sectors and when sufficient comparable positions exist.

Even with 500 or 600 occupational listings, the latitude for differences in underlying tasks is enormous. For example, the Wisconsin State Wage Survey has only a single listing for attorneys. Given the variation in the duties of lawyers in both the public and the private sector, a finding of comparability need not guarantee that similar lawyers doing similar tasks are being paid equally.

Recognizing that similar job titles need not imply similar job content has resulted in comparability studies that attempt to define positions in terms of job content. The first step is a job evaluation and the assignment of points in proportion to the nature of the tasks involved. The comparability of jobs between the sectors is then determined by the points accumulated in categories such as responsibility and level of judgment. A major study of government earnings in the Netherlands proceeds along these lines (Van der Hoek 1989). Obviously, standardizing for job content could help refine which positions are genuinely comparable, but consensus on points and weighting—a critical dimension of such measurement—is elusive.[9]

Third, different weighting schemes across sectors can yield substantially different results. One might simply weight each sector by its own employment composition. The consequence will be a misleadingly large public sector advantage. The composition of public sector employees is more heavily weighted toward higher-paid white-collar occupations. Thus, even if each occupation had exactly comparable earnings, the public sector would be paid more simply because of the difference in occupational composition. This same point applies to comparisons which measure the increase in compensation. If the public sector consists disproportionately of occupations which have larger increases, the sector as a whole will appear to have a larger increase, even if each public sector occupation has had an identical increase as its private sector counterpart.[10] In the extreme, use of each sector's own employment weights can cause a sector with lower earnings within each and every occupation to have the higher average wage. Although the typical result is less extreme, this type of problem argues against use of sector specific weights.[11]

A necessary alternative is to use a scheme which holds the weights constant across sectors. One approach is to use the total weights—the sum of observations from both sectors—to compute the average. That is, the average wage in each occupation in such sector would be weighted (i.e., multiplied) by the proportion of workers in each occupation, where that proportion is based on employment in both sectors. Using the combined weights from the public and private sector, the most recent South Dakota survey found a state sector earnings disadvantage of about 8% for wages and about 3% when fringe benefits were taken into account.[12]

An alternative to averaging across sectors is to use weights from *either* the private sector or the public sector. For example, the Wisconsin State Wage Survey presents two comparisons for the average earnings difference: one based on the public sector weights and one on the private sector weights. The differences can be substantial: The Wisconsin Wage Survey shows a 2.9% local sector advantage in 1990 using the private sector occupational weights but a 16.6% advantage with local sector occupational weights (Belman, Franklin, and Heywood 1994). The difference results from asking two fundamentally different questions. The first asks how much the local sector would earn if they had the occupational composition of the private sector, while the second asks how much the private sector would earn if they had the composition of the local sector. Obviously both are interesting, but the large difference makes a summary conclusion difficult.

Fourth, and perhaps most importantly, the averaging process and the consequent crucial canceling out can create an illusion of comparability when it does not exist. This canceling out results from the tendency of the public sector to have less disperse earnings. In position-based studies this tendency is evidenced by the low-wage occupations receiving higher earnings in the public sector and the high-wage occupations receiving lower earnings in the public sector. Even without examining occupations separately, the variance of earnings in the public sector is routinely lower than that in the private sector (Belman and Heywood 1995a). Occupation by occupation, the results can be dramatic. In 1992 private sector psychologists in Wisconsin earned nearly twice what their counterparts earned in the public sector, but the private sector paid a third less than the public sector for groundskeepers. Overall, the modest 2.9% local sector advantage in Wisconsin was actually the result of one set of occupations with a nearly 25% advantage being offset by a slightly larger group of occupations with a 20% disadvantage (Belman, Franklin, and Heywood 1994)!

The aggregate measure indicating near comparability actually disguises wide swings from comparability in both directions. To the extent that labor markets for individual occupations are separate, achieving aggregate comparability as measured by the weighted mean does little to achieve the desired policy objectives. Twenty percent earnings differences in either direction violate the equity objectives for both workers and firms. Similarly, those occupations offering 20% public sector advantages can be sure to generate more than the required supply of workers, while those with similar-sized disadvantages will face difficulties in recruiting and retaining an adequate workforce. Despite this fairly obvious point, virtually the entire research literature, both that using the position or the alternative people approach, has been concerned only with broad averages.

Concentrating on the mean difference appears to be a basic misapplication of the standard of comparability. The only appeal for such aggregate comparability is that the total public wage bill will not be overly generous if weighted mean earnings are similar. The more important objectives of equity and efficiency require an alternative measure. Comparability might be better measured by an index which classifies a public sector wage which is within a band of, say, 5% above or below the wage of an equivalent private sector occupation as comparable. The proportion of the public sector workforce and the proportion of the public sector payroll which met this definition of comparability could then be tracked to identify the degree of comparability.[13] Whatever the width of the band, such an index is a better guide to comparability than the more common average earnings measure.

Here then is the bedrock issue of public sector wage setting. If comparability is accepted as the standard, can the administrative and political processes which necessarily dominate public wage setting be sufficiently responsive to recognize not just weighted means but strive for similarity of the underlying distribution across occupations? We can hardly hold out great hope when the summary measures produced by most public and academic researchers is exactly the misleading aggregation.

Illustration from the BLS

As discussed, the Bureau of Labor Statistics does an annual survey of the private sector to establish benchmarks for comparing earnings to the eighteen General Service levels within the federal government. The survey collects annual salaries for about a 100 work levels within about 30 occupations.[14] Individual work levels are then matched to the GS levels for comparison.

As illustrated in the last row of Table 2, the average federal earnings differential steadily declined from a slight advantage in 1972 to a considerable disadvantage by 1990, with the most dramatic changes occurring over the 1970s and early 1980s. This was especially pronounced in the higher occupational levels. In 1972 there was rough overall comparability in public and private pay across almost all of the occupation groups (i.e., the ratios of public to private wages were near unity). In contrast, by 1992 federal wages were only 70% of private sector wages in the highest paying three occupation groups, but were 90% of private pay in the bottom two occupations (with the balance falling in between).

While the decline from comparability suggested by these numbers is large, they likely understate the actual decline. Responding to academic and government researchers who criticized the BLS comparability survey for a sample design that presents unrealistically high private sector

TABLE 2

Federal GS (White Collar) Earnings as a Share of That in the Private Sector

GS Level	1972	1978	1983	1987	1990
GS-1	1.04	.91	.86	.88	.92
GS-2	.99	.90	.87	.85	.88
GS-3	1.02	.86	.77	.80	.81
GS-4	1.02	.92	.82	.81	.83
GS-6	1.12	.86	.76	.77	.77
GS-7	1.05	.90	.80	.77	.76
GS-9	1.03	.90	.80	.79	.78
GS-11	.97	.90	.81	.78	.76
GS-12	1.00	.90	.79	.78	.75
GS-13	1.02	.90	.78	.72	.70
GS-14	1.04	.89	.76	.70	.67
GS-15	1.07	.90	.75	.73	.71
All GS	1.03	.90	.80	.78	.78

Source: The first three columns are taken from Freeman (1987:190) and the remainder are tabulated from U.S. Bureau of Labor Statistics. Following Freeman, GS levels 5 and 8 were excluded in order to preserve complete data for each year.

estimates, the bureau made a number of changes which have reduced the apparent wage disadvantage of federal employees (Smith 1977, 1982; U.S. GAO 1973). One change has been the use of a smaller and smaller minimum establishment size. Historically, the minimum ranged from 100 to 250 depending on the industry. In 1986 that minimum was set at 50 regardless of industry and was lowered still further to 20 workers in 1987. Starting in 1987, the survey design was broadened to include service industries that had been for the most part excluded (Morton 1987). By 1990 further expansion incorporated additional industries in agriculture, forestries, fisheries, mining, and construction. Thus the 1989–90 rotation included all industries except "farms and households."[15] The 1990 survey explicitly excluded any overtime premiums, performance or attendance bonuses, negotiated lump sum transfers, and profit-sharing forms of compensation.

The cumulative effect of these changes has been to understate the decline in federal earnings relative to the private sector. For example, the expansion of the survey to smaller establishments and into the service sector would lower the measure of the average private sector wage. The ratio of federal to private sector wages would have been lower if the private sector sample would have continued to be made up of the higher paying, larger firms not in the service sector. Likewise, exclusion of alternative wage payments from the 1990 survey—payments which are more common in the private sector and which serve as partial substitutes for straight-time earnings—may also cause an artificial increase of the ratio of federal to private earnings in that year. In essence, the fall in the ratio reported in Table 2 would have been larger had the measure of private sector wages not been expanded to include smaller firms and the service sector in the private sector comparison group or excluded benefits more common in the private sector. As such, the downward trend in Table 2 is a conservative estimate of the real trend in the ratio of federal to private sector pay. Whether comparability has been more closely attained by 1990 is a more difficult question and depends upon such factors as whether the lower federal pay is offset by higher fringe benefits and nonmonetary compensation.

By 1990 the unfavorable pay gap was recognized by the Congress and President. Despite the elaborate comparability machinery, the Office of Personnel Management admitted that the current pay system was not market sensitive (Murawski 1990). There was concern in Congress that the GS system was in jeopardy. The FBI claimed to have such trouble hiring and retaining officers, especially in large cities, that they asked for a separate pay schedule; the press reported pharmacists in the Veterans Administration remained only until eligible for positions in the private sector (Murawski 1990). There was concern that the determination of pay within each agency might revert to its appropriate congressional committee.

In an attempt to address these problems, President Bush signed the Federal Employees Pay Comparability Act of 1990. This law moved comparability to a local level and provided for "locality pay" intended to reflect the private sector wage structures in different areas of the country. The national and longstanding survey of white-collar pay was merged into the Area Wage Surveys to create the Occupational Compensation Survey. While some see this as the latest movement toward improving comparability, others contend that the new act will do little to remove the problems of a national pay system, as locality differentials can increase but will not lower wages (Johnson and Liebcap 1994). Whether such a limitation is sensible depends on the accuracy of the BLS surveys and information from other approaches, to which we now turn.

The Human Capital or People Approach

The human capital model of earnings emerged in full strength in the 1960s and 1970s. This model provides the primary alternative for testing comparability and is often summarized as the "people" approach. The notion is that although tasks might differ within and between sectors, there exists a modest set of variables that characterize the earnings potential of each worker. These variables reflect the investments that workers have made in productivity augmenting skills that generate economic returns to that investment. Thus the methodology of the people approach is to account for differences in the productivity of individual workers and examine if a sectoral difference in earnings exists after this accounting.

The first generation of human-capital-based comparability studies used a parsimonious set of explanatory variables in log wage regressions estimated separately for the public and private sectors. The estimated regression coefficients are a measure of the economic return to the human capital variables. Typically, researchers estimated separate regressions for the federal, state, and local sectors to generate an estimated wage differential for each level of government. Explanatory variables normally included years of education, a measure of actual or potential years of work experience, region of the country, veteran status, and some accounting for race and gender. Broad occupational controls were also included, highlighting that even the first people-based studies did not abandon the role of position.

The mechanics of estimating the differential involves measuring the unexplained residual from the separate regressions. The estimated coefficients from each sector are used to estimate the expected wage of workers from the other sector. This traditional Oaxaca (1973) decomposition provides two measures of the unexplained residual: (1) the difference between the mean public wage and what workers with mean public sector characteristics would earn in the private sector (public base), and (2) the difference between what workers with mean private sector characteristics would earn in the public sector and the mean private wage (private base). Smith (1977) contends the true differential lies somewhere in between, and the reader will note that these bases are simply extremes which hold the composition of wage determining characteristics constant. Thus this technique is directly analogous to using either the private or public sector occupational weights in the position-based studies. There also exists an intermediate differential that uses the mean characteristics from the public and private sector to calculate the public wage from the public equation and the private wage from the private equation.

From a theoretical point of view the accuracy of the estimated differential is only as good as the set of controls. The differential is simply the unexplained portion of the gross difference in earnings. It remains possible to exclude a variable that properly helps explain the difference or to include a variable that improperly helps explain the difference. The only tests for determining whether an explanatory variable should be included is whether it helps determine earnings and whether it is an appropriate factor on which to standardize earnings. Thus the decision to include regional variables would follow from the recognition that earnings for similarly qualified workers differ across regions of the country, that regional patterns of employment differ by sector, and that comparability should hold constant these differences. One element of the debate in the second generation of studies is exactly what should be held constant.

In the first generation of studies, the largest public sector wage differential is found at the federal level. The state differential is positive but small, and typically, the local differential is negative. Venti (1987:147) summarized the early studies suggesting that the typical estimate "indicates federal workers may be 'overpaid' relative to their private sector counterparts by as much as 15% to 20%." This large positive differential attracted the most interest, and many researchers limited their attention to the federal government (Venti 1987; Kruger 1988; Moulton 1990).

Much of the earlier work was affected by constraints on the data. In some cases the level of government had to be constructed from the industry codes. Distinct level of government codes exist only for workers in the "public administration" industry. Other public sector workers were classified in industries shared with the private sector, and their level of government was not reported. Most researchers restricted their analysis to employees in public administration excluding the majority of public employees (Quinn 1979; Smith 1976b, 1981, 1983).

Unfortunately, there exist systematic differences between the public administrators and the excluded public workers in the 1970s. The occupational composition of the two public groups differs dramatically with the public administrators tending to be lawyers, accountants, protective workers, and elected officials, and the remaining public workers being teachers, social workers, and nonprofessionals. Crucially, the vast majority of public administrators are employed in occupations that lacked private sector counterparts (Belman and Heywood 1988). Thus without explicit recognition, many of the early studies applied the people methodology on that portion of the public sector for which the position methodology provided the least guidance.

The errors from using only the public administrators to measure earnings differentials by level of government is quite large. Using a typical specification, Belman and Heywood (1988) found the public sector wage advantage over the private sector to be 4.2% for public administrators, negative 7.7% for employees outside of public administration, and zero for the aggregation of these two groups. Public administrators are then not representative of the entire public sector, tending to have larger earnings differentials. Further, the conclusion of the first generation studies—that the federal differential was between 15% and 20%—seems surely wrong with the actual differential likely smaller, by how much is unknown.

Hybrid Studies

The realization that public administrators might differ from nonadministrators stands as just one of many insights that helped create a series of second generation hybrid studies which incorporate controls for position, such as detailed occupation, in addition to human capital controls. Moulton (1990) found that after accounting for detailed positions (three-digit Population Occupation Codes) and detailed geographic location, the federal premium in traditional earnings equations fell to zero. Similarly, Belman and Heywood (1995a) found that the federal premium fell by half after excluding individuals in three-digit occupations unique to either sector. This highlights: (1) that much of the federal public sector wage advantage found in previous studies is attributable to the disproportionate distribution of federal employees in high-wage occupations, and (2) the need to explicitly control for differences in the distribution of occupations.

Belman and Heywood (1990) and Moore and Raisian (1991) also found that the federal premium was sensitive to the inclusion of employer size variables. These variables are important earnings determinants in the private sector, and since most governments qualify as large employers, including such variables causes the estimated premium to fall. Thus accounting for size causes the federal male premium to decline from 10.4% to 3.8% (Belman and Heywood 1990). Estimation of the differential by firm size finds that male federal employees earn 25% more than men employed in private sector firms with less than 25 employees, the same as those employed in firms with between 100 and 999 employees, and less than those employed in private firms of 1,000 or more. While controlling for firm size reduces or eliminates the federal public sector wage advantage, it does not affect the differential of state employees, whose premium remains positive but small, and it reduces the estimated wage disadvantage of local government workers (Brown and Medoff 1988).

The appropriateness of including firm size among the explanatory variables is not universally agreed upon. Linneman and Wachter (1990) argue that the Oaxaca decomposition misapplies comparability by holding constant certain wage related job attributes such as unionization and firm size that tend to be higher in the public sector. In essence, their argument implies that the pure public sector wage premium should include that portion of the wage differential that reflects the increased unionization and large firm size of the public sector. Implicitly, Linneman and Wachter argue that the distribution of job attributes in the private sector is "correct." To the extent that those attributes follow from a competitive market, one might sympathize with this view. Yet it is unlikely that given the different objectives and occupations of the public sector, the exact private sector distribution of job attributes would, indeed should, be duplicated. If that is true, it also seems true that replicating the return for the job attributes would be demanded by comparability. The federal government is by necessity a very large employer, but the approach of Linneman and Wachter argues that its earnings should be compared to a weighted average of the private sector distribution of firm sizes. Such a number has little claim to comparability if workers in the federal sector have working conditions similar to those in large private sector firms.[16]

In addition, Belman and Heywood (1993) have found that, even accepting the logic of Linneman and Wachter, the actual distribution of private employees across firm size understates the proportion of federal employees who would be employed in large firms in the private sector. The characteristics of federal employees make them more likely to be employed in larger firms than the average private employee. After correcting for this underweighting, the researchers found a 5.8% wage advantage for federal employees. This compares with the 3.8% advantage found holding firm size constant and the 10.2% result generated by Linneman and Wachter's methodology.

Still other approaches are hybrid in nature because of the nature of the underlying data. In a study of Houston metropolitan transit workers, Moore and Newman (1991) estimate earnings regressions across 133 occupations in the Houston area using each occupation's average wage as the dependent variable.[17] The explanatory variables include measures of education, age, and demographics by occupation. The expected wage of transit workers is estimated by placing the average characteristics of transit workers in the earnings equation. The public wage differential was measured by the difference between the actual and expected transit wage. This mimics the people approach by standardizing for human capital and demographics. It mimics the position approach by using the occupation as the unit of observation and a scheme which weights each occupation equally (regardless of the number of workers in the occupation).

The hybrid approaches have emphasized that aggregate government wage differentials conceal more diverse patterns. At the federal level, the distinction between public administrators and other workers proved important. Similarly, the federal differential varies by region and urban area (Moulton 1990). At lower levels of government, distinguishing between jurisdictions is important. Typical estimates of the state and local differentials in the U.S. are derived without regard to differences between state and local governments. This can produce a misleading average of the sort mentioned when discussing position-based studies. That in the aggregate, state workers earnings are comparable to workers in the private sector means little if it results from workers in some states earning too much while those in others earn too little.

Evidence of interstate differences in the public wage differential is reported by Belman and Heywood (1995b). Within the states examined (mostly in the Midwest), the state government wage differential ranged from 3% to -2%. The local government differential ranged from 3% to -10%. While a wider set of states might produce greater variance in the estimates, these ranges emphasize that the typical nationwide estimates hide considerable variation by state.

Another issue mentioned in the section on wage standards is the treatment of market distortions, particularly the wage consequences of race and gender discrimination. This has been a central issue in 1984 and 1991 postal interest arbitrations—one of the few instances in which regression techniques have figured in wage-setting cases. Using a single equation for all full-time employees for 1978, Perfoff and Wachter (1984) found that postal employees earned 21% more than otherwise comparable private sector employees. Asher and Popkin (1984) estimated a similar single equation model with 1979 data but allowed for differences across industries by gender and race. They find that white men in postal employment are paid comparably to white men in private employment. However, although women and minorities in the postal service were paid the same as comparable white males (in the postal service), these two groups were paid substantially less than white men in the private sector. This raises as a theoretical issue whether the postal service should pay the average private sector wage for comparable employees and thereby incorporate any discrimination which occurs in the private sector, or whether it should be paying the comparable wage calculated for the group which does not suffer discrimination. As a practical matter, the postal service is legally restricted from reproducing the discriminatory differentials which exist in the private sector.[18]

All of these hybrid approaches attempt to introduce earnings determinants not present in the first generation of people-based studies, yet they share many of the limitations of earlier studies. First, estimating wage differentials by whatever method continues to ignore potential differences in fringe benefits. Second, they assume that the characteristics of employees are not related to the wage differential being estimated. It is possible that if the public sector paid a wage above that needed to recruit an adequate labor supply, this wage would attract employees with superior productivity and characteristics. Regression estimates would find, conditional on characteristics, workers in the governmental sector were being paid appropriately and that there was no governmental differential. Still, the characteristics of the governmental sector would be more than required for the work. Given the limited number and precision of productivity related variables, it is unclear whether this issue can be addressed statistically.[19]

Third, while the hybrid approach has given increasing attention to the dimension of positions within the human capital approach, little has been done to allow for compensating differences. Thus public sector jobs in protective services may expose workers to risk of injury or death at rates different than in the private sector. Alternatively, public sector job conditions and security may be more favorable than they are other jobs. Again, little serious effort has been made to account for such potential differences, their influence on earnings and, therefore, on the public wage differential.

Fourth, it is extremely difficult to standardize for differences in worker effort between the public and private sector, even in the few studies which have data incorporating effort measures. This inability to control for effort can be particularly important if part of the public sector wage premium is an efficiency wage payment designed to encourage effort among public employees (Kruger 1988). In short, attempts to test comparability with human-capital-based earnings equations remains an imperfect art.

Issues of Self-Selection

Despite the routine application of the methodology based on the Oaxaca decomposition, it is well recognized to be incomplete. It assumes that an individual taken from one sector and placed in the other would be paid according to the wage structure of the other sector. Yet, workers may self-select into the sector where they are most suited, based on unobserved characteristics not included in the regression analysis. Consequently, each sector could consist of workers who would be disadvantaged by relocation to the other sector regardless of the estimated wage differential. Estimated parameters of the earnings equation in each sector are indeterminantly biased when such sample selection issues are left unaddressed.

Blank (1985) found that measured characteristics influence the distribution of workers between the public and private sector. The public sector was more likely to be "chosen" by women and minorities, by those with greater education, and by those with greater experience. Belman and Heywood (1989) estimated a public-private selection model which yields similar results and also reveals those with a larger predicted government wage differential are more likely to choose the public sector. Gyourko and Tracy (1988) start with a more complex choice model in which workers select across four labor markets—private nonunion, private union, public nonunion, and public union. Developing selection variables from the four-way logistic model, they proceed to estimate public wage differentials. Despite the fact that important selection effects emerge, interpretation of the estimated differentials yields few new insights.

Unfortunately, there is no way to tell if the selection effects are capturing different returns to unmeasured variables or different levels of those unmeasured variables. The former would argue that the public wage differential should be based on the sample-selected estimated wage equations but should exclude the selection term and its coefficient. The latter would argue for inclusion of the selection term and its coefficient in creating the differential. The substantial difference between the differentials that emerge from these assumptions limits the usefulness of the approach. All that Gyourko and Tracy can say is that, to the extent that selection effects account for different returns by sector to unmeasured variables, the traditional Oaxaca estimates of the wage differential are *too small*. Despite this conclusion from the work of Gyourko and Tracy, Moulton (1990) has replicated their approach with more recent data and suggests the actual differentials, both those including and ignoring the selection terms, have decreased over time.

New People-based and Hybrid Estimates

The issues of the previous section may best be understood through an illustration. In this section we provide new estimates of comparability reflecting the spirit of the contemporary literature. A variety of comparisons are made. First, for the federal workers, the difference in results between the position- and people-based approaches will be highlighted (Tables 2 and 3). Second, the difference across levels of government (federal, postal, state, and local) will be highlighted together with any differences across time (Table 3). Finally, the role of adding controls as we move toward a hybrid estimation will be explored (Table 3).

Our data come from the May 1979, 1983, 1988, and April 1993 CPS. The hybrid estimations identify factors such as firm and establishment size and tenure with the current employer as important determinants of the wage; these variables are only available from the supplemental questions for these months and years. Recognizing the profound differences in earning structures across gender, the public/private differentials and the underlying equations are estimated separately by gender.

We begin by estimating a consistent set of earnings equations for each gender and year. One problem is that the education question was changed in 1992 from identifying highest grade completed to giving only broad categorical responses to years of education but detailed information on the diplomas and degrees completed. We are forced to live with this difference in the variable and the resulting estimation. The level of government is captured by one of four dummy variables; the coefficients on these variables are used to derive the earnings differential. All equations include controls for education, age and age squared, four regional dummy variables, marital status, union membership, race, residency in an urban area, part-time employment status, and a set of one-digit occupational controls.[20] This specification is representative of those of the initial "human capital" research.

The most parsimonious estimation includes only those controls mentioned in the previous paragraph, and the resulting differentials are summarized in the first panel of Table 3. Estimates for men (shown on the left side of the table) reveal that for men, only the federal differential is consistently significant and positive between 1979 and 1993. The postal differential is significant only in 1979, when it is positive. At the state level, the differential is significantly negative in 1979 and 1988, but zero in the other two years. The sign of the local differential is consistently negative and significantly so in three of the four years. None of the four male differentials has a secular trend, although both the state and local differential is closer to zero in 1983 than either the earlier or later years. The portrait of the federal differential painted by the people approach contrasts sharply with that of the BLS surveys (Table 2). Not only is the

TABLE 3
Public/Private Wage Differentials

	MEN				WOMEN			
	1979	1983	1988	1993	1979	1983	1988	1993
Basic Human Capital								
Postal	8.1°°	1.9	3.1	6.6	42.7°°°	33.6°°°	21.1°°°	30.9°°°
Federal	13.7°°°	13.4°°°	8.7°°°	11.4°°°	18.0°°°	11.1°°°	7.9°°°	14.6°°°
State	-6.2°°°	1.4	-4.6°°°	0.0	3.7°°	4.0°	1.3	-1.3
Local	-12.1°°°	-4.5°°°	-5.4°	-1.1	-3.2°°°	-4.7°°°	-4.3°°°	-6.6°°°
Add Controls for Service Occupations								
Postal	8.1°°°	2.1	-2.2	6.8°	42.5°°°	33.8°°°	21.8°°°	30.8°°°
Federal	13.5°°°	13.1°°°	8.0°°°	12.9°°°	15.2°°°	10.7°°°	7.1°°°	14.0°°°
State	-6.6°°°	0.0	-6.8°°°	-2.5	3.5°°	3.7°°	8.0	-2.5°
Local	-13.1°°°	-6.8°°°	-8.2°°°	-4.5°°°	-3.6°°°	-5.4°°°	-5.0°°°	-8.0°°°
Job Tenure								
Postal	5.9°	3.1	-5.0	4.4	42.8°°°	35.3°°°	27.1°°°	31.0°°°
Federal	14.1°°°	10.8°°°	6.8°°°	7.8°°°	17.5°°°	6.6°°	5.8°°	11.7°°°
State	-8.3°°°	-1.4	-7.0°°°	-4.0°	3.9°°	3.1	-4.8	9.2°°
Local	-13.5°°°	-7.6°°°	-9.5°°°	-6.5°°°	-4.7°°	-6.4°°°	2.7	-9.4°°°
Firm & Establishment Size								
Postal	5.8	5.1	1.3	6.0	33.7°°°	34.2°°°	28.9°°°	28.9°°°
Federal	11.3°°°	5.0°°	2.1	3.9	12.8°°°	2.2	2.6	9.0°°°
State	-12.1°°°	-4.8°°	-10.3°°°	-7.2°°°	1.1	2.7	-3.7°°	-7.3°°°
Local	-14.0°°°	-5.1°°°	-9.4°°°	-5.7°°°	-4.5°°°	-5.6°°°	-5.3°°°	-8.7°°°

°°°-significant in a 1% two tailed 1% test; °°-significant in a 5% two tailed test; °-significant in a 10% two tailed test people-based differential positive against the negative finding of the survey, but it is relatively constant over time, contrasting with the decline indicated by the survey.

These results may be contrasted with the parallel findings for women reported on the right side of the first panel. Here the postal differential is very large and routinely positive. The federal differential is also positive and shows the same pattern as that for men, declining over the 1980s but rebounding in 1993. The state differential for women is positive and significant in the two earlier years. The local differential is negative and significant in three of the four years. Over the period under consideration, women fare better relative to their private sector counterparts than men in all but the local sector.

To illustrate how sensitive the people-based estimates are to controls for position, we modify the basic human capital model by including controls for household service and protective service employees. The controls capture substantial differences in job conditions within service occupations. Protective service workers are exposed to risks not generally experienced in other occupations, while household worker jobs are very different than those of "typical" employees. While the postal and federal differentials are substantially unchanged by this modest addition, it reduces all of the male state and local differentials and seven of the eight female state and local differentials. Thus as the second panel of Table 2 shows, the public sector wage *disadvantage* for men at the local level increased from 1 to 3.4 percentage points, depending on the year. A parallel pattern exists for women.

Estimates adding a control for job tenure to those for protective and household services are reported in the third panel of Table 3. Job tenure can capture important job-specific human capital but was not typically included in the early people-based estimates. Further, controlling for job tenure may help standardize for differences in positions as tenure may reflect responses to work requirements and conditions.[21] Inclusion of tenure causes 14 of the 16 male differentials to fall, becoming either smaller or more negative. The state and local differentials are either not significant or are significantly less than zero. The effect of job tenure on women's estimates is less easily summarized. The postal service differential has not changed much, the federal differential generally declines, and the state and local government differential generally become statistically insignificant.

The fourth panel incorporates controls for establishment and firm size. As mentioned earlier, such measures have been found to influence private sector earnings, and Brown and Medoff (1988) have confirmed such size effects among state and local workers. The estimates for men indicate that the state and local disadvantages increase once again, with all eight estimates significantly negative and with the state disadvantage now as large or larger than the local disadvantage. The 1988 and 1993 results corroborate those of Belman and Heywood (1990), who argued that inclusion of firm and establishment size cause the positive federal differential to vanish. The results for women are similar with the federal differential moderating in all estimates and losing significance in two estimates. Unlike for men, the postal coefficient remains large and significant.

The estimates in Table 3 demonstrate how sensitive conclusions from human-capital-based regressions are to the inclusion of a few key variables. The initial estimates for men suggested a large positive wage premium for employment in the federal government, no effect or a modest negative effect for employment in the state sector, and a negative effect for employment in the local sector that had vanished by 1993. With inclusion of additional controls, these conclusions change dramatically. There now appears to have been a large positive earnings effect for federal employees that was cut in half by 1983 and was virtually absent in the last two estimates. This pattern conforms with the deteriorating earnings status found in the BLS surveys. Employment in both the state and local government now appear associated with large negative earnings effects that do not reflect any secular pattern.

To further isolate position-based differences within the human capital methodology, we estimate the original human capital model from the first panel of Table 3 separately for three broad occupational groups: white collar, blue collar, and service.[22] The results support our fundamental conclusions about the standard of comparability; applying it at a mean sectoral level generates substantial misunderstanding. As shown in Table 4, we find that the differentials estimated for blue-collar and white-collar workers are generally below those estimated for the sample as a whole, while those estimated for service workers are greater than those estimated for the sample as a whole. Indeed, this pattern is so strong that for state and local workers the first two differentials are usually negative and statistically significant, while the latter differential is usually positive and statistically significant. This finding highlights the pitfalls of aggregate measures of comparability.[23] The typical human capital measure indicates comparability in both 1983 and 1993 for state workers and in 1993 for local workers. Using the same estimating equation, but estimating it separately for the three broad occupational

TABLE 4
Public-Private Wage Differentials by Occupation

	1979	1983	1988	1993
MEN:				
White Collar				
Postal	11.2°°°	-2.5	2.9	14.2°°°
Federal	11.4°°°	10.7°°°	7.0°°	12.0°°°
State	-8.9°°°	-4.0°	-9.3°°°	-6.7°°
Local	-16.4°°°	-11.3°°°	-9.9°°°	-11.9°°°
Blue Collar				
Postal	4.4	-12.2	6.2	-1.6
Federal	8.0°°	7.4°	10.6°°°	12.5°°
State	-9.5°°°	-8.1	-8.5°°	-6.0
Local	-11.6°°°	-13.3°°°	-10.2°°°	0.1
Service				
Postal	-23.5	33.0	13.4	26.8
Federal	27.4°°°	22.7°°	12.6	34.0°°°
State	22.3°°°	29.6°°°	14.5°°°	29.8°°°
Local	9.7°°°	18.9°°°	15.6°°°	26.6°°°
WOMEN:				
White Collar				
Postal	45.8°°°	64.3°	25.2°°°	30.2°°°
Federal	15.5°°°	13.9°°°	5.6°°	14.4°°°
State	1.0	3.9	1.9	-5.4°°
Local	-6.1°°°	-2.5	-7.3°°°	-11.2°°°
Blue Collar				
Postal	20.3	41.0	224.3°°	—
Federal	9.7	28.3	2.9	-8.2
State	5.5	-4.0	5.3	-16.2
Local	5.6	-6.3	8.3	5.9
Service				
Postal	7.0	—	—	—
Federal	39.7°°°	27.9°°	22.5°°	27.8°°
State	13.9°°°	22.6°°°	17.7°°°	8.6
Local	4.9°°	11.2°°°	8.8	6.9

°°° - significant in a 1% two tailed test; °° - significant in a 5% two tailed test; ° - significant in a 10% two tailed test

groups, demonstrates that those measures of comparability hide large negative differentials for white- and blue-collar employees and large positive differentials for service employees. Despite the comparability indicated by aggregate measures, no part of the governmental workforce comes close to actual comparability.[24]

Clearly then, a wide range of estimates of public/private differentials emerge from alternative specifications. While each specification may have its rationale and merits, there is a need to choose. Here, we suggest that the original emphasis on positions remains important for policy purposes. The occupation-specific results reported in Table 4 provide our preferred starting place. Indeed, these might be improved through inclusion of controls for occupation and further occupational disaggregation. Policy decisions to move the entire public earnings distribution up or down, based on aggregate differentials across all workers, make little sense. The proper application of comparability should be at as disaggregate a level as possible.

Conclusions

The bulk of this chapter has been concerned with the standard of comparability. As a concept, it has survived as the foundation of government compensation because of its perceived fairness to workers in both sectors and to private sector firms. The ability to attract appropriate quantities and qualities of workers remains an important efficiency objective, but we note that achieving this objective requires establishing employment requirements *ex ante*. Further, the notion of replicating the more general efficiency of the private labor market depends on the existence of such efficiency, otherwise the distortions of the private market are simply reproduced by comparability. In addition to these conceptual issues, there is also the empirical issue of the extent to which public sector wages are comparable to those in the private sector.

Limitations on data have restricted research to examining wage comparability, even though wages are only a portion of the total compensation package. Nevertheless, several conclusions emerge. First, comparability must ultimately be a disaggregated concept to retain either the virtues of fairness or efficiency. Aggregate measures, which indicate average comparability, achieve little if few individuals are close to the average and most receive wages substantially above or below what they would earn in the private sector. Results from both state wage surveys and human capital regressions give reason for concern with the aggregation issue. Both procedures indicate that it is easy to find large groups earning more than the private sector and large groups earning less than the private sector. This follows from the often innocuous claim that governmental earnings distributions are less disperse. The claim is true but not innocuous. It implies that even if aggregate comparability is achieved, those at the upper end of the distribution will do better in the private sector, while those at the lower end of the distribution will do better in the public sector. The second result we highlight is the profound difference between the measures of comparability that emerge from the position-based studies and the people-based studies. These differences are not just a function of the methodologies themselves. For instance, the Wisconsin State Wage Survey indicates substantial overpayment not shown in traditional earnings equations. On the other hand, the BLS survey indicates substantial underpayment of federal workers when the human-capital-based studies indicate overpayment. Much of the difference reflects the necessarily different universe of workers compared by two approaches. Position approaches exclude workers unique to either the public or private sector; people-based approaches include such workers. We have indicated that constraining the people approach to a set of similar occupations brings the estimated differentials closer together.

Third, we highlight that more recent hybrid people-based approaches have increasingly introduced controls for aspects of position such as finer occupational controls and measures of firm and establishment size. Introduction of these controls causes the measured aggregate public-private differential to move closer to zero at the federal level and become more negative for the state and local differentials.

While our focus has been on the comparability of wages, we have made clear that this dimension is too limited for drawing ultimate conclusions. Fringe benefits and differences in the nature of work may differ in cost and/or in value. The standard of comparability is largely silent on whether cost or value is the appropriate standard of comparison. Making the cost of fringe benefits comparable would be appropriate if equity with private sector employers is the paramount issue. The value of comparable fringe benefits would be appropriate if equity with private sector workers is the paramount issue.

Ultimately, comparability remains a sensible but illusive goal. Our judgment is that aggregate differentials at the federal level are relatively small and that state and local differentials are already negative (especially so at the local level). Yet, such conclusions hide a wealth of detail, and it is this detail that must influence policy. We emphasize that earnings compression is fundamentally at odds with comparability, and that as a consequence, aggregate differentials provide only very limited evidence on comparability. We suggest that responding to compression may well provide the most fruitful avenue for policy designed to achieve true comparability.

Acknowledgments

The authors thank Morley Gunderson and Douglas Hyatt for their comments and careful editorial work.

Endnotes

[1] The measurement of comparability not stipulated in the postal statute has been a source of conflict. The postal unions favor comparisons to UPS and Federal Express, while the postal service favors application of the human capital methodology.

[2] Starting in 1987, the BLS began surveying service-producing industries in odd years and goods-producing industries in even years. In 1989 the survey name was changed from the National Survey of Professional, Administrative, Technical, and Clerical Pay to the Survey of White-Collar Pay. Following the Federal Employees Pay Comparability Act of 1990, that later survey was integrated with the Area Wage Surveys.

[3] For more on the setting of pay in the federal sector, see Hartman (1983) and Ehrenberg and Schwartz (1986).

[4] See *The Staff Report of the President's Panel on Federal Compensation* (January 1976), pp. 25–7.

[5] Venti (1987:150) quotes the relevant portion of the 1962 act without comment on the near absence of an efficiency rationale. Some might claim that the second rationale suggests economic efficiency, but surely the appeal is not direct.

[6] This comparison is particularly prominent in the studies of the postal service. Perloff and Wachter (1984) present a large positive earnings differential for postal workers which Asher and Popkin (1984) claims is almost entirely a result of private sector discrimination against women.

[7] This notion of the model employer may be implicit in prevailing wage legislation. Amendments to the Service Contract Act in 1972 and 1976 added explicit language requiring prevailing wage determination to give "due consideration" to federal wage levels for comparable jobs. Congressional testimony makes clear that such language was designed to close existing gaps between the wages *and fringes* of those working for the government and those working on contract to the government. Such a strategy might make sense if the government is "protecting" its role as a model employer (see Goldfarb and Heywood 1982).

[8] Financial problems caused the District of Columbia to reduce the wages of police by 4% in 1994. Other jurisdictions responded by successfully recruiting away trained police officers from the District.

[9] Similar issues arise in comparable worth comparisons between male- and female-dominated jobs, although the issues are less complex because they are restricted to comparison within the same organization.

[10] Cox and Bruneli (1992) compute exactly these sort of aggregate increases in compensation without adjusting for the different occupational compositions of the public and private sectors. Thus they cannot distinguish between an increase in public compensation beyond comparability and an increase which merely paralleled that of comparable employees in the private sector.

[11] The extreme result can occur if the occupations with greater earnings have low weights in one sector and those with lower earnings have low weights in the other sector. This perverse outcome is known as Simpson's paradox (Thorton and Innes 1985; Samuels 1993).

[12] The authors thank Dave Hanson at the Personnel Office of the South Dakota Board of Regents for this and other helpful information.

[13] The average absolute value of deviations from comparability represents a less arbitrary measure. Using this measure, the Wisconsin data would produce a comparability measure between 20% and 25% rather than 2.9%.

[14] The exact work levels and occupations have varied over time.

[15] Starting in late 1980s, the survey was divided with goods-producing industries surveyed in even years and service-producing industries in odd years. Aggregates for all occupations were calculated each year through the use of an employment cost index.

[16] In addition, distinct treatment of job attributes and individual attributes rests on the assumption that job attributes are unrelated to productivity while individual attributes are. It is at odds with a growing literature which finds that wage differences associated with job attributes such as industry, firm size, and establishment size are associated with systematic differences in productivity (see Belman and Groshen [1996] for a review of the firm and establishment size literature).

[17] As occupations are separated by gender, there are 266 observations.

[18] Both studies use the postal service as the base of measure and incorporate dummy variables for major industry to industry specific wage effects. The industry dummies are averaged either with (Perloff and Wachter) or without (Asher and Popkin) employment weights, and these averages are used to estimate the wage advantage of the postal service. Our own research indicates that use of weighted industry dummies in place of a postal dummy variable substantially increases the apparent wage advantage of postal employees. The methodologies used by the studies also diverge from the conventional research in the use of specifications which impose constraints on certain coefficients across gender and race.

[19] For one attempt to investigate this issue by comparing the workforce characteristics of different states, see Belman and Heywood (1995b).

[20] Earnings equations using the CPS often generate a measure of potential experience that uses age minus education minus five. The lack of a continuous education variable makes this measure difficult to generate for 1993. To maintain as much consistency as possible, we simply use age itself.

[21] Obviously, one of those conditions is the compensation itself, and so longer tenure by government employees has often been taken as caused by higher compensation. On the other hand, as Ippolito (1987) points out, public earnings may come disproportionately late in work life and in retirement. This deferred compensation could be a source of greater tenure without greater total lifetime earnings.

[22] White-collar employees include managers and administrators, professionals, technical, sales, and administrative support occupations. Blue collar includes craft, operatives, transportation operatives, and laborers. Service employees are those in household, protective, food, and personal service categories of the census occupation codes.

[23] For more on alternative measures of comparability, see Belman and Heywood (1996).

[24] Further disaggregation of occupations can affect the pattern of wage differentials found by human capital approaches. For example, an estimate with 1993 data limited to male clerical employees indicates no significant differences in pay for postal, state, and local employees and approximately an 18% advantage for federal employees. Interestingly, postal workers account for 16% of all male clerical employees.

References

Asher, M., and J. Popkin. 1984. "The Effect of Gender and Race Differentials on Public-Private Wage Comparisons: A Study of Postal Workers." *Industrial and Labor Relations Review*, Vol. 38, no. 1 (October), pp. 16–25.

Belman, D., and E. Groshen. Forthcoming. "Is Small Beautiful for Employees?" *Economic Policy Institute Working Paper*.

Belman, D., and J. Heywood. 1988. "Public Wage Differentials and the Public Administration 'Industry.'" *Industrial Relations*, Vol. 27 (Fall), pp. 385–93.

_____. 1989. "Government Wage Differentials: A Sample Selection Approach." *Applied Economics*, Vol. 21 (April), pp. 427–38.

_____. 1990. "The Effect of Establishment and Firm Size on Public Wage Differentials." *Public Finance Quarterly*, Vol. 18 (April), pp. 221–35.

_____. 1993. "Job Attributes and Federal Wage Differentials." *Industrial Relations*, Vol. 32 (Winter), pp. 148–57.

_____. 1995a. "Public Wage Differentials and the Treatment of Occupation." Working Paper. University of Wisconsin-Milwaukee.

_____. 1995b. "State and Local Government Wage Differentials: An Intrastate Analysis." *Journal of Labor Research*, Vol. 16 (Spring), pp. 186–201.

_____. 1996. "Public Sector Wages: Alternative Measures of Comparability." Working Paper, University of Wisconsin-Milwaukee.

Belman, D., T. Franklin, and J. Heywood. 1994. "Comparing Public and Private Earnings Using State Wage Surveys." *Journal of Economic and Social Measurement*, Vol. 20 (May), pp. 79-94.

Blank, R. 1985. "An Analysis of Workers' Choice between Employment in the Public and Private Sectors." *Industrial and Labor Relations Review*, Vol. 38 (January), pp. 211–24.

Bloom, D., and R. Freeman. 1992. "The Fall of Private Pension Coverage in the United States." *American Economic Review*, Vol. 82, no. 2 (May).

Brown, C., and J. Medoff. 1988. "Employer Size, Pay and the Ability to Pay in the Public Sector." In R. Freeman and C. Ichniowski, eds., *When Public Sector Workers Unionize*. Chicago: University of Chicago Press.

Cox, W., and S.A. Brunelli. 1992. "America's Protected Class: Why Excess Public Employee Compensation Is Bankrupting States." *The State Factor*, Vol. 18, no. 3 (February), American Legislative Exchange Council.

Ehrenberg, R., and J. Schwartz. 1986. "Public Sector Labor Markets." In O. Ashenfelter and R. Layard, eds., *The Handbook of Labor Economics*, Vol. 2. Amsterdam: North-Holland.

Elliot, R.F., P.D. Murphy, and D.H. Blackaby. 1994. "Pay in the Public and Private Sectors: A Study Using the GHS." Discussion Paper Series, No. 94-01, University College of Swansea.

Fogel, W., and D. Lewin. 1974. "Wage Determination in the Public Sector." *Industrial and Labor Relations Review*, Vol. 27 (April), pp. 385–94.

Freeman, R. 1987. "How Do Public Sector Wages and Employment Respond to Economic Conditions?" In D. Wise, ed., *Public Sector Payrolls*. Chicago: University of Chicago Press.

Goldfarb, R., and J. Heywood. 1982. "The Economics of the Service Contract Act." *Industrial and Labor Relations Review*, Vol. 36 (October), pp. 56-72.

Gregory, M. 1990. "Public-Sector Pay." In M. Gregory and A. Thomson, eds., *A Portrait of Pay, 1970–1982: An Analysis of the New Earnings Survey*. Cambridge: Oxford University Press.

Gyourko, J., and J. Tracy. 1988. "An Analysis of Public and Private Sector Wages Allowing for Endogenous Choice of Both Government and Union Status." *Journal of Labor Economics*, Vol. 6 (April), pp. 229–53.

Hartman, Robert. 1983. *Pay and Pensions for Federal Workers*. Washington, DC: Brookings Institute.

Hill, Marvin, and Emily DeLacenserie. 1991. "Interest Criteria in Fact-Finding and Arbitration." *Marquette Law Review*, Vol. 74, pp. 399–449.

Hobt, G., and R. Weissenborn. 1980. "Total Compensation and Other Considerations for Federal Pay Reform." *Selected Papers from North American Conference on Labor Statistics*. U.S. Department of Labor, Bureau of Labor Statistics, Massachusetts Division of Employment Security (May), pp. 5–16.

Ippolito, R. 1987. "Why Federal Workers Don't Quit." *Journal of Human Resources*, Vol. 22, pp. 281–99.

Johnson, R., and G. Libecap. 1994. *The Federal Civil Service System and the Problem of Bureaucracy*. Chicago: University of Chicago Press.

Kruger, A. 1988. "Are Public Sector Workers Paid More Than Their Alternative Wage, Evidence from Longitudinal Data and Job Queues." In R. Freeman and C. Ichniowski, eds., *When Public Sector Workers Unionize*. Chicago: University of Chicago Press.

Leonard, Herman B. 1987. "Investing in the Defense Workforce: The Debt and Structure of Military Pensions." In D. Wise, ed., *Public Sector Payrolls*. University of Chicago Press.

Levitan, S., and A. Nodel. 1983. *Working for the Sovereign: Employee Relations in the Federal Government*. Baltimore: John Hopkins University Press.

Linneman, P., and M. Wachter. 1990. "The Economics of Federal Compensation." *Industrial Relations*, Vol. 29 (Winter), pp. 58–76.

Moore, W., and R. Newman. 1991. "Government Wage Differentials in a Municipal Labor Market." *Industrial and Labor Relations Review*, Vol. 45 (October), pp. 145–53.

Moore, W., and J. Raisian. 1991. "Government Wage Differentials Revisited." *Journal of Labor Research*, Vol. 12 (Winter), pp. 13–34.

Morton, J. 1987. "BLS Prepares to Broaden Scope of Its White-Collar Pay Survey." *Monthly Labor Review*, Vol. 110 (March), pp. 3–7.

Moulton, B. 1990. "A Reexamination of the Federal-Private Wage Differential in the United States." *Journal of Labor Economics*, Vol. 8 (April), pp. 270–93.

Murawski, J. 1990. "Congress Out to Cut Pay Gap, but Odds Are Against It." *Congressional Quarterly Weekly Reporter*, Vol. 48 (August 25), pp. 2710–12.

Nesbit, M. 1976. *Labor Relations in Federal Government Service.* Washington, DC: Bureau of National Affairs.

Oaxaca, R. 1973. "Male-Female Wage Differentials in Urban Labor Markets." *International Economic Review*, Vol. 14 (October), pp. 693–709.

Perloff, J. M., and M. Wachter. 1984. "Wage Comparability in the U.S. Postal Service." *Industrial and Labor Relations Review*, Vol. 38, no. 1 (October), pp. 26–35.

Phillips, D., and D. Wise. 1987. "Military versus Civilian Pay: A Descriptive Discussion." In D. Wise, ed., *Public Sector Payrolls.* Chicago: University of Chicago Press.

Quinn, J. 1979. "Wage Differentials between Older Workers in the Public and Private Sectors." *Journal of Human Resources*, Vol. 14 (Winter), pp. 41–62.

Samuels, M. 1993. "Simpson's Paradox and Related Phenomena." *Journal of the American Statistical Association*, Vol. 88, pp. 81–8.

Smith, S. 1976a. "Government Wage Differentials by Sex." *Journal of Human Resources*, Vol. 9 (Spring), pp. 179-97.

_____. 1976b. "Pay Differentials between Federal Government and Private Sector Workers." *Industrial and Labor Relations Review*, Vol. 29 (January), pp. 179-97.

_____. 1977. "Government Wage Differentials." *Journal of Urban Economics*, Vol. 4 (July), pp. 248–71.

_____. 1981. "Public-Private Wage Differentials in Metropolitan Areas." In P. Mieszkowski and G. Peterson, eds., *Public Sector Labor Markets.* Washington, DC: Urban Institute Press, pp. 81–102.

_____. 1982. "Prospects for Reforming Federal Pay." *American Economic Review*, Vol. 72 (May), pp. 273–77.

_____. 1983. "Are State and Local Workers Overpaid?" In W. Hirsch, ed., *The Economics of Municipal Labor Markets.* Los Angeles, CA: Institute of Industrial Relations, University of California, pp. 59–83.

_____. 1987. "Wages in the Public and Private Sector: Comment." In D. Wise, ed., *Public Sector Payrolls.* Chicago: University of Chicago Press.

Thorton, R., and J. Innes. 1985. "On Simpson's Paradox in Economic Statistics." *Oxford Bulletin of Economics and Statistics*, Vol. 47, pp. 387–95.

U.S. General Accounting Office. 1973. "Report to Congress: Improvements Needed in the Survey of Non-Federal Salaries Used as a Basis for Adjusting Federal White Collar Salaries." Washington, DC: GAO (May 11).

Van der Hoek, M. 1989. "Pay Differentials between the Private and the Public Sector in the Netherlands." *Public Finance Quarterly*, Vol. 17 (January), pp. 84–95.

van Ophem, H. 1993. "A Modified Switching Regression Model for Earnings Differentials between the Public and Private Sectors in the Netherlands." *Review of Economics and Statistics*, Vol. 75, no. 2 (May), pp. 215–24.

Venti, Steven. 1987. "Wages in the Federal and Private Sectors." In D. Wise, ed., *Public Sector Payrolls.* Chicago: University of Chicago Press, pp. 147–77.

CHAPTER 5

Beyond the Merit Model: New Directions at the Federal Workplace?

PETER B. DOERINGER AND AUDREY WATSON
Boston University

LINDA KABOOLIAN AND MICHAEL WATKINS
Harvard University

The federal government is the largest "internal labor market" in the United States. With nearly three million civilian employees in twelve cabinet departments, the legislative and judicial branches, and myriad independent agencies, the federal government currently accounts for about 2.3% of the civilian employment (1995), down from 2.9% in 1980 (U.S. DOL, *Employment and Earnings* 1995, 1994).

Over 90% of the full-time federal workforce is governed by some form of "merit" employment system. At the same time, the federal government is a highly unionized employer, with about 60% of total employees in exclusive bargaining units (U.S. OPM, *Union Recognition* 1992). The dominant merit system is the white-collar "General Service" that accounts for three-fourths (76%) of all full-time employment (excluding postal workers). The largely blue-collar "Federal Wage System" (FWS) accounts for another 15.7%, the elite Senior Executive Service (SES) is about 0.4% of federal employment, and there are also about 835,400 postal workers who have their own personnel system (U.S. DOL, *Employment and Earnings* 1995).

Over the years, a number of commissions and surveys have examined the performance of the federal government. They have routinely concluded that the efficiency of the federal internal labor market has been hobbled by outmoded management practices, uncompetitive salaries, and limited employee voice (National Commission on the Public Service 1989a; U.S. GAO 1991a). In response, there have been efforts to improve salaries and management incentives, and opportunities for employee voice have been expanded through presidential executive orders and legislative initiatives intended to encourage collective bargaining.

The private sector has often been used as an example of effective workplace management, and the federal government has routinely turned to the private sector for pay standards and "best practice" management techniques (Lynn 1994). For example, Robert McNamara brought the Ford Motor Company's program planning and budgeting systems to the Department of Defense, President Nixon borrowed management-by-objectives from the private sector, and President Reagan was a proponent of Total Quality Management (Lynn 1994; Barzelay and Kaboolian 1990; Kaboolian 1991).

Despite these repeated efforts at reform, fundamental systemic problems remain. Vice President Gore's 1993 National Performance Review (NPR), the most recent analysis of the performance of the federal government, concluded that bureaucratization and inadequate employee involvement continue to plague federal performance. The NPR called for a "reinvention" of the federal employment system to improve technology and work methods, thin the bureaucracy, empower the federal workforce through partnerships with unions, and focus the attention of government on meeting the needs of its "customers" (National Performance Review 1993; Kettl 1994).

This chapter reviews the performance of the federal government's employment system, with particular emphasis on developments since the 1970s. It traces the evolution of what we define as the "merit model" from its origins in nineteenth century movements to improve public management through the recent reform efforts proposed by the NPR. Despite frequent attempts to introduce collective bargaining, restructure civil service, and assure comparability of economic rewards with the private sector, we find that the federal government has failed to sustain its early lead as an innovative practitioner of progressive human resources practices.

A number of radical reforms in the provision of federal government services are now being advanced by both political parties, and steps are being taken to implement elements of the NPR. However, our assessment of many of these reform proposals is that they fail to address the underlying substance of federal performance problems. Even the most recent attempts to improve the efficiency of government through "reinvention" efforts show mixed results, suggesting that the long-term "transformation" of the federal workplace is more rhetoric than reality. We therefore conclude that more ambitious reforms in the federal employment system will be needed if the performance of the federal government is to be improved substantially.

Alternative Proposals for Reforming the Federal Government

Beginning in the 1980s, a number of proposals for radically changing the provision of government services began to surface. These can be grouped into four major strategies—privatization, downsizing, devolution, and efficiency improvement.

Privatization

The influential *Reinventing Government* (Osborne and Gaebler 1992), for example, advocated making government "competitive" by privatization wherever possible. This notion has received considerable bipartisan support, and both the NPR and the Republican party's "Contract With America" share a preference for private sector provision of government services.

Privatization of the federal sector has been increasing in recent years through both direct competition (as in the case of postal services) and the contracting of services to private sector providers (Donahue 1989). Recently, there have been proposals for new forms of privatization. For example, employee stock ownership programs are allowing employees to "purchase" selected parts of federal departments, such as the Office of Personnel Management's Office of Investigations Service (Barr 1995a), and there have been proposals to sell off entire federal businesses, such as the National Weather Service and the air traffic control system (Shoop 1995).

Downsizing

A second proposal has been to demonstrate that government should "do more with less" by making it smaller. The size of the federal workforce has always been a lightning rod for philosophical and partisan debates about the scale and scope of government; however, this rhetoric has intensified in recent years with the end of the cold war, the burgeoning attention to the budget deficit, and the public's perception that government has failed to solve pressing problems (Lynn 1994).

Devolution

The argument is often made that states and localities should take over federal government functions because they are more efficient, have better information on the preferences of their citizens, and can more flexibly tailor their services to regional conditions. This has led to various "new federalism" proposals to replace federally administered programs with block grants to states.

TABLE 1

Employment by Level of Government, 1980-95

	Federal Civilian Employment (in Thousands, Excluding Postal Service)	State and Local Government Employment (in Thousands, Excluding Education Workers)	Federal Employment as Percent of Total Government Employment	Federal Employment as Percent of U.S. Noninstitutional Population*	State and Local Government Employment as Percent of U.S. Civilian Noninstitutional Population*
1980	2,204.9	6,766.5	24.6	1.3	4.0
1981	2,111.0	6,622.9	24.2	1.2	3.9
1982	2,976.7	6,496.9	24.2	1.2	3.8
1983	2,088.8	6,506.9	24.3	1.2	3.7
1984	2,104.1	6,532.4	24.4	1.2	3.7
1985	2,132.2	6,635.2	24.3	1.2	3.7
1986	2,109.6	6,748.9	23.8	1.2	3.7
1987	2,132.7	6,882.7	23.7	1.2	3.8
1988	2,140.5	7,072.5	23.2	1.2	3.8
1989	2,155.8	7,247.6	22.9	1.2	3.9
1990	2,266.4	7,357.4	23.5	1.2	3.9
1991	2,158.6	7,532.3	22.3	1.1	4.0
1992	2,177.0	7,657.6	22.1	1.1	4.0
1993	2,127.3	7,724.3	21.6	1.1	4.0
July 1994	2,068.4	8,173.7	20.2	1.1	4.2
July 1995	2,012.1	8,240.8	19.6	1.0	4.1

* Due to changes in the methodology of the Current Population Survey, data beginning in 1986 and 1994 are not directly comparable to earlier years.

Sources: U.S. Department of Labor, Bureau of Labor Statistics, Employment, Hours and Earnings: United States, 1909-1994, Vol. II, September 1994; U.S. Department of Labor, Bureau of Labor Statistics, "Employment and Earnings," various issues.

Improving Internal Efficiency

The principle alternative to privatization, downsizing, and the devolution of federal responsibilities to state and local governments is internal reform to make the federal government more efficient. The pressures for radical reform have motivated a number of such reforms in recent years—changing federal compensation formulas, improving management, and strengthening collective bargaining—and culminated in the National Performance Review's assessment of the quality and efficiency of government.

Results

Thus far, the principal consequences of these proposals have been to shrink government in various ways. Federal employment contracted relative to the size of the American population during the 1980s and fell in absolute terms after 1992. During this same period, the federal share of government employment fell steadily from 24.6% to 20.3% (see Table 1) as direct federal grants to states and other entities increased by 4.5% annually.

This trend promises to continue. Reducing the administrative cost component of the federal budget was an express goal of President Clinton's 1993 Executive Order 12837, and both the NPR and the Congress have advocated substantial reductions in federal government employment by 1999.

The Merit Model of the Federal Government

The current problems with efficiency in the federal workplace are rooted in the evolution of the "merit model" of federal employment. The history of this merit system has been well documented (Mosher 1982; Shafritz et al. 1992; Kearney 1984; Johnson and Libecap 1994). Its evolution was shaped by four principles—merit-based employment, the "doctrine" of governmental sovereignty, "scientific" management, and pay equivalency with the private sector.

Merit-based Employment

The merit system was established in the late nineteenth century as an antidote to the inefficiencies of the "spoils" system in which political patronage, rather than competence, was the basis for staffing the federal government. While "moralistic" concerns about corruption (Mosher 1982) and class-based tensions between political elites and ethnic groups over patronage opportunities in urban areas were a factor in ending the spoils system (Painter 1987), the increasing complexity of the economy was the central motivator of reform (Shafritz et al. 1992).

Economic growth depended upon a reliable government infrastructure, particularly in areas such as postal delivery and commercial services, and a merit system was seen as central to ensuring the quality of this infrastructure. For example, early merit system reforms in the post office and New York Custom House were the result of pressure from business interests concerned about the incompetence and extraordinary inefficiency of these agencies (Shafritz et al. 1992). Similarly, the influential National Civil Service Reform League, which spearheaded legislative reform of the spoils system, was founded by "men of education and wealth," but their motive was to promote "clean, efficient government through the agency of an educated bureaucracy" (Painter 1987).

Civil service reform equated efficiency in government with the development of a professional civil service based upon merit and ability. In 1883 the Pendleton Act replaced the spoils system by creating the Civil Service Commission (CSC) with the power to establish a merit-based hiring and promotion system. Entrance to the federal civil service was to be based on competitive exams rather than patronage; the CSC was to protect civil servants from political pressure throughout their careers; and civil servants were expected to be politically neutral in their conduct at work.

The Doctrine of Sovereignty

The merit system operated under the "doctrine of sovereignty," a common law principle holding that the operation of government is the exclusive prerogative of elected officials and their designated representatives. Under the doctrine of sovereignty, direction of public institutions could not be legally shared with unions through collective bargaining (Parker, Schurman, and Montgomery 1984). As a result, the determination of wages, hours, and working conditions remained under the authority of Congress and the President; employees had no legal right to bargain collectively; and federal managers were made responsible for the day-to-day management of the workplace.

Scientific Management

The doctrine of sovereignty was reinforced by scientific management principles that were then coming into vogue. The philosophy of the merit system encouraged the incorporation of these best-practice management techniques into the public sector and federal organizations (such as arsenals and shipyards) participated in the early adoption of scientific management practices (Aitken 1960). Scientific management advocated individualistic labor-management relationships and a dominant management presence, thereby reinforcing the merit system's management prerogatives.

An important contribution of scientific management was its emphasis on the development of standards, rules, and decision-making procedures. By limiting discretion, management protected its prerogatives and nominally ensured fair and uniform treatment of the workforce.

For example, the job-based hierarchy of the federal civil service was codified by the Classification Act of 1923 to ensure that jobs of similar type were paid equitably across the federal sector. The act embodied the scientific management concept of the worker as "a human interchangeable machine part" (Shafritz et al. 1992) and gave prominence to job duties over the individual characteristics of employees in job definition and wage setting (MSPB cited in Shafritz et al. 1992).

Pay Equivalency

Pay equivalency is the final pillar of the merit system model. Recruiting and retaining able employees for the merit system depends on wage competitiveness with the private sector. As early as 1862, the federal government endorsed a compensation philosophy based on pay "comparability" with the private sector (Belman and Heywood 1996), a principle that has been largely carried forward to the present.

The Federal Pay Comparability Act of 1970 defines comparability as "equal pay for substantially equal work." In practice, this meant equating federal pay with private sector pay for a selected group of occupations. Until recently, comparability for General Service and SES salaries was based on a national survey of private sector benchmark occupations from which a single weighted average pay gap was constructed. This average benchmark was either accepted or modified by the President, who then submitted his own recommendation for congressional approval (Risher and Fay 1991).

Pay comparability for blue-collar employees under the Federal Wage System (FWS) is defined somewhat differently in that it is pegged to local prevailing wages for specific occupations (Belman and Heywood 1996). In addition, some federal sector unions, such as the Plate Printers at the Bureau of Engraving and Printing, have negotiated specific private sector benchmarks for pay comparability.

Attempts at Redefining the Merit System Model

A number of attempts were made to improve the merit system model prior to current reform efforts. Three themes were dominant in these reforms: (1) reconciling the merit system with collective bargaining as a means of introducing greater employee voice into governmental decision making, (2) promotion of equal employment opportunity, and (3) improving the quality of federal management by reforming the civil service system.

Reforms through Collective Bargaining

Despite the doctrine of sovereignty and the influence of scientific management, union organization existed before the merit system and continued alongside it. Independent craft labor organizations were to be found in Navy yards and other large construction settings as early as the 1820s (Kearney 1984), and white-collar organization dates back to the National Association of Letter Carriers (NALC) in 1888.

Unions, however, were only a weak counterweight to management prerogative because there was no legal protection of unions and no right to bargain. Even union political activity was limited through a series of presidential executive orders issued in the early 1900s that prohibited direct petitions to Congress for wage increases and the settlement of other grievances.

The passage of the Lloyd-LaFollette Act in 1912 nominally opened the merit system to greater union influence. The act recognized the right of federal employees to join unions and granted the right to petition Congress for redress of grievances. Federal unions, however, were obliged by the Lloyd-LaFollette act to renounce strikes and were still not legally permitted to bargain collectively. As a result, unions remained a marginal influence at the federal workplace.

The weak status of federal unions persisted through the collective bargaining reforms of the 1930s and World War II. President Roosevelt, for example, resisted the extension of collective bargaining to the federal sector, holding that collective bargaining "cannot be transplanted into the public service . . . it has its distinct and insurmountable limitations when applied to public personnel management. The very nature and purposes of government made it impossible to bind the employer in mutual discussions with employee organizations" (letter to NFFE President Lester C. Steward, cited in Nesbitt 1976). The prohibition on strikes by federal employees was reaffirmed in Section 207 of the 1947 Taft-Hartley legislation, and aside from the post office, union membership remained confined largely to blue-collar craft workers in industrial settings such as military installations. Only 15% of the white-collar federal workforce was unionized prior to 1962 (Mosher 1982).

Efforts to promote collective bargaining as a vehicle for reforming the merit system model met with little success until President Kennedy's Executive Orders 10987 and 10988 in 1962. These executive orders were motivated by the findings of the President's Task Force on Employee-Management Relations in the Federal Service that "the benefits to be obtained for employees and for employee organizations, while real and substantial, are limited" because "many of the most important matters affecting federal employees are determined by Congress, and are not subject to unfettered negotiations by officials of the Executive Branch" (cited in Shafritz et al. 1992).

Under these executive orders, about three-fourths of federal sector employees became eligible for union representation, and union membership increased from 19,000 to 1,416,073 between 1962 and 1969. Approximately 40% of nonpostal employees were in exclusive bargaining units by 1968 and 60% by 1978 (*Union Recognition* 1992). At the post office, 90% of eligible employees became union members (Shafritz et al. 1992).

Between 1962 and 1978, several presidential task forces recommended fine tuning this new model of federal labor-management relations, leading President Nixon to create the Federal Labor Relations Council under Executive Order 11491 (October 29, 1969). The council was to "decide major policy issues, prescribe regulations, and from time to time, report and make recommendations to the President." It also housed a Federal Service Impasses Panel empowered to "take any action it considers necessary to settle an impasse," including fact-finding and binding arbitration.

Presidential executive orders to promote "employee-management cooperation in the public service" and the sharp rise in union membership appeared to signal a transition from the management-dominated merit system to a new model based upon labor-management cooperation and employee participation. This wave of reform through collective bargaining, however, left much of the merit system model in place by preserving the doctrine of sovereignty. Management was expressly granted the right to

direct . . , hire, promote, transfer, assign, and retain employees
. . , suspend, demote, discharge or take other disciplinary

action against employees, maintain the efficiency of the Government operations entrusted to them, and determine the methods, means and personnel by which such operations are to be conducted (Executive Order 11491, sec. 12 [1969]).

Collective bargaining was confined to noneconomic issues (such as rest periods, parking, work clothing), personnel practices (including promotion policies, training, and discipline), and grievance procedures. Strikes by federal employees remained illegal. Even union security was limited by a ban on the agency shop and restrictions on dues collection (Shafritz et al. 1992), resulting in a significant "free rider" problem. In 1991, "free riding rates" in the three major federal unions ranged from 51% to 79% (the percentage of eligible employees not belonging to unions) and had generally been increasing over the previous decade (Masters and Aiken 1995).

Only postal employees were granted broad rights to bargain over economic issues. The Postal Reorganization Act of 1970—special legislation passed after an illegal strike by postal unions—gave postal workers all of the benefits of the National Labor Relations Act, except for the right to strike (Biggart 1977). The prospect of further extension of bargaining rights and impasse procedures, however, was chilled by the hiring of replacement workers during the PATCO strike in 1981.

Equal Employment Opportunity

The second, and arguably most successful, area of reform was in providing employment opportunities for minorities and women. Forty-three percent of the federal workforce is female, 17% is black, and 5.7% is Hispanic (U.S. OPM, *FEORP* 1995), and blacks of both genders have a larger share of employment in the federal government than in the civilian labor force. (Hispanics, however, are underrepresented in the federal white-collar workforce as a whole, as are white women.)

Occupation and grade levels. While the federal sector performed better than the private sector, in terms of the occupational composition of employment by race and gender, the overall performance of the merit system model is less dramatic when the level of jobs held by women and minorities is examined. Among professional workers, black males constituted 3.1% of the federal workforce, compared to 2.4% for the private sector. The corresponding shares for black females were 4.6% and 3.2%. Female employees improved their representation in professional and technical categories in the federal government, much as they did in the private sector, but there was little change in the employment share of either blacks or females in administrative jobs (See Table 2).

TABLE 2
Racial and Ethnic Composition of the Federal and U.S. Civilian Labor Forces
1980-82 and 1990-92 (in Percent)

	Professional		Administrative		Technical		All White Collar	
	1980 CLF	1982 Federal	1980 CLF	1982 Federal	1980 CLF	1982 Federal	1980 CLF	1982 Federal
White male	60.6	68.7	60.4	60.3	45.2	43.5	39.1	45.5
White female	26.9	18.5	26.6	23.1	37.0	30.5	44.3	32.9
Black male	2.3	3.0	3.6	4.8	3.5	6.6	3.5	4.8
Black female	2.8	2.9	3.1	5.9	6.3	11.6	6.2	9.7
Hispanic male	2.2	1.8	2.8	2.4	2.7	2.7	2.1	2.1
Hispanic female	1.1	0.7	1.3	1.1	2.4	1.5	2.4	1.7
Other	4.2	4.2	2.1	2.4	2.7	3.7	2.4	3.3

	Professional		Administrative		Technical		All White Collar	
	1990 CLF	1992 Federal	1990 CLF	1992 Federal	1990 CLF	1992 Federal	1990 CLF	1992 Federal
White male	54.7	56.4	42.1	49.8	36.1	32.0	37.8	41.0
White female	30.3	25.8	40.4	28.8	42.9	35.2	44.0	32.8
Black male	2.4	3.1	3.6	5.2	3.6	5.9	3.1	4.8
Black female	3.2	4.6	5.3	7.9	6.6	16.0	5.7	11.3
Hispanic male	2.1	2.2	2.6	2.9	3.2	2.8	2.7	2.6
Hispanic female	1.4	1.4	2.6	1.9	3.4	3.0	3.1	2.5
Other	5.8	6.5	3.4	3.5	4.3	5.1	3.6	4.9

Note: Percentages may not add to 100 due to rounding. Civilian labor force composition is derived from U.S. Census data.

Source: Equal Employment Opportunity Commission, *Annual Report on the Employment of Minorities, Women, and People with Disabilities in the Federal Government*, 1990 and 1992.

Similarly, blacks and females are underrepresented in the higher GS grades (relative to their overall share of federal government employment), although this grade distribution is becoming less skewed (Kellough 1990). In 1972 the average GS grade for white workers was 3.0 grades higher than that for black workers, but by 1982 the black-white grade difference had leveled out at 2.1 (OPM, *Occupations* 1983; EEOC 1990:Table 3). Grade differences between men and women are more pronounced than those between blacks and whites (see Table 4).

TABLE 3

Average GS Grade by Race and Ethnic Group: 1972, 1982, 1992

| | | | | Grade Difference: | |
	White	Black	Hispanic	White-Black	White-Hispanic
1972	8.5	5.5	6.5	3.0	2.0
1982	8.6	6.5	7.1	2.1	1.5
1992	9.8	7.7	8.5	2.1	1.3

Source: Equal Employment Opportunity Commission, *Annual Report on the Employment of Minorities, Women, and People with Disabilities in the Federal Government*, various years.

In 1983, for example, women averaged 3.62 grade levels below men (the male average grade was 10.04, while the female average grade was only 6.42). By 1992 the grade gap had fallen to 2.64 grade levels.[1]

TABLE 4

Average GS Grade Level by Gender: 1983-93

	Men	Women	Total	Male-Female Grade Difference
1983	10.04	6.42	8.37	3.62
1985	10.03	6.58	8.40	3.45
1987	10.09	6.81	8.51	3.29
1989	10.24	7.16	8.75	3.08
1991	10.38	7.50	8.97	2.88
1993	10.55	7.91	9.26	2.64

Source: Office of Personnel Management, *Occupations of Federal White-Collar and Blue-Collar Workers*, various years.

Earnings differentials. Comparisons of grade differences by race and gender, however, can be misleading if they reflect differences in education, experience, and other human capital variables. Even after controlling for such differences, however, earnings differentials between blacks and whites and men and women were narrower in the federal government than in the private sector during the 1970s and 1980s (Moulton 1990). For example, estimated earnings of female high school graduates with five years of experience in the federal sector were 88% of those of males in 1979 (controlling for differences in human capital) and 93% of male earnings in 1988. In the private sector, wages for similar females rose from 77% to 86% of male wages during the same period (derived from Katz and Krueger 1991). For college-educated workers, equality of pay in the federal government was even more pronounced, with earnings in 1979 for females with five years of experience being equal to those of males in the federal government. The comparable gender gap in the private sector was 23% (derived from Katz and Krueger 1991).

Restructuring through Civil Service Reform

The marginal changes in the merit system model resulting from the spread of collective bargaining and fair employment practices did little to change the persistent sense of inefficiency in government. By 1978 President Carter concluded that there was no longer "enough merit in the merit system" (cited in Shafritz et al. 1992). The federal personnel system had become a "bureaucratic maze which neglects merit, tolerates poor performance, and permits abuse of legitimate employee rights, and mires every personnel action in red tape, delay and confusion." (Shafritz et al. 1992) The proposed solution was the Civil Service Reform Act of 1978 (CSRA).

The CSRA was designed to replace "a system created by one hundred years of accretion and tinkering" (Ingraham and Rosenbloom 1992) with a statutory system that codified the bargaining rights of employees and established formal governmental machinery for implementing these rights. At the same time, it sought to strengthen the effectiveness of federal managers and to improve executive compensation (Mosher 1982).

The CSRA separated the Civil Service Commission's conflicting missions of protecting employees through the merit system, facilitating labor-management relations, and representing management interests (Shafritz et al. 1992). The Office of Personnel Management (OPM) was created to "develop the personnel policies governing civilian employment in executive branch agencies" (Campbell 1978). A new Federal Labor Relations Authority (FLRA) was to be the federal analog of the National Labor Relations Board, exercising administrative and adjudicatory function over labor-management relations. The merit system functions of the CSC were ceded to an independent Merit Systems Protection Board (MSPB) that was to hear employee grievances and be the neutral arbiter of merit and efficiency ratings (Vaughn 1992). Lastly, the CSRA provided for enhanced dispute resolution mechanisms, including the negotiation of grievance procedures and the provision of multiple avenues for resolving impasses.

However, the extension of union rights was limited and the scope of bargaining largely unchanged by the CSRA because many issues stipulated by statutes, rules, or agency regulations remained nonnegotiable. Agencies could elect to bargain over staffing, grades, and means of performing work, but any union proposal that prohibited an agency from "acting at all" was mandated to be nonnegotiable (Rosenbloom 1992). The act's emphasis on managerial reforms and on strengthening management may have actually reinforced the bureaucratized merit system model, while the reforms designed to strengthen employee voice remained limited (Mosher 1982).

Slippage in the Merit System Model

Despite its ambitious rhetoric, the passage of the CSRA failed to correct the underlying problems of the federal employment system. Federal salaries failed to become competitive with those in the private sector, recruitment and retention problems arose, there was a surge in unfair labor practice charges against the government, employee dissatisfaction was rising, and there were signs of declining quality in the federal workforce.

Declining Wage Competitiveness

Government surveys comparing private sector and federal pay by broad occupations continued to find that federal employees received much lower pay than their private sector counterparts during the 1970s and 1980s. For example, a General Accounting Office study of ten occupations (primarily clerical and technical) in over 60 metropolitan statistical areas found an average overall wage gap of 20.3% (1988) in favor of the private sector. Median private sector pay was higher than federal pay in 90% of the cases examined, and disparities tended to be largest in high-wage localities (GAO 1990a).

The wage gap also appeared to be growing. Presidential proposals and congressional authorizations for federal sector wage increases were routinely below those indicated by comparability wage surveys in every year between 1978 and 1990 (GAO 1990a). The overall gap between federal and private sector pay rose from 2.9% to 25.02% during this period, as shown by the difference between actual pay increases and the recommended increases based on private sector pay, as shown in Figure 1 (GAO 1990a). For example, in 1978 an increase in pay of 8% was needed to achieve comparability with private sector, while only a 5% increase was actually awarded. By 1990 the cumulative effect of repeated shortfalls in actual increases meant that an increase of 28% was needed to achieve comparability, while only a 4% increase was approved. There has also been a widening of local and regional differences between federal and private sector pay during the 1980s (Katz and Krueger 1991).[2]

FIGURE 1

History of General Schedule Pay Adjustments
1978-90

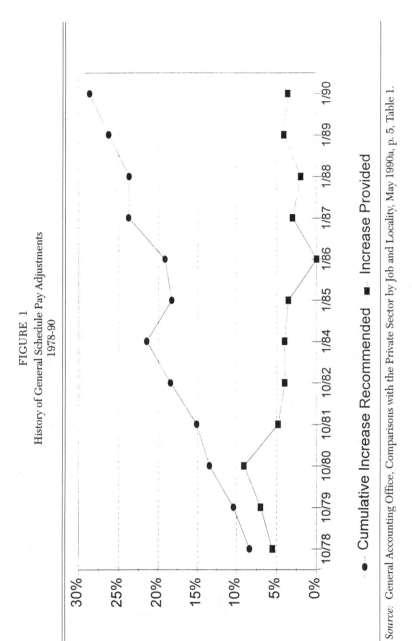

● — Cumulative Increase Recommended   ■ — Increase Provided

Source: General Accounting Office, Comparisons with the Private Sector by Job and Locality, May 1990a, p. 5, Table 1.

The problem of pay competitiveness is accentuated at the higher rungs of the occupational ladder. The combination of relatively higher wage increases for blue-collar workers, relatively greater "grade creep" in the lower wage grades (Table 5), and salary caps affecting the top pay grades (National Commission on the Public Service 1989b) has resulted in the compression of wage differentials by skill and salary grade.

TABLE 5

Distribution of GS Employees by Grade Ranges: 1983, 1993 (Percent)

GS Grade	1983	1993
1-4	17.5	9.0
5-8	31.9	31.0
9-12	36.3	41.0
13-15	14.3	19.0
	100.0	100.0

Source: Office of Personnel Management, Federal Civilian Workforce Statistics: Occupations of Federal White-Collar and Blue-Collar Workers, various years.

Alternative measures of pay competitiveness. The extent of this gap, however, is very sensitive to the way that it is measured. If the earnings of federal and private sector employees are compared within a human capital framework—asking what a worker with given skill, experience, and demographic characteristics (for example, a white male high school graduate with fifteen years of experience) would earn in the private sector versus the federal sector—the finding has often been that federal workers receive a pay premium over similar workers in the private sector (Linneman and Wachter 1990; Belman and Heywood 1990; Moore and Raisian 1991).

These estimates, however, often fail to compare similar public and private employment settings. For example, 34% of federal workers are employed in establishments of 1,000 or more employees, compared to about 11% of private sector workers (Belman and Heywood 1990). Since large private sector firms tend to pay higher wages than small ones (Brown, Hamilton, and Medoff 1990), it may be more appropriate to compare federal pay with that in large private sector establishments.[3]

When controls for size of enterprise, occupation, and location are included in human capital models, the federal wage premium falls substantially. For example, one study that included both establishment and firm size found that the federal wage premium became statistically insignificant (Belman and Heywood 1990) and that federal workers in the largest establishments (1,000 or more workers) actually earned less than their private sector counterparts. The introduction of detailed occupational and geographic controls also substantially reduces, and even erases, the federal premium (Moulton 1990).

Recent work by Belman and Heywood (1996) that simultaneously controls for occupational categories, size of establishment, and location, as well as human capital characteristics, finds no federal pay premium for male workers in the late 1980s and early 1990s. They also find that there was no significant premium for female employees in the 1980s.

While occupational wage comparisons and human capital analyses continue to disagree on the extent to which federal workers are paid differently from those in the private sector, recent research tends to reconcile the apparent inconsistency between the two sets of findings. The effects of adding additional control variables, as described above, suggest both that earlier estimates of the federal pay premium should be revised downward and that the premium has become quite small in recent years (Moulton 1990; Belman and Heywood 1996). The introduction of still finer controls for occupation, workplace location, and hard-to-observe worker attributes should reduce estimates of the federal pay premium even further. In addition, although they differ in their estimates of the relative levels of federal pay, human capital and occupational studies depict similar trends: Both sets of studies suggest that the position of federal employees deteriorated relative to that of those in the private sector during the late 1970s and 1980s.

Limited Advancement Prospects

Currently, the General Schedule system provides for fifteen salary grades defined by job content, responsibility, and qualifications. Within each grade, there are ten wage steps through which employees advance according to years of service, with employees in grades 13-15 also being eligible for merit pay. The grade structure "pyramid" does not narrow dramatically at higher grade levels within the GS structure (see Table 5), and there has also been a gradual upward drift in the average grade level from 1983 to 1993 (OMP, *Occupations* various years).[4]

If grade structure and trends in average grade level are any indicator of promotion opportunity, career advancement should be relatively good in the federal sector and could explain part of the inconsistency between occupational comparability and human capital studies of federal pay.

However, the actual amount of upgrading is limited by outside hiring (of both civil servants and political appointees) and by "bottlenecks" at lower and middle GS grades 8, 10, and 14, where the number of positions declines by 45% from that in the previous grade (National Commission on the Public Service 1989a; OPM, *Pay Structure* 1993).[5]

Recruitment and Retention

The declining wages and limited promotion opportunities of federal employees relative to those in the private sector have raised concerns about the recruitment and retention of qualified federal workers. Surveys report that differences in wages, promotion, and personal growth opportunities between the federal and private sectors are a deterrent to recruitment (GAO 1994a). For example, many recent college graduates felt that the private sector offered better opportunities than the federal sector, and pay differences are routinely cited by federal employees as a reason for not encouraging young people to work for the government (MSPB 1994a, 1994b).

Other obstacles to recruitment include bureaucratic procedures, tight security measures, rude and poorly informed staff (MSPB 1994a, 1994b), and long delays in notification about recruiting decisions (GAO 1992b, 1994a). These factors, along with pay compression, coincided with a fall in application rates for white-collar federal jobs between 1979 and 1986, a time when application rates were rising for blue-collar federal jobs (Katz and Krueger 1991).

While declining relative wages may have adversely affected the federal labor supply, quit rates in the federal government have traditionally been low (running less than 6% annually during the 1980s and 4.4% in 1994) (MSPB 1989; OPM, *Employment and Trends* 1995), and a recent study (MSPB 1994b) reports that 72% of federal employees are satisfied with their jobs (1992), compared to 68% in 1986, and 59% in 1983.

However, pay is the major source of employee dissatisfaction (MSPB 1994b). A 1989 exit survey (MSPB 1990) found that pay ranked among the most important reasons for leaving federal employment. Pay was a particularly important reason to decline or leave federal employment among professional workers (GAO 1990b).

Workforce Quality

Problems of recruitment and retention translate directly into lower worker quality in the federal sector. Krueger (1988), for example, finds that the quality of employees is directly correlated with changes in the federal wage gap, in that a 1% decline in the federal wage relative to the private sector results in a 2% decrease in the number of applicants judged minimally qualified for their prospective jobs. This finding, coupled with the evidence on wage compression, suggests that quality of applicants may have fallen during the 1980s, particularly for more highly skilled white-collar jobs in high-wage areas. Limited direct evidence on federal workforce quality, mainly from studies of engineers and scientists at the Department of Defense, also confirms that the quality of highly skilled workers has declined since the late 1970s (Alderman 1984, cited in Katz and Krueger 1991).

Retention problems have affected workforce quality in a similar way. Seventy-one percent of those who left the federal government took a higher paying job, and a study of the Department of Defense found that quit rates were 50% higher for those with math Scholastic Aptitude Test scores above 650 than for those with scores below that level (GAO 1992a; Alderman 1984, cited in Katz and Krueger 1991). Federal employees also believe pay to be a leading cause of the "brain drain" from government, and pay was particularly correlated with the decision to quit among employees who were ranked as "outstanding" by their supervisors (MSPB 1990). This evidence confirms the repeated conclusion from direct observation of quality declines in the federal workforce (National Commission on the Public Service 1989a, 1989b).

Reconciling the Findings

While no single piece of research is conclusive, our reading of wage comparisons, hiring studies, employee surveys, and exit interviews is that the weight of evidence points to a decline in the quality of federal employees relative to those in the private sector. That is, in any given occupation, worker "quality," as measured by observable human capital characteristics, is lower in the federal sector than in the private sector. This interpretation would reconcile the apparent inconsistency between the occupational comparability data and the human capital analyses of federal-private sector wage differences (Hartman 1983, cited in Moulton 1990). Factoring in the probable decline in the quality of the federal workforce that is "unobservable" in human capital and occupational comparison studies would further reinforce this conclusion.

Reinventing the Federal Government

The workforce quality implications of declining labor market competitiveness, limited employee voice, and employee dissatisfaction with the quality of federal managers prompted further proposals for reform in the federal employment system during the late 1980s and early 1990s. Three attempts are particularly noteworthy—restoring wage competitiveness, the introduction of Total Quality Management, and the proposals of the National Performance Review to "reinvent" government.

Reforms in Federal Compensation

In 1989 concern that declining relative pay levels were turning the federal government into the "employer of last resort," the Office of Personnel Management commissioned a comprehensive review of the GS salary program (Wyatt Co. 1989). The result was the passage of the Federal Employees Pay Comparability Act of 1990 (FEPCA) that reaffirmed the principle of wage comparability by occupation and sought to make wages more responsive to market comparisons.

A number of steps were taken to narrow occupational pay gaps by raising top salaries and introducing greater flexibility in wage determination. Senior Executive Service and other high-level employees were given substantial raises (ranging from 22% to 30%), and wage rates were replaced with a single salary "band" to make wages more competitive for workers in super grades (OPM, *Pay Structure* 1993). FEPCA also permits the payment of recruiting, retention, and relocation bonuses and allows new hires to start above the first step of their grade level. Beginning in 1992, annual increases for most white-collar employees were to be based on formulas that were tied to changes in the "Employment Cost Index" in the private sector.

A second major provision of the act was to extend locality-based pay to all federal employees whose pay was more than 5% below the prevailing local level. Locality pay was scheduled to begin in 1994 and was to be phased in gradually so that GS salaries would be no more than 5% behind those of the private sector by the year 2003 (Risher and Fay 1991).

Total Quality Management

The Reagan and Bush administrations attempted to reinforce the merit model by introducing Total Quality Management (TQM) techniques—an emphasis on customer satisfaction, continuous improvement in quality and productivity, and employee involvement—into the federal government. Experimentation with TQM began during the mid-1980s in agencies such as NASA, the Internal Revenue Service, Naval Aviation Depots, and the Postal Service (Burstein and Sedlak 1988; Burstein 1989). It spread more widely through the federal government in the late

1980s and early 1990s under the aegis of a productivity improvement program initiated by the Office of Management and Budget (OMB) designed to emulate the quality movement that was emerging in the private sector (Burstein and Sedlak 1988:122).

A Federal Quality Institute (FQI) was also established in 1988 to "promote and facilitate the implementation of Total Quality Management throughout the Federal Government in order to improve the quality, timeliness and efficiency of Federal services to the American people." FQI supported the diffusion of TQM ideas and methodologies through training programs and sponsored the President's Award for Quality to recognize exemplary quality efforts (Barzelay and Kaboolian 1990).

The penetration of TQM principles into federal sector organizations, however, varied widely. Some agencies (notably the Department of Defense, the Social Security Administration, and the Internal Revenue Service) adopted TQM as their principal approach to managing organizational improvement, whereas others adopted only the superficial rhetoric of TQM (Barzelay and Kaboolian 1990). Improving employee involvement under TQM, by reducing the number of management levels and by delegating authority from top management to lower level employees, proved to be particularly problematic (Radin and Coffee 1993).

The National Performance Review

The assessment of the federal workplace provided by Vice President Gore's National Performance Review (NPR), completed in the fall of 1993, resonated with the same themes of poor service to customers, inflexible management, and unempowered workers as prior examinations of governmental performance. The NPR, however, proposed far more ambitious reforms than previous efforts. Its recommendations focused both on improving managerial efficiency—decentralizing personnel and procurement functions, eliminating redundant services and regulations, reducing the size of the federal workforce, and encouraging "an army of reinventers throughout the federal government" (Kettl 1994:vii)—and on improving the labor-management relationship, which had been characterized by GAO in 1991 as too adversarial and clogged by litigation over trivial matters (GAO 1991a).

The NPR reform model saw stronger unions, a greater role for collective bargaining, and increased empowerment of employees as central to achieving high-performance government. As part of the implementation strategy for the NPR, President Clinton signed Executive Order 12871, establishing a "National Partnership Council" (NPC) to set guidelines for agency-level labor-management partnerships to implement the NPR's recommendations (National Partnership Council 1994). Membership included the national presidents of the largest unions representing federal employees; the AFL-CIO public employees department; and federal officials, such as the heads of the Office of Management and Budget, the Federal Labor Relations Authority, the Federal Mediation and Conciliation Service, and a representative of the Secretary of Labor. Executive Order 12871 also required agencies to bargain with its unions on all permissive topics not expressly reserved to the President or Congress.

Has Reform Changed the Federal Employment System?

Despite the lofty ambitions of the NPR, the expansion of the scope of collective bargaining by executive order, and the successful implementation of partnership programs in some federal agencies, there are signs that the reform movement is in trouble. At one level, the NPR has been hobbled by the political shifts following the 1994 elections. Moreover, the NPR was based on the faulty assumption that negative influences on performance—uncompetitive wages, threat of job loss, and unfair employment practices—would not be an impediment to the formation of effective partnerships.

The failure to address long-term systemic problems, however, is at the heart of the NPR's difficulties. In grafting greater employee voice onto a merit model that was grounded in management prerogative, the NPR model did not resolve the inherent contradictions between management prerogative and employee voice. Instead, the resolution was entrusted to the untested capacities to bargain on a broader range of issues and to form effective agency-level "partnerships" between labor and management (National Partnership Council 1994).

Continued Erosion of Federal Pay

Some progress appears to have been made in narrowing the pay gap for federal employees by 1993 (Belman and Heywood 1996), and this was accompanied by an improvement in the perceived quality of new hires (MSPB 1994b). This progress in achieving FEPCA's goals of moving towards parity with private sector pay and improving employee quality, however, was soon undermined by presidential and congressional actions.

Beginning in 1994, federal employees were to receive both general increases (based on the Employment Cost Index) and locality pay increases designed to reduce the "target gap" between federal and private sector pay by 20% in the first year and 10% in succeeding years until federal pay levels were within 5% of those in the private sector (Clark 1994). This formula would have awarded most federal white-collar employees an across-the-board increase of 2.2%, augmented by locality pay adjustments averaging nearly 4% of federal salaries. Congress cancelled the general increase at the request of the administration, approving only the locality pay increases (Clark 1994).

Subsequent increases approved for 1995 and 1996 were also substantially below those defined by the FEPCA formula. In 1995 the general increase was 2%, compared to 2.6% projected under FEPCA, and locality pay was also reduced from the level anticipated by FEPCA (Causey 1994a, 1994b). For 1996 the President submitted to Congress a pay plan calling for an average 1996 increase of 2.4%, 2% of which was across the board, while the FEPCA formula would have yielded a 2.4% general pay increase and an increase in locality pay estimated between 2.7% to 3.5% (Barr 1995b:A4; BNA 1995).

This pattern of wage increases puts the federal government behind schedule in making federal pay competitive with the private sector (Clark 1994). It also contributes to the perception that the cost-cutting objectives of the National Performance Review take precedence over those of workplace reform.

Downsizing the Federal Government

The National Performance Review recommended the reduction of 252,000 FTE positions by 1999, and Congress increased this number to 272,000 under the Federal Workforce Restructuring Act 1994 (FWRA)—a reduction of almost 13% from 1993 employment levels. In particular, the NPR urged a focus on administrative and supervisory positions at the agency level to reduce supervisory ratios from 1:7 to 1:15. By the end of FY 1995, 105,672 buyouts had been accepted—68,837 at the Department of Defense and 36,835 at other executive agencies (King 1995). The bulk of buyouts (70%) came from middle and upper-level grades, and 40% of the departing employees (in agencies other than the Department of Defense) vacated overhead positions (King 1995). It is, however, doubtful that the goal of reducing middle managers was fully achieved because the GS 11-15 grades consist primarily of professional positions (Light 1995).

Reduced Employment Gains for Women and Minorities

Although human capital studies continue to show larger federal pay premiums for female and nonwhite workers than for white male workers

(Moulton 1990; Belman and Heywood 1996), other information suggests that the leadership position of the federal government in equal employment opportunity has also begun to decline. For example, one study indicates that the gap between male and female wages decreased more rapidly in the private sector than in the federal government in the 1980s; this pattern was particularly pronounced for young college-educated women, for whom the gender gap in the federal government actually increased. In addition, the promotion of women within the federal government still remains problematic. A study of promotion by gender, for example, concluded that men and women had comparable rates of promotion once they reached GS-11 grade. However, women were promoted less frequently than men into the "gateway" GS-9 and GS-11 grades that are critical for entry to the highest graded jobs, even though performance evaluations by gender were relatively equal (MSPB 1993).

A similar pattern can be discerned in data on earnings by race. For example, one study of racial earnings differences in the federal sector partitioned the wage gap into a portion due to human capital differences and a portion attributed to "the cost of being black," defined as receiving lower wages for the same human capital characteristics (Zipp 1994). In 1980 blacks of both genders faced a higher cost of being black in the private sector than in the federal government. By 1990, however, this "cost" for blacks was markedly greater in the federal sector than in the private sector (Zipp 1994). Overall, the evidence, although mixed, suggests that while the federal government may retain some advantages for female and minority employees, such advantages are being gradually eroded in the face of more rapid progress by these groups in the private sector.

Adversarial Labor-Management Relations and Partnerships

It is premature to reach any overall judgment about whether the NPR's "bargaining and partnership" model is improving the efficiency of the federal government. Nevertheless, the evidence is mixed. In spite of the positive posture towards federal unions in the NPR—the creation of agency-level labor-management partnerships, the commitment to broaden the scope of bargaining, and the emphasis on developing alternative methods of dispute resolution—the rate of unfair labor practice filings by federal unions continued to increase through 1993 (See Table 6). While this trend may reflect other slippages in the federal employment system, such as deterioration of pay and job security, it is unlikely to be a sign of more harmonious labor-management relations.

TABLE 6

Number of Unfair Labor Practice Cases Filed
(Per Thousand Employees Covered by Collective Agreement)
1980-83

	ULP Cases Per 1000 Employees under Agreement
1980	4.31
1981	5.52
1982	4.22
1983	4.69
1985	4.53
1987	4.81
1989	5.34
1991	6.09
1993	7.14

Sources: Federal Labor Relations Authority, *Annual Report of the Federal Labor Relations Authority,* various years; OPM, *Union Recognition in the Federal Government,* various years.

A second cause for concern is the limited number of agencies that are cited by federal officials as "best practice" success stories of partnership efforts. However, the experiences of two such agencies—the Internal Revenue Service (IRS) and the Bureau of Engraving and Printing (BEP)—provide an indication of the strengths and weaknesses of the partnership approach.

Radical reinvention at the IRS.[6] In the early 1980s, the Internal Revenue Service (IRS) appeared to be a well-run agency successfully employing the merit model of public management. A highly professional management staff in Washington exerted strong central control over a large array of field offices and service centers—setting policy, assessing performance, and dealing with Congress. The service centers, which processed returns, were run as "paper factories" with performance measured by "cost-per-thousand returns processed."

Strong assertion of managerial rights had resulted in a highly adversarial relationship between IRS management and the National Treasury Employees Union that represented over 70% of its workforce. In the 1960s and early 1970s, the IRS had effectively fragmented union influence by dealing one on one with the individual NTEU locals. In 1977, however, the Federal Labor Relations Authority ruled that NTEU could bargain with the IRS as a single national unit. During the next two years, the union and the agency bargained over more than 220 issues but in a climate where management held firmly to its prerogatives, while the NTEU engaged in picketing and instigated congressional investigations of IRS practices.

The negative consequences of strong, centralized management and weak employee voice became evident when the IRS unilaterally installed a new computerized processing system during the 1985 tax-filing season. There was a complete breakdown of returns processing. Waiting times for refunds skyrocketed, and in some instances, employees reacted to management pressures to reduce the growing processing backlog by "losing" or destroying tax returns.

The IRS initially responded to congressional and public outrage by applying traditional merit model methods. The breakdown was attributed to short-term problems with new computer programs that had not been fully debugged and to inadequate training of employees. Accordingly, software systems were rewritten, computer hardware upgraded, and employees retrained.

Senior managers eventually came to conclude, however, that structural flaws in the IRS's management systems and collective bargaining relationships had rendered the agency vulnerable to major performance problems. One diagnosis of the 1985 failure, for example, concluded that the service centers had become "so compartmentalized that people couldn't see to the left or right" and that the emphasis on performance indicators (such as cost-per-thousand returns processed) rewarded efficiency but at the cost of flexibility, quality, and improvements in performance.

Between 1987 and 1994, the IRS management and the NTEU began a radical reinvention of the agency by adopting (and adapting) private sector approaches to organizational improvement. During this period, an organizationwide Total Quality Management (TQM) program was implemented. The IRS simplified forms and procedures, upgraded taxpayer assistance systems, introduced electronic filing, and completely redesigned and automated the tax collection system.

Management's early efforts to change the organization coincided with a push by the National Treasury Employees Union (NTEU) for greater involvement in decision making at the agency. The union had come to realize that negotiating through litigation and lobbying had its limits and argued that greater union participation in determining the methods of work could have prevented the 1985 disaster. For its part, management understood that agencywide adoption of TQM could be accomplished only with the unifying force of the union as part of the plan.

As a result, management and union leaders agreed to form a partnership to renew the IRS in the belief that it would lead to both higher employee satisfaction and significant productivity increases for the agency. The new approach was codified in a 1987 IRS-NTEU agreement establishing a Total Quality Organization (TQO) program to create a workplace based upon labor-management consensus.

The framework for TQO began with the formation of a labor-management National Quality Council to support and direct the program. Counterpart joint councils were also established in each IRS field location and were vested with the authority and responsibility to establish Quality Improvement Process teams (QIPs). In a 1993 follow-on agreement, the NTEU and IRS recognized the need to supplement the incremental total quality approach with more fundamental process redesign efforts.

The IRS's reinvention effort yielded impressive results. Between 1990 and 1993, the processing workload increased somewhat from 112.5 million to 113.5 million returns per year (GAO 1994b). In the same period, however, total staff fell from 130,000 to 121,000 (U.S. Government, Internal Revenue Service, *Annual Report*, various years), implying an increase in productivity of 8.4%. In key measures of service, such as error resolution, telephone accuracy, and refund timeliness, the IRS also realized significant improvements in performance. In processing telephone tax law inquiries, for example, accuracy increased from 63% in 1989 to 89% in 1994 (GAO 1994b).

By the early 1990s, the IRS was widely recognized as a leader in reinvention in the federal government. The IRS's service center at Ogden, Utah had won a Presidential Quality Award, and senior IRS personnel, including the head of the Ogden service center, were assigned to key planning and policy-making positions in the NPR effort.

"Hybrid" reinvention at the Bureau of Engraving and Printing.[7] While the IRS embraced a radical approach to reinvention, other federal agencies responded to the demands of the late 1980s and early 1990s with more incremental change strategies. The result was a "hybrid" approach that combined elements of the traditional merit model with mechanisms for incorporating greater employee voice through collective bargaining.

The experience of the Bureau of Engraving and Printing (BEP) illustrates this approach. Founded during the Civil War, the BEP is the only authorized printer of U.S. currency and the primary supplier of stamps sold by the U.S. Postal Service. In 1990 currency production at BEP still operated much as it had in the late 1950s using updated versions of 1950s rotary press technology.

The legacy of scientific management was also very much in evidence at BEP. Operations were highly compartmentalized, with each stage of production occurring in a different room under the jurisdiction of a different union. The operations directorate was the dominant force within management, and attainment of monthly production plans was the driving organizational objective. A steep managerial hierarchy exerted strong top-down control over a workforce of about 3,500, and employees were restricted to narrow job classifications which impeded cross-training and management development.

The bureau's employees were represented by 17 unions, reflecting the traditional craft and occupational structure of the printing industry, and labor-management relations at the bureau were fragmented and adversarial. Senior executive staff characterized unions as a disruptive force, impeding efficiency by refusing to abandon outmoded work rules and jurisdictional boundaries; front-line workers asserted that management's authoritarian style and union-bashing orientation was at fault; and the unions routinely countered management initiatives with grievances and unfair labor practices claims.

Adversarial relations had resulted in a very restrictive set of staffing practices and work rules at BEP. Strict complements for staffing presses continued to apply long after changes in press control systems had reduced the demands on operators, while long rest periods and generous overtime provisions reduced productivity and drove up costs.

During the 1980s, BEP faced an enormous increase in worldwide demand for U.S. currency that required it to more than double production. Constrained in its ability to hire new staff, BEP met the increase in demand largely through the use of overtime in its Washington facility. A new printing plant in Fort Worth eased the capacity crunch somewhat, but forecasts indicated that the bureau would once again have insufficient capacity to meet demand by the mid- to late 1990s. The bureau then opted to expand capacity further by investing in a new currency technology that produced currency in an integrated, continuous-flow process. It was estimated that this technology would raise productivity by a factor of four compared to the traditional system.

Management recognized that the new technology would require different skills, staffing arrangements, and organizational structures, if its full potential were to be realized. In the face of union unwillingness to give ground on craft jurisdictions and other work rules, however, management decided to circumvent union restrictions by replacing its skilled union workers with a small team of technicians trained in systems engineering and electro-mechanical maintenance. It initially proposed introducing this staffing arrangement on an experimental integrated printing system but contemplated a "parallel organization" strategy for transforming production at the bureau. Under this strategy, the "old" compartmentalized craft union production organization would be allowed to wind down slowly, while the "new" production organization would be progressively built up around an integrated technology system operated by teams of nonunion engineers and technicians.

The unions objected to this strategy, and following threats of litigation, an interim compromise was struck. Union members became part of the experiment but were allowed to operate only the printing units, while technicians controlled the rest of the technology. The situation remained in an uneasy state of truce.

Senior management learned from this experience that technological change in the bureau could cause severe labor-management relations and human resource problems that would undermine the productivity advantages of the new technology unless a more collaborative approach was taken. Bureau management, therefore, moved to accept the BEP unions as partners at the workplace by encouraging union voice, opening the agency to employee involvement in operating decisions, and expanding the scope of collective bargaining.

The director began to open up dialogue with the union leaders, a Joint Partnership Council was established with elected union members, and the unions became involved in a wide range of bureau initiatives, including the new technology. Senior management also explored the potential for instituting bargaining over wages as a way of trading economic benefits for support in implementation of new technologies and relaxation of restrictive work rules.

Efforts to involve the unions were complemented by other management changes. Top management began to engage in comprehensive strategic planning, human resources planning was more closely linked to strategic planning, comprehensive skills assessments and training program development initiatives were undertaken, and mechanisms for improving downward and upward communications were introduced.

Although it is too early to observe the results of the incremental approach to reinvention in terms of operational performance, there is evidence of substantial improvement in BEP's organizational climate. Comparisons of the results of organizational climate surveys administered in 1993 and 1994 showed significant improvements in the areas of communications, labor-management relations, quality of management, and perceived integrity of decision-making processes.

Strengthening the Federal Employment System

This review of recent reforms in the federal employment system finds that the legacy of the nineteenth century merit system remains very much in evidence today. Executive and congressional prerogatives are largely untouched, the scope of collective bargaining remains limited to noneconomic issues, and private sector management techniques have been routinely introduced without corresponding improvements in the opportunity for employee voice at the workplace. There is only scattered evidence that the federal government is developing high-performance workplace practices.

What has changed is the competitive position of the federal workplace. The relationship of federal to private sector pay has slipped in the last two decades, particularly for middle managers and professional occupations and in high-wage areas. Recruitment has become more difficult as a result of pay and downsizing efforts, and the more capable employees tend to leave government. While FEPCA promised to reverse this slide in competitiveness, federal pay continues to lag behind that in the private sector, and the NPR's ambitions for constructive employee involvement and higher productivity have been eroded by cost-cutting, downsizing, and lack of congressional support.

The persistent difference between the rhetoric and the reality of reforming the federal employment system, in our view, lends credence to current proposals for radical change in government—privatizing federal government functions, introducing greater political accountability, and transferring federal programs to state governments. Nevertheless, with the possible exception of privatization, none of these proposals addresses the central problem of how to achieve a high-performance workplace, an area in which even the private sector has made only limited gains in this direction (Osterman 1994; U.S. Department of Labor-U.S. Department of Commerce 1994a).

Our case studies, however, point to the promise of an alternative approach that directly addresses performance. The examples of the Internal

Revenue Service and the Bureau of Engraving and Printing demonstrate the capacity for innovation in the areas of improved management and the unlocking of employee voice. They also document substantial grassroots support for improving governmental performance and the willingness of management and unions to work together for such improvement.

In each of these cases, key executives and union leaders responded constructively to the challenges posed by a political environment that demands more competitive performance. Even though there was often skepticism about reform efforts, labor and management grappled successfully with the most pernicious legacies of the merit model—unilateral management prerogative, centralized control, and limited scope for employee voice.

Furthermore, the cases demonstrate that there need not be a single formula for reinventing government. Instead, it is possible to tailor approaches to high-performance government to the specific circumstances of each agency. The Internal Revenue Service successfully undertook a radical reinvention based on principles of Total Quality Management and business process reengineering, supported by a labor-management partnership. A hybrid approach to reinvention—incorporating new technology, improvements in key planning systems, and greater employee voice—achieved significant improvements at the Bureau of Engraving and Printing.

While these may be the exceptional cases of improvement, they are not atypical of federal government workplaces. The IRS is a mainstream government agency in that its activities span both the delivery of services and the monitoring of compliance with regulations, and the BEP is not unlike other government production facilities—naval shipyards, the Government Printing Office, and the Mint. Therefore, these examples can be influential in demonstrating that fundamental reform of the merit system model is achievable within the federal system.

In addition, we see the potential for such agencies providing leadership in creating "best practice" workplace models for the wider American economy. The size and diversity of the federal government and its nonprofit status make it an ideal testing ground for best practice. The resources that are now devoted to personnel rule-making, administration of regulations, and litigation of labor-management disputes could be better used to foster experimentation in collective bargaining, human resources management, employee development, and workforce involvement.

This was the role that the federal government played in the late nineteenth century when it was at the forefront of developing merit systems and scientific management practices. Since then, the federal government has occasionally done pioneering work in areas such as pensions and equal employment opportunity, but it has largely ceded its position of leadership over the last century.

While the failure of the federal government to retain its leadership role in developing high-performance workplace practices is often blamed on bureaucratic inertia and the lack of market incentives, we believe that the main impediments are the strongly held prerogatives of federal sector management and the limited scope for employee involvement. For a variety of reasons, we see collective bargaining as the most practical vehicle for addressing these problems.

First, the federal government has demonstrated its inability to adhere to stated policies of pay comparability with the private sector. Collective bargaining over wages, hours, and working conditions, backed by either the right to strike or final and binding impasse procedures, provides a way of helping the federal government to compete on an even footing with the private sector in the market for high-performance employees.

Second, empowered unions are important for building effective employee voice, particularly in situations where management sovereignty has traditionally been strong (Appelbaum and Batt 1994). For example, in the U.S. Postal Service where authoritarian management and adversarial labor relations were commonplace (Walsh and Mangum 1992), unions are now recognized as the channel for employee voice on all issues related to efficiency and labor-management cooperation (GAO 1995).

Third, one of the unique features of the U.S. industrial relations system in the private sector has been the ability of collective bargaining to tailor wages and working conditions to the needs of specific firms and workgroups (Slichter 1961). Our case studies demonstrate a corresponding need for such flexibility in the public sector and show how collective bargaining can be an effective vehicle for bringing this about. Strengthened collective bargaining can further contribute to flexibility by reducing the need to regulate employment rights through detailed civil service procedures.

There are always downside risks to strengthening collective bargaining, and efforts to move from adversarial to participatory labor-management relations in the federal sector have not yielded either quick or painless improvements in workplace performance. However, the potential gains to be realized from recasting collective bargaining relationships appear to be high (U.S. Department of Labor-U.S. Department of

Commerce 1994a, 1994b), and the alternative reform proposals are hardly risk free.

Endnotes

[1] Race and gender grade differences are exceptionally large for technical occupations and, in general, appear to be widest in higher-level occupations. In 1992 the black-white grade difference was 30% of the average technical grade, while the male-female grade difference was 25.9% of the average technical grade. Male-female grade differences for professional employees were 9.1% of the average professional grade; the corresponding figure for administrative workers was 8.3%, while female clerical workers actually had a slightly higher average grade level than their male coworkers. The grade difference between blacks and whites was equal to 5.8% of the occupational group average at the professional level and 5.0% at the administrative level, falling to 4.0% for clerical workers (U.S. Government EEOC 1992).

[2] Belman and Heywood (1996) argue that this decline may have been understated because of changes in the design of the comparability survey. However, the cost of fringe benefits in the federal sector has been rising relative to the private sector since the late 1970s (Katz and Krueger 1991:5), although this does not necessarily equate with rising value of benefits. There is no evidence in surveys of federal employees that their fringe benefit package is perceived as more favorable than alternatives in the private sector.

[3] Some analysts (Linneman and Wachter 1990) question this conclusion, arguing that the inclusion of variables such as establishment and firm size controls represent "job-descriptive" rather than "skill-descriptive" variables. As such, they are unlikely to be transferable between sectors and their inclusion in human capital analyses will bias downward estimates of the federal premium. However, others have demonstrated that large private sector firms are the most likely alternative employers for federal workers, so that it is appropriate to recognize "size-of-firm" effects when making federal-private pay comparisons (Belman and Heywood 1993).

[4] The Civil Service Reform Act of 1978 replaced most GS salary grade 16-18 positions with a six-grade Senior Executive Service.

[5] One study found that only 22% of the professional and administrative appointments in 1992 were done through internal selection (MSPB 1994a). Promotion rates, however, were substantially higher after controlling for the educational qualifications of applicants.

[6] This section draws upon "Management and Labor United for Quality at the Internal Revenue Service," a case study written by Madeline Marget under the direction of Peter B. Doeringer and Michael D. Watkins.

[7] These materials are based upon Geri Augusto, H. James Brown, Peter B. Doeringer, and Michael Watkins, "Managing Change at the Bureau of Engraving and Printing: Final Report of the Harvard Study Team on Strategic Analysis of Technological and Organizational Change," January 1995.

References

Aitken, Hugh G.J. 1960. *Taylorism at Watertown Arsenal: Scientific Management in Action.* Cambridge, MA: Harvard University Press.

Alderman, Karen C. 1984. "Using Labor Market Indicators as a Gauge for Setting Pay for Federal Employees: Review of the Issues." Mimeo, U.S. Department of Defense.

Appelbaum, Eileen, and Rosemary Batt. 1994. *The New American Workplace: Transforming Work Systems in the United States.* Ithaca, NY: ILR Press.

Asher, Martin, and Joel Popkin. 1984. "The Effect of Gender and Race Differentials on Public-Private Comparisons: A Study of Postal Workers." *Industrial and Labor Relations Review*, Vol. 38, no. 1 (October), pp. 16–25.

Augusto, Geri, H. James Brown, Peter B. Doeringer, and Michael Watkins. 1995. "Managing Change at the Bureau of Engraving and Printing: Final Report of the Harvard Study Team on Strategic Analysis of Technological and Organizational Change." Mimeo, John F. Kennedy School of Government (January).

Barr, Stephen. 1995a. "Plan To Turn Program Into Employee-Owned Company Draws Criticism." *Washington Post* (June 16), p. A 23.

_____. 1995b. "Clinton Plans 2.56% Raise for Area Employees: Pay Boost Would Be Lowest in Recent Years." *The Washington Post* (September 2), p. A4.

Barzelay, Michael, and Linda Kaboolian. 1990. "Total Quality Management in the Federal Sector: Discourse, Practices and Movement." Paper presented at the Association for Public Policy Analysis and Management (APPAM) Research Conference, San Francisco, CA (October).

Belman, Dale, and John S. Heywood. 1988. "Public Wage Differentials and the Public Administration Industry." *Industrial Relations*, Vol. 27, no. 3 (Fall), pp. 385–93.

_____. 1990. "The Effect of Establishment and Firm Size on Public Wage Differentials." *Public Finance Quarterly*, Vol. 18, no. 2 (April), pp. 221–35.

_____. 1993. "Job Attributes and Federal Wage Differentials." *Industrial Relations*, Vol. 32, no. 1 (Winter), pp. 148–57.

_____. 1996. "The Structure of Compensation in the Public Sector." In D. Belman, M. Gunderson, and D. Hyatt, eds., *Public Sector Employment in a Time of Transition.* Madison, WI: Industrial Relations Research Association.

Biggart, Nicole W. 1977. "The Creative-Destructive Process of Organizational Change: The Case of the Post Office." *Administrative Science Quarterly*, Vol. 22 (September), pp. 410–25.

Brown, Charles, James Hamilton, and James Medoff. 1990. *Employers Large and Small.* Cambridge, MA: Harvard University Press.

Bureau of National Affairs (BNA). 1995. *Government Employee Relations Reporter* (September 11).

Burstein, Carolyn. 1989. "Total Quality Management in Federal Agencies." *National Civic Review*, no. 78 (March-April), pp. 103-11.

Burstein, Carolyn, and Katherine Sedlak. 1988. "Federal Productivity Improvement Efforts: Current Status and Future Agenda." *National Productivity Review* (Spring), pp. 122-33.

Campbell, Alan K. 1978. "Civil Service Reform: A New Commitment." *Public Administration Review.* (March/April), pp. 99–103.

Causey, Mike. 1994a. "The Pay Perception Gap." *The Washington Post* (December 15), p. C2.

_____. 1994b. "Richmond Is On Its Own." *The Washington Post* (October 11), p. B2.

Clark, Paul S. 1994. "Pay Reform Under Siege." *Government Executive* (January), pp. 27–31.

Congressional Budget Office. 1993. "Reducing the Size of the Federal Civilian Work Force." Washington, DC: Government Printing Office.

Doeringer, Peter B., et al. 1991. *Turbulence in the American Workplace.* New York, NY: Oxford University Press.

Donahue, John D. 1989. *The Privatization Decision: Public and Private Means.* New York: Basic Books.

Federal Labor Relations Authority. Various years. *Annual Report of the Federal Labor Relations Authority.* Washington, DC: Federal Labor Relations Authority.

Hartman, Robert. 1983. *Pay and Pension for Federal Workers.* Washington, DC: Brookings Institution.

Hundley, Greg. 1991. "Public- and Private-Sector Occupational Pay Structures." *Industrial Relations*, Vol. 30, no. 3 (Fall), pp. 417–34.

Ingraham, Patricia W., and David H. Rosenbloom, eds. 1992. *The Promise and Paradox of Civil Service Reform.* Pittsburgh, PA: University of Pittsburgh Press.

Johnson, Ronald N., and Gary D. Libecap. 1994. *The Federal Civil Service System and the Problem of Bureaucracy.* Chicago: University of Chicago Press.

Kaboolian, Linda. 1991. "Ruthless with Time, Gracious with People?: Teleservice At SSA." Mimeo, John F. Kennedy School of Government Case Program, Cambridge, MA.

Katz, Lawrence F., and Alan B. Krueger. 1991. "Changes in the Structure of Wages in the Public and Private Sectors." NBER Working Paper no. 3667 (March).

Kearney, Richard C. 1984. *Labor Relations in the Public Sector.* New York: Marcel Dekker.

Kellough, J. E. 1990. "Federal Agencies and Affirmative Action for Blacks and Women." *Social Science Quarterly*, Vol. 71, no. 1, pp. 83–92.

Kettl, Donald F. 1994. *Reinventing Government? Appraising the National Performance Review.* Washington, DC: Brookings Institution.

King, James. 1995. Director of the U.S. Office of Personnel Management, testimony before the U.S. House of Representatives Government Reform and Oversight's Subcommittee on Civil Service. Chairman John L. Mica, R-Fla. (May 17).

Kochan, Thomas A., Harry C. Katz, and Robert B. McKersie. 1986. *The Transformation of American Industrial Relations.* New York: Basic Books, Inc.

Krueger, Alan B. 1988. "The Determinants of Queues for Federal Jobs." *Industrial and Labor Relations Review*, Vol. 41, no. 4 (July), pp. 567–81.

Light, Paul C. 1995. *Thickening Government: Federal Hierarchy and the Diffusion of Accountability.* Washington, DC: Brookings Institution.

Linneman, Peter D., and Michael L. Wachter. 1990. "The Economics of Federal Compensation." *Industrial Relations*, Vol. 29, no. 1 (Winter), pp. 58–76.

Lynn, Lawrence. 1994. "Government Lite." *The American Prospect*, No. 16 (Winter), pp. 135–44.

Marget, Madeline. 1994a. "Building the Workplace of the Future at AT&T." Mimeo, case study written under the direction of Peter B. Doeringer and Michael D. Watkins, John F. Kennedy School of Government.

_____. 1994b. "Management and Labor United for Quality at the Internal Revenue Service." Mimeo, case study written under the direction of Peter B. Doeringer and Michael D. Watkins, John F. Kennedy School of Government.

Masters, Marick F., and Robert S. Atkin. 1995. "Bargaining, Financial, and Political Bases of Federal Sector Unions: Implications for Reinventing Government." *Review of Public Personnel Administration* (Winter), pp. 5–23.

Mohanty, Madhu S. 1994. "Union Premiums in the Federal and Private Sectors: Alternative Evidence from Job Queues." *Journal of Labor Research*, Vol. 15, no. 1 (Winter), pp. 73–81.

Moore, William J., and John Raisian. 1991. "Government Wage Differentials Revisited." *Journal of Labor Research*, Vol. XII, no. 1 (Winter), pp. 13–31.

Mosher, Frederick C. 1982. *Democracy and the Public Service.* Oxford: Oxford University Press.

Moulton, Brent. 1990. "A Reexamination of the Federal-Private Wage Differential in the United States." *Journal of Labor Economics*, Vol. 8, no. 2 (April), pp. 270–93.

National Commission on the Public Service. 1989a. *Leadership for America: Rebuilding the Public Service, The Report of the National Commission on the Public Service.* Washington, DC: Government Printing Office.

_____. 1989b. *Leadership for America: Task Force Reports to the National Commission on the Public Service.* Washington, DC: Government Printing Office.

Nesbitt, Murray B. 1976. *Labor Relations in the Federal Government Service.* Washington, DC: Bureau of National Affairs.

Osborne, David E., and Ted Gaebler. 1992. *Reinventing Government: How the Entrepreneurial Spirit Is Transforming the Public Sector.* New York: Plume.

Osterman, Paul. 1994. "How Common is Workplace Transformation and Who Adopts It?" *Industrial and Labor Relations Review*, Vol. 47, no. 2 (January), pp. 173–88.

Painter, Nell I. 1987. *Standing at Armageddon.* New York: W.W. Norton.

Parker, Donald F., Susan J. Schurman, and B. Ruth Montgomery. 1984. "Labor-Management Relations under CSRA: Provisions and Effects." In P.W. Ingraham and C. Ban, eds. *Legislating Bureaucratic Change: The Civil Service Reform Act of 1978.* Albany, NY: State University of New York Press, pp. 161–81.

Radin, Bery, and Joseph Coffee. 1993. "A Critique of TQM: Problems of Implementation in the Public Sector." *Public Administration Quarterly* (Spring), pp. 43–54.

Risher, Howard, and Charles Fay. 1991. "Federal Pay Reform: A Response to an Emerging Crisis." *Public Personnel Management*, Vol. 20, no. 3 (Fall), pp. 385–95.

Risher, Howard, and Bridget W. Schay. 1994. "Grade Banding: The Model for Future Salary Programs?" *Public Personnel Management*, Vol. 23, no. 2. (Summer), pp. 187–99.

Rosenbloom, David H. 1992. "The Federal Labor Relations Authority." In P.W. Ingraham and D.H. Rosenbloom, eds., *The Promise and Paradox of Civil Service Reform.* Pittsburgh, PA: University of Pittsburgh Press, pp. 141–56.

Shafritz, Jay M., Norma N. Riccucci, David H. Rosenbloom, and Albert C. Hyde. 1992. *Personnel Management in Government.* New York: Marcel Dekker.

Shoop, Tom. 1995. "Going, Going, Gone." *Government Executive* (June), p. 18.

Slichter, Sumner H. 1961. "The American System of Industrial Relations: Some Contrasts with Foreign Systems." In John T. Dunlop, ed., *Potentials of the American Economy: Selected Essays of Sumner H. Slichter.* Cambridge, MA: Harvard University Press.

U.S. Department of Labor (U.S. DOL), Bureau of Labor Statistics. Various years. *Employment and Earnings.* Washington, DC: Government Printing Office.

_____. 1994. *Employment, Hours and Earnings: United States 1909–1994,* Vol. 2. Washington, DC: Government Printing Office.

U.S. Department of Labor—U.S. Department of Commerce. 1994a. Commission on the Future of Worker-Management Relations, *Fact Finding Report.* Washington, DC: GPO (May).

_____. 1994b. Commission on the Future of Worker-Management Relations, *Report and Recommendations.* Washington, DC: (December).

U.S. Equal Employment Opportunity Commission (EEOC). 1990, 1992. *Annual Report on the Employment of Minorities, Women and Handicapped Individuals in the Federal Government.* Washington, DC: Government Printing Office.

U.S. General Accounting Office (GAO). 1990a. *Federal Pay: Comparisons with the Private Sector by Job and Locality,* GAO/GGD-90–81FS. Washington, DC: Government Printing Office.

_____. 1990b. *Recruiting and Retention: Inadequate Federal Pay Cited as Primary Problem by Agency Officials,* GAO/GGD-90–117. Washington, DC: Government Printing Office.

_____. 1991a. *Federal Labor Relations: A Program in Need of Reform,* GAO/GGD-91–101. Washington, DC: Government Printing Office.

_____. 1991b. *Federal Pay: Private Sector Differences by Locality,* GAO/GGD-91–63FS. Washington, DC: Government Printing Office.

_____. 1992a. *Federal Employment: How Federal Employees View the Government as a Place to Work,* GAO/GGD-92–91. Washington, DC: Government Printing Office.

_____. 1992b. *Federal Recruiting: College Placement Officials' Views of the Government's Campus Outreach Efforts,* GAO/GGD-92–48BR. Washington, DC: Government Printing Office.

_____. 1993. *Affirmative Employment: Assessing Progress of EEO Groups in Key Federal Jobs Can Be Improved,* GAO/GGD-93–65. Washington, DC: Government Printing Office.

_____. 1994a. *Federal Employment: How Government Jobs Are Viewed on Some College Campuses,* GAO/GGD-94–181. Washington, DC: Government Printing Office.

_____. 1994b. *Tax Administration: IRS Can Strengthen Its Efforts to See That Taxpayers Are Treated Properly,* GAO/GGD-94–14. Washington, DC: Government Printing Office.

_____. 1995. *Performing Remote Bar Coding In-House Costs More Than Contracting Out,* GAO/GGD-95–143. Washington, DC: Government Printing Office.

U.S. Internal Revenue Service. Various years. *Annual Report of the Internal Revenue Service.* Washington, DC: Government Printing Office.

U.S. Merit Systems Protection Board (MSPB). 1989. *Who Is Leaving the Federal Government: An Analysis of Employee Turnover.* Washington, DC: Government Printing Office.

_____. 1990. *Why Are Employees Leaving the Federal Government: The Results from an Exit Survey.* Washington, DC: Government Printing Office.

_____. 1993. *Questions of Equity: Women and the Glass Ceiling in the Federal Government.* Washington, DC: Government Printing Office.

_____. 1994a. *Entering Professional Positions in the Federal Government*. Washington, DC: Government Printing Office.

_____. 1994b. *Working for America: An Update*. Washington, DC: Government Printing Office.

U.S. National Partnership Council. 1994. "National Partnership Council: A Draft Report on Implementing Recommendations of the National Performance Review." Mimeo (January). Washington, DC: U.S. NPC.

U.S. Office of Personnel Management (OPM). Various years. *Federal Civilian Workforce Statistics: Employment and Trends*. Washington, DC: Government Printing Office.

_____. Various years. *Federal Civilian Workforce Statistics: Occupations of Federal White-Collar and Blue-Collar Workers*. Washington, DC: Government Printing Office.

_____. Various years. *Federal Civilian Workforce Statistics: Pay Structure of the Federal Civil Service*. Washington, DC: Government Printing Office.

_____. 1995. *Federal Equal Opportunity Recruitment Program: Annual Report to Congress, FY 1994*. Washington, DC: Government Printing Office.

_____. Various years. *Union Recognition in the Federal Government*. Washington, DC: Government Printing Office.

U.S. Vice President. 1993. "Creating A Government That Works Better and Costs Less: The Report of the National Performance Review." Washington, DC: Government Printing Office (September).

Vaughn, Robert. 1992. "The U.S. Merit Systems Protection Board and the Office of the Special Counsel." In P.W. Ingraham and D.H. Rosenbloom, eds., *The Promise and Paradox of Civil Service Reform*. Pittsburgh, PA: University of Pittsburgh Press, pp. 121–40.

Walsh, John, and Garth Mangum. 1992. *Labor Struggle in the Post Office: From Selective Lobbying to Collective Bargaining*. New York: M.E. Sharpe Inc.

Wyatt Company. 1989. "Study of Federal Locality Pay." Sponsored by the U.S. Office of Personnel Management. Washington, DC: Government Printing Office.

Zipp, John F. 1994. "Government Employment and Black-White Earnings Inequality, 1980–1990." *Social Problems*, Vol. 41, no. 3 (August), pp. 363–81.

CHAPTER 6

Workplace Innovations and Systems Change in the Government Sector

ANIL VERMA
University of Toronto

JOEL CUTCHER-GERSHENFELD
Michigan State University

At the beginning of this century, employment relations in the public sector in Canada and the United States were dramatically transformed by the rise of the civil service. Driving the change were both internal forces in the rejection of the patronage political machines and the availability of external innovations, such as the bureaucratic organizational form and the principles of scientific management. Though there have been a number of subsequent waves of reform, it is only within the past half dozen years that we are beginning to see fundamental challenges to the century-old set of principles and assumptions that have been guiding employment relations at federal, state/province, and local levels.[1]

Today numerous organizational changes are under way challenging key features of the bureaucratic civil service model, including the flattening of hierarchy, the empowerment of employees, the streamlining of processes and procedures, the broadening of governance to include new stakeholders (especially citizens, workers and unions), and the privatization of specific operations or services. Some of these initiatives operate under the total quality management or continuous quality improvement umbrella. Other initiatives use the rubric of "reinventing government" or eliminating "government waste." Many of these changes are labor-management initiatives while others may be broader collaborations involving citizens and other stakeholders.

Underlying the many initiatives, however, are two very different competing sets of assumptions and principles guiding the change efforts. From an employment relations perspective, the two general approaches embody a longstanding debate in the field—whether labor should be viewed primarily as a cost to be reduced or as a source of value to be enhanced. For example, many of the privatization initiatives treat labor almost exclusively as a cost to be reduced. At the same time, the rhetoric and—to varying degrees—the reality of many quality initiatives focuses on the effective harnessing of employee ideas and energy around continuous improvement in operations.

In most cases, in practice, there are concurrent initiatives rooted in the two alternative approaches operating side by side or even intertwined with one another. For example, a total quality change effort may emphasize employee-led process improvement as a way of adding value, but it may also be used as a platform for restructuring that is seen by the same employees as draconian in nature.

The alternative organizational models in the public sector do not directly map onto the emerging private sector models, based on flexible specialization (Piore and Sable 1984), nonunion innovation (Kochan, Katz, and McKersie 1986), or lean manufacturing (Womak, Jones, and Roos 1990). However, they are comparable in scope and implications to many public sector initiatives for organizational change. Both the cost-based model and the value-added model fundamentally alter the traditional roles of managers, unions and employees, as well as the dynamics of the employment relations system.

In this chapter we review a selection of illustrative cases in order to identify the dynamics associated with the two change models. This is not a comprehensive review of public sector innovations in Canada or the U.S.—comprehensive data of this sort is scarce. Rather, it is an initial step toward a framework for thinking about workplace innovations in the public sector. This is a hypothesis generating exercise, not a hypothesis testing study. In that spirit, we conclude the paper with a set of propositions that are informed by these cases.

Scope and Definitions

Our focus in this chapter is on workplace innovations such as work redesign, team-based work systems, employee participation, joint training initiatives, total quality initiatives, labor-management partnerships, and dispute resolution systems. These are a subset of the many possible innovations, but together they are sufficient to illustrate key dynamics and underlying assumptions associated with workplace change in the public sector. While our analysis will begin with a focus on separate innovations, we find in each of our cases that the mix of changes underway quickly become entwined. Indeed, our own prior work in the private sector highlights the interconnections among different forms of work-place innovations (Cutcher-Gershenfeld, Kochan, and Verma 1991; Verma and Cutcher-Gershenfeld 1993).

Determining the extent of such innovation in the public sector is difficult. A number of surveys have been carried out in the last few years to determine the extent to which certain workplace innovations have diffused across Canadian and U.S. workplaces (Betcherman and McMullen 1986; Betcherman et al. 1994; Lawler, Mohrman, and Ledford 1992; Osterman 1994), but all have focused on the private sector. The lack of focus on the public sector may reflect various factors: the assumption that there were few if any changes in public sector establishments; the difficulty in defining the establishment in the public service (e.g., a whole government department or a given geographical location or both); and the lack of emphasis on workplace change because it does not directly relate to productivity and competitiveness. As such, it is difficult to assess the degree to which the cases examined here are (or are not) representative of public sector employment relations generally. Indeed, we know at the outset that our analysis is based on leading cases that are illustrative of the dynamics facing parties pursuing workplace innovation.

Another issue that needs clarification is articulation of the goals of workplace change. As noted earlier, parties will often initiate change for very diverse reasons. In the present era we are examining workplace change in the context of government spending cuts and the need to deliver better services—a situation that is parallel to, but not the same as, the competitive pressures driving change in the private sector. The analysis also takes as a point of departure a much higher level of unionization in the public sector in comparison to the private sector in the U.S. and Canada.

Normatively, we value workplace changes with goals centered both on achieving greater efficiency in the workplace and creating better jobs (i.e., safer, more interesting, well paying, and with more opportunities for advancement). Here we draw on a long industrial relations tradition, centering on the assumption that employment relations are mixed-motive in nature featuring a mixture of common and competing interests (Walton and McKersie 1965). Although both objectives may be theoretically compatible, we recognize that in practice the parties to the employment relationship may not always pursue both objectives with equal vigor. Further, as noted earlier, the two may even be manifest as counter-posed alternative avenues for change.

Toward a Framework

The literature on employer-employee relations in the public sector has emphasized many unique aspects of this sector relative to the private sector. It has been argued, for example, that the differential process and outcomes of collective bargaining can be explained, at least in part, by such unique features of the public sector as the absence of a market, the difficulty in measuring quality and output, the ambiguity and multifaceted nature of the employer, the use of voters and legislatures for "end runs," and the relative importance of an underlying mandate to serve the public (Taylor 1948; Kochan and Katz 1988). Although these "traditional" arguments have been updated in the 1990s (we discuss the updates in a later section), some of the factors are discussed below to highlight the effect they continue to have on the likelihood of workplace change and adoption of innovations.

Ambiguity Surrounding the Definition of Employer

In the public sector, there isn't one sole representative of the employer who has authority in the collective bargaining process as in the private sector. Responsibility for labor relations decisions is shared between professional managers and elected officials (Ponak and Thompson 1995). The latter often lack labor relations experience and have their own political agenda. This results in ambiguity surrounding the definition of employer. As well, the government has the dual role of acting both as an employer and a protector of public welfare (Swimmer and Thompson 1995).

Change processes in the private sector often begin with a vision and mission statement. Using the marine analogy, it is assumed that there is a captain of the ship who is charting the course and providing leadership for the team. The ambiguity surrounding the identity of the employer is likely to make workplace change more difficult to propose, design, and implement. For elected officials, workplace change can also pose a political risk. If the delivery of services is snagged during the implementation of a new workplace system, a complaining public could get practices reversed quickly to a traditional mode.

Ownership and Multilateral Decision-making Structure

In the private sector, private investors own the companies. In the public sector, however, the funds and resources come from a number of different sources (municipal, public, provincial), and therefore each source has a claim in the collective bargaining process which results in a timely and complex decision-making process (Ponak and Thompson 1995). Furthermore, if parties reach impasse during negotiations, union power is not sufficient to ensure a successful strike since a strong and determining factor in the union's success is public opinion (Lewin, Feuille, and Kochan 1992; Kearney 1984). This factor leaves the union and management each trying to make its case to the public in hopes of securing its support. In this environment it is very difficult to introduce and sustain change which needs a clear consensus among the parties and some local control over decisions that would lead to speedy decisionmaking.

Profit Motive is Absent

In the private sector the profitability of the firm is the primary output that is easily measured and evaluated. In the public sector, however, economic outcomes are not a high priority, and political outcomes such as public opinion take precedence. Workplace change, therefore, does not always have well-defined objectives such as profits or costs which can severely compromise its effectiveness and, in hindsight, its efficacy as a vehicle for organizational change.

Ability to Legislate

In the public sector the government has the ability to legislate, and this results in its unusual ability to influence labor relations and workplace affairs. The public employer can frequently resort to wage controls, back-to-work legislation, or "essential services" designation to achieve its desired goals rather than relying on the negotiations process (Panitch and Schwartz 1984; Thompson and Ponak 1992; Ponak and Thompson 1995). Some theorists question whether collective bargaining as it was intended still exists in the public sector given these government prerogatives (Swimmer and Thompson 1995). This situation deters the parties at the workplace level from engaging in ideas about workplace reform. Problems can be solved more expeditiously by resorting to controls and to legislation.

Public Sector Has a Monopoly on Its Services

Since the employers in the public sector are providing services for which their organization is the sole provider, there is little need to be concerned with quality because there is no competition or threat of the public using other services. In this regard the public does not put pressure on the agencies to improve the quality of the services provided. Government agencies also do not have a comparison group against which to be evaluated when decisions about restructuring are made. Thus the competitive pressure that often persuades private firms to introduce workplace change is often absent.

Centralized vs. Decentralized

In the Canadian public sector the nature of employer representation, be it on a sector-by-sector basis, or for the public sector as a whole, varies from province to province. For example, the public sector in Ontario is decentralized relative to British Columbia, Alberta, and to a lesser extent to Saskatchewan, Manitoba, New Brunswick, Nova Scotia, and PEI (Swimmer and Thompson 1995). As a result, one can conclude that the outcomes of collective bargaining in Ontario are less visible and the government is, therefore, less accountable for the results relative to collective bargaining in centralized provinces. One of the perceived consequences of this decentralization is that the government loses direct control over its budget (Derber 1988). This is perceived as a negative outcome given the government's current desire to control expenditure.

The private sector experience shows that workplace change is quite often a limited local "experiment" to see how new ideas work in practice. Rather than introduce changes such as teams or pay for knowledge company wide, firms introduce them in selected plants or divisions. Local management plays an important role in these decisions. In a highly centralized public service there may not be enough local autonomy either at the bargaining table or at the workplace to introduce reform in a limited context. The decentralized nature of successful workplace change efforts suggests that local buy-in and local control for fine tuning during implementation are critical to adoption and sustainability of workplace innovations. In general the public sector workplace may be handicapped in this area.

The "New" Public Management and Workplace Change

Since the 1980s a number of books and studies have promoted the idea of rethinking the role and activities of government (Levin and Sanger 1994; Savoie 1994; Borins 1994a, 1994b, 1995a; Osborne and Gaebler 1992; Pollitt 1988). The pressures of privatization, deregulation, technological change, and devolution of public decision making have all added up to questioning the scope and the methods of government activities. To put these new ideas in context, it is advisable to take stock of the historical context that has shaped the government sector.

In the post-World War II years, government spending increased rapidly in Canada and the U.S., often outracing growth in public revenues. In this kind of environment there was little emphasis on workplace efficiency and, hence, few initiatives were undertaken to move away from traditional workplace practices. The dramatic growth of public sector unions largely served to reinforce the existing system, replacing or supplementing civil service procedures with a parallel set of rules.

There was a flurry of public sector innovations in the late 1970s and early 1980s following the rise of the quality-of-work-life movement in the private sector. In this context there were numerous experiments with labor-management committees, quality circles, alternative pay systems and even some work redesign initiatives (Greiner et al. 1981). In some cases the experiments served to challenge the fundamental assumptions embodied in the civil service system, but most were "add-ons" to the existing system, modifying the rigid rules of bureaucracy through mechanisms for consultation and joint problem solving.

Beginning in the 1980s and extending into the 1990s, growing pressure was exerted on governments to slow the growth of, or even cut, public spending and to balance budgets. The International Monetary Fund, alarmed at the growing trend in budget deficits, set guidelines for budget deficits (3% of annual revenue) and for public debt (60% of GNP). These pressures can be likened to competitive pressures that force workplace change in the private sector. As these pressures mount through global financial markets, bond rating agencies, and domestic public opinion, public employers are more prone to examining workplace practices and introducing change.

Of course, improving efficiency is not the only response to the need to cut public spending. In the U.S., Vice-President Al Gore's 1993 National Performance Review called for reinventing government by introducing extensive changes in technology and work methods. This followed the central theme of Osborne and Gaebler's book, *Reinventing Government* (1992). Had these initiatives been announced a decade earlier, they would have likely been seen as dramatic in their scope and reach. Set in a world where many nations are privatizing entire sectors of government and rethinking core socialist assumptions, the reinvention theme seems almost modest in its ambitions. This was vividly illustrated in the United States after the 1994 mid-term elections, when the Republican party's so-called *Contract with America* shifted the emphasis from making service delivery more efficient to eliminating many government services.

A government budget crisis can be addressed through a number of responses from the public manager. First, the government can try to raise revenues through user fees, especially for those citizens who are most able to pay, and they can offer new services for which people may be willing to pay. Second, the government can cut costs by cutting services and programs. This may prove unpopular in some cases and, in others such as health and education, very difficult to achieve without compromising principles of universal access and minimum standards. Third, the public manager can respond by cutting costs. Since there are a variety of costs, these approaches would vary. Cutting wages and benefits (i.e., through concession bargaining) would be one response which has been tried with variable success in the private sector. Generating efficiencies through innovations in workplace organization is another way to cut costs (Savoie 1993; Borins 1995a, 1995b).

Our analysis is premised on the assumption that public managers would try to generate new efficiencies in government work through workplace innovations. Our point of departure is the traditional organizational form—the bureaucratic, civil service model (Johnson and Libecap 1994; Shafritz et al. 1992). It is important to recognize that this model emerged as an antidote to what was known as the "spoils" or the patronage system, which was in turn a response to a political system dominated by farmer elites. The virtues of the civil service system were its promise of clearly delineated job definitions, procedures for merit-based promotions, the ostensible linking of greater authority with greater knowledge and expertise, and the mitigation of the patronage system (Doeringer et al., this volume). Of course, the need to move away from a patronage system was aided by principles of scientific management. The result was a system that relied heavily on job descriptions and on standardization as opposed to individual creativity and flexibility in rules.

We highlight two emerging alternative models. Both approaches represent significant departures from the traditional, bureaucratic civil service model. The first, which we will refer to as the value-added model, emphasizes the way front-line employees are the primary source of added value in the operation. The second, which we will refer to as the cost-focused model, emphasizes labor's status as the single most expensive factor input in most government agencies.

The value-added model turns the hierarchical ordering of authority and expertise on its head. It holds that the most important knowledge and skill resides at the point of service delivery and that the rest of the organization needs to be reoriented around providing the necessary support and resources to the front-line employees. Issues of integration and capability are frequently resolved through the parallel creation of cross-functional service delivery teams, which run directly counter to the structure and control systems build into traditional government operations. For example, a service delivery team in a social service office may involve people from different government agencies working together to deliver whole activities that are funded out of a variety of federal, regional, and local sources. Yet, if they are sharing resources, such as files, telephone lines, and field visits, separate accounting by each source of funding for each activity may become quite complex to track and allocate.

The cost-focused model is also a significant departure in that it is premised on the reduction or elimination of bureaucracy. While solutions under this approach may also result in cross-functional teams, the primary aim is the elimination of hierarchical layers and the identification of alternatives to government providing various services. For example, in 1995 the governor of Massachusetts proposed providing people with lifetime drivers licenses, arguing that substantial savings are possible if people were not required to process license renewals. The primary research question driving our analysis concerns how the alternative models of government are manifest in selected examples of labor-management innovation.

Selected Workplace Innovations

Six types of workplace innovations are highlighted here: work redesign in a greenfield context, work redesign in a downsizing context, empowered work teams, labor-management partnerships, continuous quality improvement, and new dispute resolution systems. The general nature of each innovation in the public sector is discussed, followed by an illustrative case study. While the cases have been presented as illustrations of a given type of innovation, we highlight in each case the interconnections among multiple concurrent innovations. The cases are summarized in Table 1.

The Canadian cases have been collected from nominations for awards of excellence, received by the Institute for Public Administration of Canada. We picked those cases where several or all of the above mentioned aspects of workplace change formed the bulk of changes introduced. The U.S. cases were selected to span both state and federal sectors and to illustrate a diverse mix of change initiatives. As was noted earlier, these are all leading examples of workplace innovation which

TABLE 1

Selected Cases of Workplace Innovations in the Public Sector

Site, Organization/Union		Start Year	Coverage	Union Involvement	Part of Col. Agmt.	Description of Innovation	Outcomes
Office of the Registrar General, Govt of Ontario	OPSEU	1987	Whole department	Limited-staff redeployment, joint memorandum of understanding	No	Organization of Work—redesign, STS approach	Productivity—increased by 55% over the 1991 low
						Information, Consultation, Employee Involvement—teams, partnerships	Decreased salary costs
							Improved service
						Labor Relations—employment equity	Better jobs—job rotation, knowledge-based pay
						Training & Development—multiskilling	Employment Equity—women and minorities were 60% of the new workforce
						New Technology—Auto Imaging Technology	
CFB Shearwater	UNDE	1988	Construction Engineering	Yes	Yes	Organization of work—STS approach	Increased customer satisfaction
							Increased employee job satisfaction, those affected by the re-design
							Decrease in down-time

TABLE 1 (*Continued*)
Selected Cases of Workplace Innovations in the Public Sector

Site, Organization/Union		Start Year	Coverage	Union Involvement	Part of Col. Agmt.	Description of Innovation	Outcomes
B.C. Hydro	IBEW	1988	Electric business	Yes	No	Information, Consultation, Employee Involvement— teams	Employee ratings of management have increased
						Employee involvement— hiring, scheduling, and ordering	Employee ratings of job have increased
							Decline in turnover, absenteeism, and accident rates
							Concluded fiscal year with the highest net income in its history
MI DNR	UAW, OPE, SEIU, and others	1992	All Agency Employees	Extensive	No	Continuous Quality Improvement	Process improvement in many operations
							Development of pilot service delivery teams
							Development of cadre of trained facilitators of change

TABLE 1 (*Continued*)
Selected Cases of Workplace Innovations in the Public Sector

Site, Organization/Union	Start Year	Coverage	Union Involvement	Part of Col. Agmt.	Description of Innovation	Outcomes
National Partnership Council	AFGE, NFFE, NTU, and others	1993	All federal sector employees	Extensive	No	Labor-Management Partnership	Creation of a network of joint forums for managing change
							Initiation of a host of workplace reform experiments under the partnership framework
U.S. Post Office Lansing Mail Sorting Center	APWU	1989	All APWU bargained-for employees	Extensive	Yes	Alternative Dispute Resolution System	Reduction of a backlog in grievances and movement to resolution at lower levels
							Development of an internal process of grievance mediation

provide lessons for workplace parties as they head down these paths but are not necessarily representative of all or most public sector workplaces. Some of the cases are also discussed in other chapters of this volume, but our focus here is on the underlying principles relative to the two models presented at the outset of the chapter.

Work Redesign in a Greenfield Context

Most of the literature on workplace redesign is based on private sector experiments in what are known as "greenfield" settings, literally factories build in rural green fields (Rankin 1990; Trist 1981; Walton 1980). These settings frequently are designed to operate on a nonunion basis and have proven highly influential on employment relations in existing operations, both union and nonunion (Kochan, Katz, and McKersie 1986). There is comparatively little written, however, about the experience with greenfield settings in the public sector. In large part, this reflects the relative infrequency with which entire new operations are established and the even smaller subset of new facilities that are approached from a sociotechnical systems work redesign framework.

The redesign of a government operation provides a powerful opportunity to explore the relative importance of the two alternative organizational models highlighted at the outset of this chapter. The use of sociotechnical work redesign principles signals a likely emphasis on the value-added approach, with the potential for the new operation to represent a fundamental departure from the bureaucratic, civil service model. The key challenge in this context involves the degree to which the value-added approach also delivers on anticipated cost savings.

Case Example: Office of the Registrar General[2]

In 1987 the provincial government of Ontario announced its intention to relocate some government functions to communities in northern Ontario. The primary aim of the government's Northern Relocation Project was to utilize modern communications technology to move certain operations from downtown Toronto in an attempt to provide new public service job opportunities in Ontario's northern communities. The Office of the Registrar General (ORG), which has the responsibility for registering vital statistics (e.g., births, deaths, marriages, etc.) for the Province of Ontario, was part of the relocation program. It was to be moved from Toronto, a metropolis of 3 million, to Thunder Bay, a small regional city (population: 100,000) 1375 km from Toronto, and made operational by April 1991. Prior to the relocation the ORG employed

137 employees who were members of the Ontario Public Service Employees Union (OPSEU) which represents the bulk of all unionized employees of the government of Ontario.

The assistant deputy minister of the Ministry's Registration Division saw the move as a "greenfield" opportunity to plan, design, and implement an entirely new operation that would incorporate modern technology, promote learning and diversity, and solve some of the structural inefficiencies that were inherent in the operations at the Toronto location. A number of workplace innovations were undertaken such as the reorganization of work, information sharing, consultation, employee involvement, training and development, and introduction of new technology.

Organization of work. The records held in the ORG dated back to 1869 and were among the oldest retained by the province. They totalled about 20 million, a quantity which made work flow quite cumbersome and resulted in continual service backlogs. For example, if a mail request arrived it would pass through six separate units before the request was fully processed, and some customers were required to make two visits over at least a three-day period to gain access to their records.

An organizational review revealed that the Office of the Registrar General reflected a typical bureaucratic structure. It consisted of six layers of management from the director to the front line with very detailed job classifications. There were 147 staff and 41 job descriptions within 23 general job classifications. Communication between departments was restricted to the bureaucratic chain of command.

The ORG saw a need to redesign the office and did so through the sociotechnical systems (STS) perspective. This process includes both technical analysis which evaluates the operations involved in transforming inputs to outputs and social analysis which coordinates the activities that people perform in the transformation process. Three key STS principles guided the redesign. The first, multi-skilling, was key to the redesign because it equipped employees with broad skills and enabled them to perform different tasks as required. This was accompanied by a change in the pay system such that once a full-time training program was completed by clerical workers, their pay could increase by two pay grades. Second, jobs were enriched and the 23 classifications were condensed into three which meant less detailed job descriptions and more generic positions requiring greater judgment and creativity. The third principle required that the design process be continuous.

The redesigned structure integrated the twelve functional units into one multifunctional department that consisted of seven teams and was directed by the deputy registrar general. Each team consisted of twelve multiskilled team representatives and one team manager. The restructuring eliminated two levels of the management hierarchy and seven levels of clerical hierarchy. The redesign allowed for more independent decision making at the lower level, fewer reporting chains, and job enrichment, since the 41 original job descriptions were reduced to three (team representative, team manager, and the deputy registrar general).

Alternate work-time arrangements were available to the staff to accommodate individual needs. These included regular part-time, regular part-time night shift, a compressed work week, and flexible work hours. Workplace child care was also provided.

Innovations in technology. New technology was implemented in order to facilitate the redesign. Prior to the move to Thunder Bay, only about 5% of the information gathered at the ORG was stored and processed using information technology. The majority was stored in hard copy form, implying expensive storage, risk of losing records to fire or other natural disasters, and considerable space. The need for new information technology became evident. Auto Imaging Technology (AIT) was chosen, allowing for the storing of documents on optical platters which are similar to compact discs. The STS approach facilitated the integration of the employees with the new technology.

Innovations in training. The new ORG fosters a culture of continuous learning with knowledge acquisition being key to advancement within the branch. Job rotation serves as the mechanism for learning, and it is required of all employees. When clerical workers complete the full training program, as stated earlier, their pay may advance by two pay grades.

Innovations in partnership. In order to facilitate the move to Thunder Bay, the ministry pooled resources from outside groups through establishing partnerships with the private sector, nonprofit organizations, and the union.

ORG partnered with Arthur Andersen Consulting to work with Goodwill Industries, representing a multi-party public/private partnership. The task was to convert the paper records to electronic form using scanning technology. The ministry provided the user/system requirements and handled cost scheduling and contract management. Goodwill trained the scanners and supervisory personnel to operate 18 scanner work stations on two shifts, seven days per week. Arthur Andersen Consulting provided the technology, configured the environment, and supported the scanner personnel. The new staff consisted of 86 workers who had not had any previous computer experience and who had previously been on social assistance. The ORG reported that the project was completed on time, under budget, and at a savings of $750,000 in welfare benefit payments.

It was the goal of the ministry to recruit a workforce that was reflective of the local demographics. Of the 110 new recruits, 60% represented targeted groups (such as women, aboriginals, etc.) and 50 recruits were graduates from training programs through agencies sponsored by the federal Canadian Employment and Immigration Commission—an interagency partnership. This partnership reduced welfare and other social assistance costs by an estimated $1 million per annum.

There was concern that the lack of legislative support for union involvement in workplace change may have diminished union involvement throughout the process; however, an unsigned agreement between Ontario Public Employees' Union (OPSEU) and the ministry guided both parties throughout the redesign and encouraged union involvement. The ORG relied on OPSEU for input in managing the redeployment of non-relocating staff from downtown Toronto. Only six of the staff from the Toronto office relocated. Those who did not relocate were offered various forms of assistance to find other jobs, including favored access to certain job competitions, skills upgrading programs, job interview skills training, and psychological counseling. This partnership was also important in compiling the Memo of Agreement between the union and management which outlined parameters for a new philosophy statement, equity recruitment, a training plan, and alternate work strategies. This partnership reinforced and further developed the ongoing and consultative relationship between ORG and OPSEU.

Innovations in hiring. In the relocation project, the ORG's goal was to target members of underrepresented groups. Of the 110 new recruits, 60% came from the designated groups: 10% aboriginal, 14% physically challenged, 5% Francophones, and 6% visible minorities. Of the new recruits altogether, 81% were female. A committee comprised of designated group members was established to assist in the recruitment of employees represented by these groups, and a development program was established to train native Canadian managers. The ORG also expanded the category of underrepresented groups to include social assistance recipients and single parents.

Outcomes. Immediately after the relocation, the ORG experienced delays and poor customer service; however, these problems were only temporary. By the following year productivity improved and costs decreased. The redesign achieved a number of results for the ORG. The number of requests processed per employee went from 5,000 per year at an average cost of $5.42 to 7,200 at an average cost of $4.75. The turnaround time for mail-in requests went from six weeks to four weeks. Auto-imaging service times for in-person[3] requests went from days to minutes, serving to benefit individuals who are in need of birth or death certificates on the spot.

The redesign also led to the creation of more meaningful jobs. Recognition and advancement became tied to knowledge acquisition. Job rotation is standard. There is no status differentiation between different jobs within the team, and communication is improved by the fact that there is only one level in the hierarchy.

The ORG redesign combined new technology with the STS approach to create an enriched work environment and to improve service. It provided new public service opportunities for communities in northern Ontario; and it allowed the ministry in the process of moving to plan, design, and implement an entirely new operation. Through the redesign, the ORG formed a number of partnerships with the government, community, and the union, and in so doing, employed members of traditionally underrepresented groups and those on social assistance. This, in turn, saved millions of dollars in welfare benefit payments. Improvements occurred in productivity, service, and production costs. The success of the redesign inspired other departments, such as the Personal Property Security Division, to conduct similar technological change projects (which do not necessarily involve greenfield sites).

The savings and efficiency improvements reported above clearly required new investments in technology and incurred other personnel costs such as moving, severance, etc. Although expenditures for the department as a whole were available for the years when the move took place, costs directly attributable to the reorganization were difficult for the researchers to track. Information provided by key informants, however, did establish that personnel costs were minimal as most dislocated employees found alternate employment within the government or outside. Thus unemployment or other welfare costs arising out of the move were negligible. The amount of investment in new technology at the new location was roughly $6 million; however, it is difficult to estimate what portion of this cost was attributable to the move itself. Most of this cost would have been incurred even if the move had not occurred. Although a full cost-benefit analysis would be illuminating, the purpose of this brief overview of the case is not to suggest that efficiency considerations alone were the driving factors of change in this organization.

Clearly, this case is illustrative of a dramatic departure from the traditional bureaucratic model. Given that the innovation was centered on a set of value-added assumptions, employees and the union were able to take on very different roles centered on high involvement and partnership. The diffusion of the model will be important to trace, however, given that there are still likely to be comparatively few additional greenfield opportunities.

Work Redesign in the Context of Downsizing

While greenfield opportunities may be rare in the public sector, work redesign in the context of downsizing has become quite commonplace in the public and private sectors. Many of the redesign opportunities are nothing more than new ways to make do with fewer hands and less resources. In other cases the combination of necessity and opportunity created by the downsizing becomes the foundation for fundamental rethinking of the underlying assumptions about how government operations should be structured.

In the context of the two alternative models highlighted in this chapter, it might be expected that the cost-focused model would dominate, given that labor costs are typically the primary factor driving a downsizing. In this context the key challenge involves the degree to which the pursuit of cost savings does not undercut employee motivation and commitment to add value.

Case Example: CFB Shearwater/UNDE Local 80409[4]

In the fall of 1990, shrinking budgets, Treasury Board directives to reduce employment, and the union and management's search for an effective change strategy paved the way for work redesign efforts at Canadian Forces Base (CFB) Shearwater. This base is located just outside of Dartmouth, a community near Halifax, Nova Scotia. The base provides Sea King helicopters and trains crews to support naval vessels attached to the Maritime Command. Approximately 2,000 military personnel and civilians worked at the base in 1990 when the work redesign initiative began. Of the 475 civilians, 375 were members of the Union of National Defense Employees (UNDE), Local 80409.

Although the Shearwater base was not explicitly threatened with downsizing or closure at the time the work redesign process began, there was a general threat of downsizing facing all CFBs. At Shearwater the management and the union agreed to a clause in their collective agreement providing for an employment security guarantee against any layoffs that could result from the work redesign process. If personnel were rendered surplus as a result of work redesign, they were to be offered alternate employment and retraining if needed.

Pressure especially hit the Construction Engineering (CE) section because it had a reputation of being inefficient. The CE section is responsible for the design, construction, and maintenance of all structures on the base, from single-family homes to aircraft runways. This section had 200 employees, 125 of whom were union members. Most of the employees were tradespeople and some were military and civilian managers, engineers, draftspeople, clerks, and laborers.

The UNDE and Air Command reached an agreement to undertake a joint change initiative at two bases, beginning at CFB Shearwater. It was believed that a joint initiative was necessary for the redesign to be successful and to ensure employee commitment to the changes. The sociotechnical systems (STS) approach was chosen as it was most suited to their needs. The workplace innovation at CFB Shearwater is an example of an innovation relating to the organization of work and will be described as such.

The work redesign was carried out under a three-level committee system: a Senior Review Team (SRT), a Quality of Work Life (QWL) Steering Committee, and a Redesign Team. There was union representation at all levels of the committee system. A representative from the UNDE National Office was on the SRT; the internal coordinator of the QWL steering committee was a union member; and the union vice-president was on the redesign team. Union representation at all levels reinforced management's commitment to a joint change initiative.

At the beginning of the redesign process, the redesign team observed the current operating system, analyzed the process, and then recommended changes. CE employees, senior managers and union officials outside the base, and customers' opinions about problem areas or suggested improvements were solicited. Efficiency data were collected prior to the redesign to provide baseline productivity measures. The greatest gain in performance resulted from changing how the material was delivered to the work site.

After gathering and analyzing the data, the team recommended seven areas for in-depth analysis. Separate study groups were formed to further investigate each of the seven areas. It became evident that reworking the overall approach to construction engineering was necessary. The redesign team developed 41 integrated recommendations and an implementation plan from the information collected to date. Some of the changes included a move from nine single-trade shops and five levels of management to four mixed-trade zones and four levels of management; from centralized work control to three-zone work control; from hit-and-miss training to a full-time civilian trainer and a training committee; from management unilaterally hiring staff, ordering shop stock, and scheduling customer visits to worker involvement in hiring, ordering their own shop stock and scheduling customer visits.

Outcomes. The redesign produced noticeable outcomes. Results were compared to data obtained by the redesign team prior to the change process. Improvements in service were noted by customers almost immediately. The percentage of customers who were either satisfied or very satisfied with the overall performance of CE nearly doubled from 50% to 90%. Efficiency measures increased by 25% to 30%. At mid-trial, employee satisfaction also increased from a mean of 5.1 to 6.9 (measured on a 10-point rating scale), while the satisfaction of those not involved in the redesign decreased. Job satisfaction was assessed via interviews and focus groups, and at the end of the trial period it was found that 90% to 95% of the employees who had been directly affected by the STS redesign reported increased job satisfaction.

Other evidence suggests that there was a decrease in first-stage grievances, a drop from two to zero, and that tradespeople were spending 28% more time, on average, doing productive work, as opposed to, for example, waiting for directions and supplies. Work was consistently completed under budget in the 1992 trial period, and this was not the case in 1991, a comparison year.

The case of CFB Shearwater is an example of work redesign in the context of a downsizing.[5] The main vehicle for these changes was the STS approach to job redesign. The project was characterized by extensive employee involvement throughout the whole process, as well as being a joint union-management initiative right from the beginning. In these regards the case illustrates key steps toward the construction of a new work system even where the downsizing was primarily driven by cost factors. This suggests that the context alone does not necessarily determine the model of workplace change that is adopted.

Empowered Work Teams

The burgeoning literature on work teams is primarily focused on the private sector, though implications for the public sector are often noted (Katzenback and Smith 1993; Tjosvold 1991). However, most discussions of teams in the public sector say little about the degree to which they are part of a fundamental departure from the bureaucratic, civil service model. It is possible, of course, for the traditional model to feature work to be organized around work groups even with a measure of job rotation. However, to the degree that the team has increasing responsibility and authority, it represents a shift toward the value-added view that the most important expertise in the organization is at the point of service delivery.

Case Example: B. C. Hydro[6]

In the spring of 1988, B.C. Hydro, Canada's third largest electric utility, unveiled a dramatic new Corporate Strategic Plan designed to reshape and rejuvenate the organization. The mission of the organization was "to support the development of British Columbia through the efficient supply of electricity." Its gas and rail divisions were accordingly sold off.

Corporate objectives were created that focused on being the most efficient utility in North America, maximizing its contribution to the economic development of British Columbia, being a superior customer service company, being one of the best employers in British Columbia, and minimizing the impact of its activities on the natural environment. Corresponding corporate values and business principles were established to guide work processes. The organizational structure was changed to reflect key business units, and the hierarchy was flattened to an average of 4.6 layers between the chairman and front-line management.

The new corporate vision was communicated to every employee through the work group leaders who met with their groups and reviewed a video explaining the company objectives and its new vision. The employees provided feedback on the new objectives during a discussion session and through the completion of surveys. The critical issues raised by employees included employment security, training, the operating styles of managers, and communications to employees. The company responded to these issues through the establishment of an employment security policy, the quadrupling of training investments and the empowerment of supervisors in making training decisions, the initiation of an intensive management-style change process, and the establishment of an electronic-mail-based newsletter. The empowerment of managers through a confidential feedback-based experiential change process allowed them to focus on personal behavior changes required to develop a management style that was more suited to the new corporate vision. These managers established contracts that outlined behavior changes. Adherence to the contract would directly affect their results-based pay.

Managers were empowered to do their own strategic planning. The concept of empowered work teams was introduced as a means of increasing productivity and job satisfaction and improving customer service. The implementation of workteams was strictly voluntary. If they were to be adapted, managers and their employees would jointly decide on new ways of redrawing the traditional boss-subordinate "contract" and transferring some of the "position power" of the boss to the team. Interested managers were trained in advance on how to empower their employees and how to change their role from decisionmaker/director to supporter/coach. Performance-based bonuses are paid to the empowered workteams. Those work units that decided on empowered workteams participated in a two-day change workshop which provided the members with the appropriate direction. The workshop covered how the work unit supported the key business unit's mission, the customers' needs and how the work team could satisfy the needs, possible impediments to success, analysis, action plans, agreements for change, measures of success, and follow-up plans.

A "Statement of Principles" had been signed with the International Brotherhood of Electrical Workers, Local 258, which provided for the establishment of a Joint Implementation Team to ensure effective consultation during the implementation phase. It also ensured that IBEW-affiliated employees would be represented on the team of empowered workteam workshop facilitators.

Outcomes. In nine months about 25% of the managers and employees had voluntarily chosen the empowered workteam approach. By December 1990, 162 separate teams were functioning. Most of the teams are in the early stages of a three- to five-year maturing process. The trust and communication levels are up, and employees report that they are working more effectively. About 10% of the teams have started to develop new ways to improve their operations and measure changes and are clearly starting to impact the bottom line.

B.C. Hydro is slowly starting to see the benefits of the New Corporate Strategic Plan. Employee ratings of managers and of the job, in general, have improved; turnover, absenteeism, and accident rates have decreased; and the organization is accomplishing all of its targeted industry efficiency comparisons.

Although the employer and the union are making progress toward a team-based model that truly harnesses employees' capability to add value, they are still a long way from this ideal. At this stage they are still vulnerable to changes made under the auspices of the cost-based approach. This applies equally to the union-management partnership governing the process. Indeed, as a public utility, B.C. Hydro is subject to a host of competitive business pressures that are likely to focus attention on labor cost. If the initiative can survive these test events, then it is on the way toward becoming a robust alternate to the traditional bureaucratic model.

Continuous Quality Improvement

Modern quality principles build on a set of statistical principles forged in the United States during World War II and then extended to the organizational level in Japan during the post-war recovery (Deming 1986; Ono 1988). At their core the principles take as a given the fact that there will be variation in performance at all levels of the organization. They suggest the point of service delivery or product manufacture as the places to begin reducing variation and identify the front-line employee as most important in accomplishing this task. As such, these initiatives are in principle unambiguously rooted in the value-added model. In fact, however, many cost-cutting initiatives are cloaked in the rhetoric of quality, with the implication that cynicism and distrust are reinforced. Direct cuts in labor in this case are not just unwelcome, they are seen as a violation of the stated quality principles. This tension can be found in the private sector as well. In fact, public sector managers who propose a quality initiative are typically confronted with the baggage that TQM has accumulated in the private sector.

Case Example: The Michigan Department of Natural Resources and Five Unions[7]

At the end of 1992 a strategic planning study of the Michigan Department of Natural Resources urged the adoption of a Total Quality Management initiative. Among the agency's top leaders there was a broad range of reactions from enthusiastic support to vocal opposition. Moreover, there was an even broader range of understandings around just what this concept meant.

In order to better understand the concept and its implications for the DNR, a design team was assembled. Consisting of about a dozen middle and top managers, the team spanned the three major segments of the agency: environmental protection, parks/recreation, and administration. The design team worked closely with faculty and staff from Michigan State University to explore quality principles and potential applications in the public sector. At the conclusion of the study it was recommended that the umbrella term "Continuous Quality Improvement" (CQI) be utilized and that a coordination team be established to oversee the work of eight implementation task forces targeted at issues such as communications, training, rewards, and stakeholders. While some members of the design team strongly urged that the five unions who represented DNR employees should be involved early on in the process, the top management leadership team was reluctant to reach out to unions until it had made some progress sorting out its own internal disagreements about the concept and its implications.

Initial efforts centered on the development of a common process improvement model, a set of guidelines for Quality Action Teams, and the development of a week-long Facilitator Institute in partnership with MSU. Within the first year approximately eighty CQI facilitators were trained in process improvement and group facilitation skills. Combined with another twenty facilitators who had been trained in conjunction with the federal Park Service or other efforts, this represented a substantial cadre of people, each of whom was able to devote up to four hours per month assisting Quality Action Teams who were applying quality principles. Some of the initial group of facilitators also developed and delivered a series of orientation sessions for managers and employees around the state.

One early success, for example, involved a Quality Action Team that examined the time and attendance policies. It conducted a process map of the procedure by which employee hours are recorded and processed in order to generate payroll checks. For about half of the divisions there were comparatively few steps involved. For the remaining divisions, however, there were approximately three times the number of steps in which paper was handled and then passed along to someone else. A preliminary analysis indicated that there was no functional distinction among the divisions that would account for the extra steps. A root cause analysis revealed that the extra steps had been added bit by bit over the years in response to various special case problems, even though those problems may have been infrequent or one time events. Thus the analysis enabled the organization to eliminate many unnecessary steps, speed turn-around time in payroll, and re-allocate freed up staff.

Concurrently, the stakeholder task force became increasingly vocal in insisting that the five unions be brought into the process. When they were approached, however, the unions expressed resentment at not having been included at the outset and skepticism about the quality principles. A series of briefings and constructive discussions ensued, combined with separate, off-line meetings of the union leaders. Within three months some of the unions were expressing cautious enthusiasm about the quality principles, while others continued to be highly skeptical. Still, they all agreed that it was better to take on joint responsibility for the process than to let it happen without their input. Accordingly, they asked for five seats on the coordination team. Management was initially only willing to grant one or two seats. It took a joint session of the top union and management leaders for management to be persuaded of the resolve and constructive approach taken by the union leaders, as well as the impossibility of allocating two seats among these five unions. Ultimately, the coordination team was disbanded (concurrent with the completion of initial work by many of the implementation task forces), and a new guidance team was established with five union seats, four management seats, and two seats for nonmanagerial, nonrepresented employees. Also, a new management position was created for the Director of Continuous Quality Improvement, which was filled by the former personnel director for the agency who had been instrumental in the initiative.

One series of events is particularly instructive in illustrating the dynamics around the integration of the unions in the quality initiative. When the first group of eighteen facilitators was attending the week-long training institute, it had been arranged for there to be a Thursday afternoon panel consisting of the leadership of the five unions and labor relations officials from the department and the state office of the employer. The purpose of the panel was for facilitators to understand and help manage the boundary between collective bargaining matters and quality issues. At this point the panel members were all still new to quality principles. When the panel was asked about this issue, all the panelists (union and management) were in agreement. They told the facilitators that the quality action teams must limit their activities just to issues covered by the management rights clause of the contract. The facilitators, most of whom were bargaining unit members, were furious, contending that solving systems problems would not be possible with what they saw as artificial constraints. The issues remained unresolved by the end of the session.

About three months later the panel was convened at MSU's next Facilitator Training Institute. The same issue came up early, but this time the panelists were more encouraging. They cautioned against quality action teams taking on any active grievances or attempting to renegotiate any contractual rights. Still they acknowledged the potential value of applying quality principles to problems that might be solved before they became the source of grievances. Over the course of the next couple of meetings, the basic guideline remained, but many of the union leaders became even more encouraging as they came to see the use of quality principles as another way to address the interests of their members.

Around this time it became clear that the splits among top management around CQI were symptomatic of much deeper divisions, especially between the environmental and recreational parts of the agency (which contrasted in culture and whether the function was regulation or service provision). The new guidance team became a strong voice for the process with the unions now playing a key role in partnership with the management members of the guidance team. Together they provided support for the facilitators and the Quality Action Teams at a time when this support was less solid among top management. A divisional strategy emerged as well, where targeted support was provided to divisional managers anxious to apply quality principles in their division. Under the CQI umbrella there began to be experiments in the complete restructuring of field offices and the use of multi-disciplinary service delivery teams. Still the spread of diffusion has fallen short of what was implied at the statewide employee-orientation sessions, at least partly due to the lack of unified support at the top management level.

A series of strategic planning sessions for top management leadership helped to identify a complementary strategic framework centered on what was termed "eco-system management." Instead of pulling the top labor and management leadership together, this became one more point of contention. The director responded to pressure for results from the governor by unilaterally announcing a major downsizing. Ultimately, in the summer of 1995, Michigan's governor announced the split of the organization with creation of a new agency devoted to environmental protection and a reduced mandate left for the Department of Natural Resources. At present both organizations have expressed continued support for the CQI concept, but there are already indications that each will be applying the principles in its own way.

Outcomes. Many specific process improvements have been made throughout the organization. Concurrently, the institutional role of the unions has been expanded and relations among the unions have improved dramatically. As well, a cadre of talented facilitators has been developed. At the same time, some of the delays in diffusion have reinforced a preexisting deep cynicism about change in the agency, and the larger organizational tensions overrode the value-added spirit of the CQI initiative.

In this case, the tensions between the two models are acute, and both run against the inertia of the existing, bureaucratic civil service model. While the successes point toward fundamental restructuring of work and labor-management relations, the tensions at the top level have led to concurrent cost cutting and distributive splits in the operations. In many ways this is a case poised at the crossroads of the two alternative models but unable to continue traveling down a combination of the two paths.

Labor-Management Partnerships

The concept of labor-management partnerships dates back at least to the turn of the century in the United States and Canada with numerous public and private sector examples in the intervening hundred years. These partnerships have historically been debated relative to collective bargaining with the general conclusion that the partnerships can be vital complements to the collective bargaining process but poor substitutes for bargaining (Cutcher-Gershenfeld 1985; Gomberg 1967; Golden and Parker 1955; Douglas 1921). More recently, however, research in the private sector points to emerging partnerships that represent fundamentally new relationships between labor and management—social contracts premised on employee commitment and labor-management cooperation (Walton, Cutcher-Gershenfeld, and McKersie 1994). While there is not a well-developed literature on these partnerships in the public sector, the partnerships would be most likely to emphasize the value-added organizational model. A clear question arises around the capability of public sector partnerships to manage concurrent cost-cutting initiatives.

Case Example: U.S. National Partnership Council and Agency Partnerships[8]

On October 1, 1993, President Clinton issued Executive Order 12871 which established clear top leadership support for the principle of labor-management partnerships. The executive order was drafted to reinforce a National Performance Review which mandates that every federal agency identify its customers and assess how well it is meeting its customer's needs. The order stated, in part:

> Only by changing the nature of Federal labor-management
> relations so that managers, employees, and employees' elected
> union representatives serve as partners will it be possible to
> design and implement comprehensive changes necessary to
> reform Government. . . . Labor-management partnerships will
> champion change in Federal Government agencies to trans-
> form them into organizations capable of delivering the highest
> quality services to the American people.

In the short period since this executive order, a number of new partnerships were established: a national Partnership Council, agency partnerships in nearly all major federal agencies, and countless mid-level and
local-level partnerships under the auspices of the agency partnerships.
The initial executive order had a two-year time frame, and this was recently extended to September 30, 1997.

Under the partnership structure, for example, the U.S. Department
of Agriculture has an agency-level partnership council consisting of the
top agency officials as management and representatives from all unions
with exclusive representation rights for agency employees. As well,
there are a number of mid-level partnerships such as the partnership
council in Food and Consumer Services, which includes the management leadership from this division of the agency and the relevant union
officials. At the facility level there are union-management partnerships
at a number of Food and Consumer Services locations.

Guiding the partnership initiatives are two basic principles, pushing
decision making to the lowest possible level and utilizing interest-based
bargaining principles. From a process point of view, the partnerships
have proven an important source of innovation. For example, at the
Norfolk Navy Yards the most recent collective bargaining agreement
was negotiated in 23 days, in comparison to a drawn out three-year-long
negotiations over their last contract.

Many of these partnerships have become forums where difficult
issues are being addressed concerning maintaining services in the face
of budget cuts and other constraints on resources. Parties report that
many of the seemingly win-lose issues can be transformed in constructive ways when they keep the focus on pushing decisions to the lowest
levels and when the interest-based negotiations principles are applied.
For example, the Red River Army Depot operates with a number of
clear performance measurables which enable it to calculate direct cost
savings from improvement ideas. By jointly negotiating and implementing a gainsharing program, the partnership at this location has provided

a constructive framework for cost savings. The bottom line is that $1.5 million in gainsharing payments have been made, reflecting a successful harnessing of employee ideas and energy.

One interesting implication of the overall partnership initiative concerns the institutional roles of federal sector unions. Traditionally, these unions have had a constrained role, with many economic issues outside the scope of bargaining and other institutions (such as the civil service) providing parallel forums for channelling disputes. The executive order is explicit, however, in making a number of permissive subjects of bargaining mandatory issues for discussion in the partnership forums. Consequently, unions are motivated to enter the partnerships since they represent a unique avenue to expand their capability to represent their members. Concurrently, many managers are finding that the union leadership brings new ideas and a capacity to help marshall the collective energies of federal employees.

Outcomes. Although the initiative is still comparatively new, the federal partnerships have already altered the landscape of federal sector labor relations. They have helped to expand the role and influence of federal sector unions, served as a forum for addressing a number of complex and contentious issues, and begun to build a lasting infrastructure of local-, agency-, and national-level councils.

Preliminary evidence regarding the U.S. federal partnerships suggests that they have been surprisingly robust in dealing with highly divisive issues. Their apparent success is traceable to three interrelated factors: the clear top leadership support from the President's office, the worse alternative of having the change imposed through a cost-cutting process, and the institutional opportunity for unions to expand the scope of their influence.

Dispute Resolution Systems

Following the publication of the book, *Getting to YES* (Fisher and Ury 1983), there has been a dramatic growth in scholarship and field experiments with alternative dispute resolution (ADR) systems (Ury, Brett, and Goldberg 1988; Rowe 1984). Most of this literature is focused on workplace disputes in the private sector. In the public sector the ADR literature has centered mostly on alternative approaches to public disputes (such as environmental disputes, neighbor-to-neighbor disputes, public rule-making disputes, etc.) (Singer 1994; Susskind and Cruikshank 1987). While the overall literature talks extensively about transforming the nature of disputes, there is relatively little said about transforming the nature of organizations.

In fact, a close look at ADR principles reveals important parallels with both of the alternative models emerging. The emphasis on resolving disputes close to the source matches nicely with the value-added focus on the front-line employees. At the same time the recognition of distributive or claiming aspects to a dispute (Walton and McKersie 1965) provides a useful theoretical framework to explore the nature of the cost-based approach.

Case Example: U.S. Postal Service Lansing Mail Sorting Center and APWU[9]

In 1990 the U.S. Postal Service's Lansing Mail Sorting Center received national sanction to be one of six pilot experiments under national contract language for labor and management partnerships (LAMPs). At the time the parties were locked in a highly contentious relationship driven by extensive changes in technology, combined with a culture of distrust and even antipathy between employees and first-line supervisors. In this one setting with about 400 employees, for example, there was a backlog of over 2,000 unresolved grievances and a total of 31 grievances going to arbitration in the eighteen months prior to the LAMPs initiative. Under the LAMPs language a labor-management committee was formed. It should be noted that the APWU at the national and local levels chose the committee format in direct rejection of the quality-of-work-life language and approach embraced by some of the other postal unions at this time.

One of the first agenda items tackled by the LAMPs group was the grievance backlog. A set of union and management appointees were selected and empowered to jointly investigate and resolve backlogged grievances. At the same time these individuals were designated as step A in the grievance procedure as a screen before a grievance was passed out of the hands of the supervisor and steward. Within the first year the individuals worked with the committee and successfully eliminated most of the backlog. While there was also an increase in resolutions at the early stages of the grievance procedure, the LAMPs appointees quickly recognized that a long-term solution would have to reach beyond any set of appointees.

As a next step, a special union-management task force was established to collect data on the five most frequent types of grievances. For example, overtime issues were a common source of contention. Then on a joint basis, sample grievances were examined, and the task force developed consensus agreements on how to interpret the contract language. These recommendations were then presented in a training session for all supervisors and stewards along with training in communications and problem-solving skills.

There continued to be a decline in grievances, and the grievances that were filed were generally resolved at lower levels with only two arbitration cases in the two years following the initiation of the LAMPs program. However, the daily contentiousness remained between labor and management. Not only were there still a number of grievable issues, it was increasingly evident that many of the grievances filed had root causes that went far deeper than the contract provision specified. Deep conflicts might exist between a supervisor and an employee based on noncontractual issues, but the dispute would show up as a grievance since that was one of the few forms of voice available. In response to this complex reality, the parties embarked on an ambitious next step in the LAMPs process.

By this time there had been three successive pairs of LAMPs appointees, all of which had demonstrated the value of joint data collection and informal mediation of workplace disputes. The parties decided to extend the idea of mediation considerably by introducing the notion of peer mediation. To support this process a draft social contract was developed by the leadership which featured shared understandings of what people in the workplace might expect of one another. Then, all of the represented employees and their supervisors/managers attended a series of training sessions where they were briefed on the history of LAMPs, the task force interpretations of the commonly contested parts of the contract, and the content of the proposed social contracts. The employees in each work area were then afforded the chance to modify the language and come to consensus on this social contract. Concurrently, they were provided some mediation training and told that any employee could (under the social contract) request mediation assistance from any other employee in order to help resolve a dispute.

Following the training, a number of employees indeed served as peer mediators, and some work areas began to report the early signs of a more constructive workplace climate. However, a major restructuring of the organization resulted in the transfer of key managers associated with the initiative. Further, major budget cuts raised new tensions between the union and the employer. Within the union there was also a growing split between advocates of even closer partnership (on the one hand)

and those who were increasingly concerned that the union was too close to management already. In this climate some of the momentum of the LAMPs effort was dissipated, especially as the union leadership in power became more vocal in its challenges to management.

A year later, however, the 1995 local union elections turned on this issue with a new leadership slate elected on a platform of working more closely with management. Indeed, the newly elected president had been one of the initial LAMPs mediators appointed to the step A position. Today these efforts are being revived and linked to broader quality and work restructuring initiatives, though the ultimate success depends on the still very complicated task of untangling the underlying contentious and sometimes abusive culture.

Outcomes. The most direct outcomes of the initiative have been a dramatic reduction in the backlog of unresolved grievances, an equally dramatic reduction in the inflow of new grievances, and the virtual elimination of lengthy appeals to arbitration. Concurrently, increased capability has been built among a number of union and management officials. Finally, some progress has been made in reducing the most abusive features of the shopfloor climate.

The experience in the Lansing Mail Sorting Center illustrates the potential reach of an initiative designed to improve the resolution of disputes. What started as a relatively simple experiment in grievance mediation at the early steps of the grievance procedure came to include training for supervisors and stewards, joint task forces on contract interpretation, and the forging of a social contract to govern relations. The sustainability of the initiative was tested, however, by agencywide layoffs and other cost-based actions. At this point the election of the new union leaders represents a pivotal event that is pointing toward a redoubling of efforts around the value-added model.

Learning from the Cases

Despite the limited scope and number of cases examined in this chapter, the evidence points to several factors that may be critical in thinking about introducing and implementing workplace innovation in the public sector. Each will be addressed in turn.

Alternative Models for Change

At the outset, it is clear that all of the change initiatives examined represent important alternatives to the bureaucratic civil service model.

Further, they all draw primarily on the value-added model identified at the beginning of this chapter. Yet, aspects of the cost-based model are interwoven with these cases. Thus this analysis has pointed to what might be called a debate in progress—the relative merits and limitations of these alternative models are being sorted out in real time.

In some cases, such as the Office of the Registrar General in Ontario, we saw the early signs of the value-added model taking hold. In other cases, such as the Michigan Department of Natural Resources, the diffusion of this model has been circumscribed by internal management politics and other factors. A clear issue for further research would center on the degree to which the present mix of change initiatives in the public sector do represent a fundamental alternative to the traditional civil service model (as we have argued they do) and, if so, the degree of diffusion of this model. As a possible aid to such research, we offer the following proposition which is derived from our case examples (and other experiences of each author):

> *Proposition 1:* The present forces of change in the public sector will drive the emergence of alternative models of government service that are fundamentally different from the bureaucratic, civil service model.

Impetus for Change

As is often the case in the private sector, many of these cases of workplace reform have been driven by a crisis of some sort. For example, the Lansing Mail Sorting Center faced a crisis in the form of an escalating set of battles around the grievance procedure, while the Canadian Forces base faced the crisis of a closing of the facility. We know from the private sector experience that innovation best flourishes in a middle domain where the crisis is neither so severe as to stifle innovation nor so mild as to enable complacency. We also know that the diffusion of innovation depends on leadership, relationship building, and other factors, not just a continued state of crisis (Verma and Cutcher-Gershenfeld 1993). This preliminary analysis of cases suggests parallel dynamics between the public and private sectors, even if the specifics of the crises are different.

It should be noted, however, that not all cases were driven by crisis at the outset. This was the case at the Michigan Department of Natural Resources, for example, where the primary driver was a comprehensive strategic planning task force report that looked to private sector innovation in Total Quality Management as a model. Similarly, the U.S. partnership initiative is driven primarily by the top leadership and a perceived need to align labor-management relations with an overall performance review in government. In these cases the driver is clearly grounded in the value-added model, and success depends on how well subsequent cost-cutting or political crises are managed. There are important advantages and limitations of each type of driving force, which are reflected in the following two propositions.

> *Proposition 2:* Where workplace innovations are driven primarily by a crisis, effective implementation will depend on the crisis being neither too severe nor too mild, while subsequent diffusion will depend on leadership, relationship building, and other drivers in addition to the crisis, similar to the experience in the private sector.

> *Proposition 3:* Where workplace innovations are driven primarily by planning and leadership, effective implementation and diffusion will depend on establishing a perceived compelling need for change and avoiding derailment by subsequent crises.

Local Autonomy and Increased Interdependency

The need for local autonomy and the importance of increased interdependency is well established in all the cases reported in the literature and in this chapter. Increased autonomy is one of the defining features of the value-based model when it is combined with the concurrent management of increased interdependency. Either element alone can be accommodated to some degree by the traditional civil service model, but not both together.

The need for local autonomy may mean that collective bargaining should be flexible enough to allow for local-level contracts or addenda. Certainly, union and management officials need to be prepared to manage increased variation in practice at the facility and work group levels. There are many industries where a central agreement is supplemented with local contracts. We speculate that the public service can not fully explore the potential value inherent in local agreements so long as it remains embedded in the more centralized civil service model. As such, the local bargaining (and subsequent agreements) must be sufficiently broad in their mandate to be able to address the kinds of changes that many of these workplace innovations require. A local agreement with a very limited mandate is unlikely to meet the needs of workplace reform under either the cost-based or value-added model.

Proposition 4: Workplace reform is more likely in government departments where managers have greater local autonomy over workplace practices.

Proposition 5: Workplace innovations are more likely to be introduced in those government departments where local collective agreements, formal or informal, can be negotiated without destabilizing the master collective agreement that covers all government employees.

Management Skills for Change

The development of the internal labor market in the civil service, the lack of external benchmarking for efficient operation, and the fact that the ultimate leadership is politically elected might have led to a focus on system maintenance rather than on system innovation skills for managers. Thus we speculate that the average public sector manager receives less training and education in change management and new innovations than his or her private sector counterpart. It is not clear if the same is true of union leaders. The private sector experience points strongly to identifiable "process champion(s)" in many cases of successful workplace reform. If workplace reform comes more slowly to the public sector, we have to ask if senior managers have been trained in the skills needed to champion change in their respective organizations. It is an unfortunate irony that the use of these skills runs directly counter to the demands of the traditional system which emphasizes stability and avoidance of risk. Note that this is a dilemma under both the cost-based and value-added models. Accordingly, we offer the following proposition for further research.

Proposition 6: The effective implementation of innovations in the public sector will depend on managers and union leaders mastering process change skills while still being effective in a system that resists the use of these skills.

Multiple Objectives

The public service does not enjoy a single dominant objective like the private sector does in its goal of seeking profits. We suggest that given the multiplicity of objectives before a government department, a single objective such as improving efficiency may not be sufficient for workplace reform to happen. The ORG case shows that the relocation provided the government with an opportunity to achieve several objectives: (1) improving efficiency, (2) supporting smaller communities by relocating government departments, (3) promoting employment equity for disadvantaged groups, (4) fostering partnerships between labor, management, and community groups, and (5) reducing social assistance costs. The possibility of achieving all of these objectives simultaneously gave the ORG the impetus and the resources they needed to introduce fundamental system change.

> *Proposition 7:* Fundamental workplace reform is more likely in those government departments where the need for improving efficiency can be linked to achieving other objectives of government.

Role of Unions

The role of unions in successful public sector workplace change comes across in all the cases as being critical for a number of reasons. The higher rate of unionization in the public sector means that unions are a more important stakeholder in the workplace change process than in the private sector. Public sector unions are more political and are attuned to the complexities of the political process. They are skilled in protecting their interests within the system of political decision making. Thus when managers have tried to implement workplace change without the approval or involvement of unions, they have found it very tough to sustain performance. In a number of cases discussed here and in other chapters, workplace change did not really begin to move forward until the union was engaged effectively.

In the process, however, the role of unions has expanded and changed. In these cases, for example, we see that increased union partnership in change can expand the scope of bargaining for the union but requires it to be effective in nontraditional forums, such as joint committees and employee teams. Ultimately, we see unions taking on the political risks associated with co-leading a change initiative in exchange for the potential benefits of being able to claim credit for successes achieved through the change initiative. As such, we offer the following two propositions:

> *Proposition 8:* Unless the union becomes involved in and supports change initiatives, fundamental workplace change in unionized settings can not be implemented effectively.

Proposition 9: Unions' involvement in driving fundamental change in the workplace will expand and transform their role in workplace representation and governance.

Conclusions

The rise of the civil service bureaucratic model was driven by functional needs. This model provided stability and clarity of roles in a system dominated by two prior models rooted in elitism and favoritism. Inevitably, however, yesterday's solutions have become today's barriers (Senge 1990). What was once stability is now seen as ossification, and what was once clarity of roles is now seen as a set of restrictive rules.

In response, we observe a growing number of public sector change initiatives that all reject the traditional model but that draw on highly divergent assumptions and principles. These initiatives are substantively distinct from debates about transformation in the private sector but comparable in scope and implications. All of the cases examined here represent innovations largely rooted in the value-added model but impacted in a variety of ways on the concurrent changes rooted in the cost-based model.

In all such examinations of the transformation of the public sector, it is important to keep in mind that the public service will remain answerable to political masters, and hence, the kind of isolation from political interference that workplace innovations sometimes need will never be realized completely. Innovations must be carried out in this sector in the full glare of political debate. This may hinder workplace innovations at times, but it may also facilitate them at other times. A skillful public manager will blend workplace innovation objectives with other objectives of the government to achieve success.

These cases suggest that the two alternative organizational models are inevitably intertwined in the public sector. As these models continue to diffuse, the tensions and dilemmas will continue to present themselves. While all parties may agree on the importance of not returning to the bureaucratic civil service model, we are still in the early stages of a debate in practice over what will emerge as the new model or set of models underlying public sector labor relations.

Acknowledgment

We are much indebted to Maria Rotundo at the University of Toronto and to Peter Seidl in Vancouver for excellent research assistance. Also, we would like to thank Jack Knott of Michigan State University for helping to stimulate thought about current innovations in government. Finally, we are indebted to Betty Barrett, Sandford Borins, Rick Chaykowski, Kevin Ford, Rick Herrera, Tom Rankin, Mark Thompson, and the editors of this volume for comments and feedback on earlier drafts of this chapter.

Endnotes

[1] The term public sector will be used in this chapter to refer largely to the civil service at federal, state or provincial, and municipal levels of government. The quasi-public sectors of education and health are excluded because of the need to limit the scope of the paper and for reasons of lack of comparability across Canada and the U.S. The education and health sectors are predominantly in the public domain in Canada whereas they are spread across the public and private sectors in the U.S. This restriction notwithstanding, two cases examined in this chapter are a public utility and the postal service—both of which are government owned operations but subject to many of the same market forces as the private sector.

[2] For a more detailed description of this case, see Hebdon and Hyatt (forthcoming).

[3] In-person visits could be made initially in Toronto where an on-line terminal provided instant access and, of course, in Thunder Bay. Although there were no immediate plans to do so, the technology was available to expand in-person services to many other locations across the province.

[4] See Rankin and Gardner (1994) for more information on this case.

[5] There were no layoffs at Shearwater until 1994 when a new round of budget cuts forced many bases to close, while Shearwater was downsized to roughly half its civilian complement.

[6] Data for the case were collected through a series of key informant interviews.

[7] The material presented in this case is based on three years of direct involvement by co-author Joel Cutcher-Gershenfeld, who was a lead consultant to the initiative (along with Kevin Ford and Donna Winthrop) under the auspices of the Program on Innovation Employment Relations Systems (PIERS) at the School of Labor and Industrial Relations at Michigan State University.

[8] Information based on telephone interviews with federal officials responsible for partnership activities and various reports of the National Partnership Council.

[9] For more information on this case, see Cutcher-Gershenfeld and Barrett (1992) and Barrett, Fleming, Harcus, Mossberg and Stefanick (1992).

References

Aaron, Benjamin, Joyce M. Najita, and James L. Stern, eds. 1988. *Public Sector Bargaining*, 2d ed. Industrial Relations Research Association. Washington, DC: Bureau of National Affairs.

Barrett, Betty, William Fleming, Joyce Harcus, Jesse Mossberg, and Mary Stefanick. 1992. "Creating a New Way to Disagree: The LAMPs Dispute Resolution Project." In C. Cutrona, D.M. McCabe, and W. Wilkins, eds. *Beyond Borders*. 19th

Annual International Conference of the Society of Professionals in Dispute Resolution. Washington, DC: SPIDR.

Betcherman, G., and K. McMullen. 1986. *Working with Technology: A Survey of Automation in Canada*. Ottawa: Ministry of Supply and Services.

Betcherman, G., K. McMullen, N. Leckie, and C. Caron. 1994. *The Canadian Workplace in Transition*. Kingston, ON: INC Press.

Borins, Sandford. 1994a. *Public Sector Innovation: Its Contribution to Canadian Competitiveness*. Kingston: Queen's University.

_____. 1994b. *Government in Transition: A New Paradigm in Public Administration*. Toronto: Commonwealth Association for Public Administration and Management.

_____. 1995a. "The New Public Management Is Here to Stay." *Canadian Public Administration*, Vol. 38, no. 1, 122–32.

_____. 1995b. "Public Sector Innovation: The Implications of New Forms of Organization and Work." In B.G. Peters and D.J. Savoie, eds. *Governance in a Changing Environment*. Montreal: McGill-Queen's University Press.

Cutcher-Gershenfeld, Joel. 1985. "The Emergence of Community Labor-Management Cooperation." In Woodworth, Whyte, and Meek, eds., *Industrial Democracy: Strategies for Community Economic Revitalization*. Beverly Hills: Sage Publications.

Cutcher-Gershenfeld, Joel, and Betty Barrett. 1992. "Transforming Workplace Dispute Resolution by Expanding the Scope of Grievance Mediation." In C. Cutrona, D.M. McCabe, and W. Wilkins, eds., *Beyond Borders*. 19th Annual International Conference of the Society of Professionals in Dispute Resolution. Washington, DC: SPIDR.

Cutcher-Gershenfeld, Joel, Thomas Kochan, and Anil Verma. 1991. "Recent Developments in U.S. Employee Involvement Initiatives: Erosion or Diffusion." *Advances in Industrial Relations*, Volume 5.

Deming, W. Edwards. 1986. *Out of the Crisis*. Cambridge, MA: Massachusetts Institute of Technology, Center for Advanced Engineering Study.

Derber, Milton. 1988. "Management Organization for Collective Bargaining in the Public Sector." In B. Aaron, J.M. Najita, and J.L. Stern, eds., *Public Sector Bargaining*, 2d ed., Industrial Relations Research Association. Washington, DC: Bureau of National Affairs.

Doeringer, Peter B., Linda Kaboolian, Michael Watkins, and Audrey Watson. "Beyond the Merit Model: New Directions at the Federal Workplace?" This Volume.

Douglas, Paul. 1921. "Shop Committees: Substitute for, or Supplement to, Trade Unions?" *The Journal of Political Economy* (February).

Fisher, R., W. Ury, and B. Patton. 1983. *Getting to YES: Negotiating Agreement Without Giving In*, 2d ed. New York: Penguin Books.

Golden, Clint, and Valerie Parker. 1955. *Causes of Industrial Peace under Collective Bargaining*.

Gomberg, William. 1967. "Special Study Committees." In J. Dunlop and N. Chamberlain, eds., *Frontiers of Collective Bargaining*. New York: Harper and Row.

Greiner, John M., Harry P. Hatry, Margo P. Koss, Annie P. Millar, and Jane P. Woodward. 1981. *Productivity and Motivation*. Washington, DC: The Urban Institute Press.

Hebdon, Robert, and Douglas Hyatt. Forthcoming. "Workplace Innovation in the Public Sector: The Case of the Office of the Ontario Registrar General." *Journal of Collective Negotiations in the Public Sector*.

Johnson, Ronald N., and Gary D. Libecap. 1994. *The Federal Civil Service System and the Problem of Bureaucracy*. Chicago: University of Chicago Press.

Katzenback, Jon R., and Douglas Smith. 1993. *The Wisdom of Teams*. Boston: Harvard Business School Press.

Kearney, Richard C. 1984. *Labor Relations in the Public Sector*. New York: Marcel Dekker.

Kochan, Thomas, and Harry Katz. 1988. *Industrial Relations and Collective Bargaining*, 2d ed. Homewood, IL: Richard D. Irwin, Inc.

Kochan, Thomas, Harry Katz, and Robert McKersie. 1986. *The Transformation of American Industrial Relations*. New York: Basic Books.

Levin, Martin, and Mary Sanger. 1994. *Making Government Work*. San Francisco: Jossey-Bass.

Lawler, Edward E., III, Susan A. Mohrman, and G.E. Ledford. 1992. *Employee Involvement and Total Quality Management*. San Francisco: Jossey-Bass.

Lewin, David, Peter Feuille, and Thomas Kochan. 1988. *Public Sector Labor Relations: Analysis and Readings*, 3d ed. Lexington, MA: Lexington Books.

Ono, Taiichi. 1988. *Toyota Production System: Beyond Large-Scale Production*. Cambridge, MA: Production Press.

Osborne, D., and T. Gaebler. 1992. *Reinventing Government*. Reading, MA: Addison-Wesley.

Osterman, P. 1994. "How Common Is Workplace Transformation and Who Adopts It?" *Industrial and Labor Relations Review*, Vol. 47, no. 2, pp. 173–88.

Panitch, Leo, and Don Swartz. 1984. "From Free Collective Bargaining to Permanent Exceptionalism: The Economic Crisis and the Transformation of Industrial Relations in Canada." In M. Thompson and G. Swimmer, eds., *Conflict or Compromise: The Future of Public Sector Industrial Relations*. Montreal: Institute for Research on Public Policy, pp. 403–35.

Piore, Michael, and Charles Sabel. 1984. *The Second Industrial Divide*. New York: Basic Books.

Pollitt, Christopher. 1988. *Managerialism and the Public Service: The Anglo-American Experience*. Oxford: Basil Blackwell.

Ponak, Allan, and Mark Thompson. 1995. "Public Sector Collective Bargaining." In M. Gunderson and A. Ponak, eds., *Union-Management Relations in Canada*. Toronto: Addison-Wesley, pp. 415–54.

Rankin, Tom. 1990. *New Forms of Work Organization: The Challenge for North American Unions*. Toronto: University of Toronto Press.

Rankin, Tom, and Archie Gardner. 1994. "New Forms of Work Organization in the Federal Public Service: The Case of CFB Shearwater/UNDE Local 80409." *OPTIMUM: The Journal of Public Sector Management*, Vol. 24, no. 4 (Spring).

Rowe, Mary. 1984. "Are You Hearing Enough of Your Employee's Complaints?" *Harvard Business Review*.

Savoie, Donald. 1993. "Innovating to Do Better with Less." *Public Sector Management*, Vol. 4, no. 1 (Spring), pp. 15–7.

_____. 1994. *Thatcher, Reagan, Millrun: In Search of a New Bureaucracy*. Pittsburgh: University of Pittsburgh Press.

Senge, Peter M. 1990. *The Fifth Discipline: The Art and Practice of the Learning Organization*. New York: Doubleday.

Shafritz, Jay M., Norma N. Riccucci, David H. Rosenbloom, and Albert C. Hyde. 1992. *Personnel Management in Government*. New York: Marcel Dekker.

Singer, L. 1994. *Settling Disputes: Conflict Resolution in Business, Families, and the Legal System*. Boulder: Westview Press.

Swimmer, Gene, and Mark Thompson. 1995. "Collective Bargaining and the Public Sector: An Introduction." In G. Swimmer and M. Thompson, eds., *Public Sector Collective Bargaining in Canada*. Kingston: IRC Press, pp. 1–19.

Susskind, L.E., and J. Cruikshank. 1987. *Breaking the Impasse: Consensual Approaches to Resolving Public Disputes*. New York: Basic Books.

Taylor, George. 1948. *Government Regulation of Industrial Relations*. New York: Prentice-Hall.

Tjosvold, Dean. 1991. *Team Organization: An Enduring Competitive Advantage*. Chichester: John Wiley & Sons.

Trist, Eric. 1981. *The Evolution of Socio-Technical Systems Theory*. Toronto: Ontario Quality of Working Life Center.

Thompson, Mark, and Allan Ponak. 1992. "Restraint, Privatization and Industrial Relations in the 1980s." In R. Chaykowski and A. Verma, eds., *Industrial Relations in Canadian Industry*. Toronto: Dryden Press, pp. 284–322.

Ury, W., J. Brett, and S. Goldberg. 1988. *Getting Disputes Resolved: Designing Systems to Cut the Cost of Conflict*. San Francisco: Jossey-Bass.

Verma, Anil, and Joel Cutcher-Gershenfeld. 1993. "Joint Governance in the Workplace: Beyond Union-Management Participation and Worker Cooperation." In B. Kaufman and M. Kleiner, eds., *Employee Representation: Alternatives and Future Directions*. Madison, WI: Industrial Relations Research Association.

Walton, Richard E. 1980. "Establishing and Maintaining High Commitment Work Systems." In Kimberly and Miles, eds., *The Organizational Life Cycle*. San Francisco, CA: Jossey-Bass.

Walton, Richard E., and Robert B. McKersie. 1965. *A Behavioral Theory of Labor Negotiations*. New York: McGraw Hill.

Walton, Richard E., Joel E. Cutcher-Gershenfeld, and Robert B. McKersie. 1994. *Strategic Negotiations: A Theory of Change in Labor-Management Relations*. Boston: Harvard Business School Press.

Womack, James P., Daniel T. Jones, and Daniel Roos. 1990. *The Machine That Changed the World: The Story of Lean Production*. New York, NY: Rosen Associates.

CHAPTER 7

Canadian Public Sector Employment Relations in Transition

MORLEY GUNDERSON
University of Toronto

DOUGLAS HYATT
*University of Wisconsin-Milwaukee, University of Toronto,
and Institute for Work and Health*

In the previous IRRA volume on public sector bargaining, Shirley Goldenberg (1988:266) stated: "The public sector is an area in which Canadian labor relations have broken new ground, in contrast to the private sector where they have developed in large measure on the pattern established in the United States. Collective bargaining in the public sector, broadly defined, has a considerably longer history in Canada than in the United States and is currently more varied and more extensive." This statement provides an important motivation for examining labor relations in the Canadian public sector.

The longer history of bargaining and the considerable variation in legal structures and procedures across the different jurisdictions and elements of the Canadian public sector means that there is considerable "time series and cross-section variation" from which to draw inferences and test hypotheses. The more extensive degree of bargaining and the associated high degree of unionization in the Canadian public sector means that the inferences are based on a meaningfully large group of employees. The extensive degree of innovation and breaking of new ground provides lessons to be learned from such experimentation. Canada has an industrial relations system much like that of the United States, but it has gone much further down the road of public sector collective bargaining. As such, there are potentially important lessons to learn from that experience.

Employment relations issues in the public sector are taking on increased importance in Canada for a variety of other reasons. Public concern over government budget deficits and a reluctance to raise taxes to reduce these deficits have led to pressure to contain government expenditures, with public sector payrolls being an obvious target. This is especially true since labor costs often make up the bulk of the total cost of providing public services. There has been increased emphasis on the importance of certain public infrastructures (e.g., education, training, transportation, and communications, including the "information high-way") to facilitate competitiveness. This has led to an emphasis on effi-ciency in the public sector in delivering its outputs. As well, the emerg-ing pressures to "reinvent government" have obvious implications for public sector labor relations. There is considerable interest in whether public sector labor relations in Canada is based on an outdated Wagner model and, if so, whether it can adjust its human resource and work-place practices to the new environment.

It is well known that political constraints guide decision making in the public sector, just as profit constraints guide decision making in the private sector. With the emphasis on deficit reduction and competitive-ness, the political constraint in the public sector is becoming more bind-ing. Previously, the success of public sector managers was gauged in terms of the size of their department and how fast they grew (often independent of any growth in their services). Increasingly, it is now based on how much they cut (again, often independent of the reduction in services). Whereas political capital was once garnered by adding new programs, it is now garnered by cutting them. Similarly, it seems politi-cally acceptable, if not popular, for governments to completely bypass the bargaining process and to dictate the terms and conditions of employment through such mechanisms as wage controls, back-to-work legislation, designating employees as not having the right to strike, and simply abrogating the collective agreement. What the state gives, the state can clearly take away. These trends in the political arena have obvi-ous implications for public sector labor relations and compensation.

There was often a strong emphasis on the public sector as a model employer, providing wages, fringe benefits, and working conditions to set an example for the private sector. Legislative initiatives like pay and employment equity, for example, have been largely initiated in the pub-lic sector (Weiner 1995). Now the emphasis is increasingly placed on the public sector as a model of restraint, to constrain costs both to enhance competitiveness and to facilitate macroeconomic stability, especially the control of inflation. While there always has been a con-cern that public sector settlements will have costly spillover effects if emulated by the private sector, increasing attention is now being placed on that issue. As well, increased emphasis is placed on ensuring that the public sector follows the private sector with its emphasis on quality, customer orientation, and flexibility and adaptability. Deregulation, privatization, subcontracting, and user fees are important instruments in this process (Thompson 1995).

Global competition and capital mobility have enhanced the importance of market forces in constraining political decision making with respect to legislative initiatives and social policy. Political jurisdictions must now pay more attention to the implications of these policies for costs and competitiveness. In essence, different jurisdictions increasingly compete for business investment and the jobs associated with that investment. Such competition can be on the basis of reducing government expenditures and regulations, as well as on emphasizing government programs and infrastructures that can enhance competitiveness. This, in turn, can have important implications for the size and function of the public sector.

In addition, demographic and environmental changes place new demands on the public sector. As the population ages, different demands have been placed on different elements of the public sector, including the education and health care sectors. Similarly, the continued increase in the labor force participation of women and the associated dominance of the two-earner family have placed increased demands on the government as an employer as well as a regulator and provider of services like day care.

These environmental changes obviously are not unique to Canada (Beaumont, this volume). Nevertheless, they are particularly prominent in this country because of its federal-provincial division of powers and because Canada is particularly influenced by the global economy and especially the United States. These factors have important implications for employment relations in the public sector, which in turn have important feedback effects on the functioning and role of governments.

The purpose of this chapter is to analyze the recent trends and current situation in Canadian public sector employment with respect to three main dimensions: (1) the legal structure; (2) dispute resolution procedures, especially strikes and arbitration; and (3) compensation outcomes. Prior to addressing each of these areas, some basic background information is also presented on the size and growth of the public sector and unionization in that sector. The chapter concludes with a discussion of the new and emerging issues associated with public sector restructuring and reinventing government.[1]

Background

Table 1 indicates that 27% of the Canadian workforce is employed in the public sector, broadly defined.[2] If employees in government enterprises were included, approximately one-third of the workforce would be in the public sector. Within the public sector, the largest category is health and welfare (social services), followed closely by education. Federal, provincial, and local administration (commonly called government employment or civil service) are fairly similar in size. When the three levels of government are combined, this narrow definition of "civil service" constitutes about one-quarter of the public sector, or 7% of all employment.

TABLE 1

Public Sector Employment in Canada, 1985 and 1995

Sector	% of Total Employment		% Change in Employment 1985-1995
	1985	1995	
Federal government	2.9	2.5	0.8
Provincial government	2.4	2.2	6.5
Local government	2.1	2.0	13.7
Education	9.0	9.4	23.3
Health and welfare	9.7	11.2	37.6
Total public sector	26.1	27.3	23.7
Private sector	73.9	72.7	16.6
Public and private	100.0	100.0	18.4
Total employment (000)	8697.8	10,301.8	18.4

Source: Calculated from data given in Statistics Canada, *Employment Earnings and Hours*, No. 72-002, February 1985 for 1985 data and February 1995 for 1995 data (both referring to January of the respective years).

In the past ten years, the Canadian public sector has grown by about 24%, compared to the 17% growth in employment of the private sector. All three levels of civil service have experienced slower growth than the private sector, with federal government employment not growing at all over that period. The broader public sector has grown more rapidly than the private sector. This is especially the case for health and welfare and to a lesser extent for education. In essence, in the past decade the growth of employment in the more narrowly defined civil service of government has been slower than in the private sector, while the growth of employment in the already large education and health sectors has been

considerably higher, so that overall employment growth in the total public sector growth has outstripped that of the private sector.

Union density[3] (i.e., union members as a percentage of paid workers) is approximately 80% in public administration in Canada. This is
over twice the 35% union density for all workers (including the public
sector) and about four times the density rate of 20% for the private sector alone. Over half of all union members in Canada are in the public
sector, and the two largest unions are public sector unions. In descend-
ing order, union density rates for the different elements of the public
sector are provincial government, 95%; education, 75%; federal government, 73%; local government, 68%; and health and social services, 51%.
In virtually every industry, workers who are employed by governments
are much more likely to be union members than are workers who are
not employed by governments.

Although this high degree of collective bargaining in the public sector was established mainly between 1965 and 1975, it was built on three
main foundations that were established earlier.[4] First, municipal workers
(except for police and firefighters) had a long history of being covered
under the private sector labor relations legislation of each jurisdiction.
This means that this important group of public sector employees had the
same bargaining rights, including the right to strike, as did private sector
workers. Since municipal workers were often in essential service sectors
(transportation, garbage collection, water, and sewage) and employed by
local governments, they provided the "thin edge of the wedge" for further expansion of collective bargaining in the public sector.

Second, the thin edge of the wedge was further widened by the fact
that a socialist party (the predecessor of the New Democratic party) in
Saskatchewan broke precedent and included its own civil service under
the coverage of its original labor legislation when it was established in
1944. Essentially, that gave its own civil servants the same collective bargaining rights, including the right to strike, that were granted to private
sector employees.

The third foundation for the subsequent and rapid development of
collective bargaining in the public sector was the fact many employees in
that sector had a long history of consultation with their employers
through employee associations. Dominated by professionals and white-
collar employees, such associations were reluctant to behave as traditional
unions, especially with respect to utilizing the strike weapon. Similarly,
public sector employers strongly resisted collective bargaining as anath-
ema to the sovereignty of the state. This is perhaps best illustrated by the

oft-cited quote of the premier of Quebec: "The Queen does not negotiate with her subjects" (Goldenberg 1973). While both employee associations and public sector employers were generally loath to engage in traditional collective bargaining, the fact remains that the employee associations had a structure and leadership in place ready to make the transformation from "collective begging" to collective bargaining. Furthermore, employers had some exposure to the negotiation process, at least as it occurred through the consultation procedures.

While the foundations were in place for a transformation to collective bargaining, the rapid transformation that occurred had to be precipitated by certain events. The events were a series of legislative changes that essentially granted bargaining rights to government employees. The legislative changes first occurred in 1965 when the Quebec government granted its own employees broad collective bargaining rights, including the right to strike. This was followed by the Public Service Staff Relations Act of 1967, which did the same for federal government employees (based on promises made by the prime minister in 1963). These innovative changes had important demonstration effects on other provinces, which followed suit with collective bargaining rights, although not always with the right to strike (as documented later).

While the legislative changes were the intervening variables that fostered collective bargaining in the public sector, the legislative changes themselves were not exogenous events. They were spawned by the cumulation of other events. As indicated by Ponak and Thompson (1995:422), "Also helping the transition was the general climate of social change characteristic of the 1960s. It was the era of the civil rights movement, anti-Vietnam War protests, the Quiet Revolution in Quebec, and campus militancy. The public sector was in a period of rapid growth, and newly hired employees brought campus attitudes to their employment. Thus the social environment was conducive to challenges of authority and of the status quo in general, making the time particularly propitious for public employees to undertake major changes in norms."

In essence, in the mid-1960s in Canada a rapid expansion of collective bargaining in the public sector was precipitated by the conflux of a series of interrelated events: the changing social norms of the 1960s; the snowballing of legislative changes; and the foundations laid earlier by municipal bargaining, the Saskatchewan precedence of giving private sector bargaining rights to its own employees, and the history of consultation through employee associations. By the mid-1970s the basic structure was in place. Collective bargaining had not only come to the public sector, it dominated the public sector and was more prominent in the public sector than in the private sector.

Legal Structure

The legal structure governing collective bargaining in the public sector in Canada is complicated by the dominance of provincial jurisdiction in labor relations matters, with only about 10% of the workforce under the federal jurisdiction. The federal jurisdiction covers workers in sectors that span the different provinces, such as banking, postal service, transportation, communication, and the federal civil service. As such, a "crazy quilt" pattern of legal structures has emerged since the ten provinces and the federal jurisdiction (as well as the Yukon and the Northwest territories which follow the federal jurisdiction) have different elements of the public sector covered under different labor relations statutes, often with quite different dispute settlement procedures.

Statutes Governing Public Sector Collective Bargaining[5]

As discussed previously, municipal employees in all jurisdictions are covered by the private sector labor relations legislation of each jurisdiction and have the right to strike. The same usually applies to employees of government-owned enterprises, although in some jurisdictions they are covered by separate legislation and do not have the right to strike, or that right is limited to employees who are not designated as essential. Civil servants are usually covered under a separate statute, although in Saskatchewan they are covered under private sector collective bargaining legislation. Police and firefighters have a mixture of legislative regimes: separate legislation for each of those sectors; special sections within the general private sector labor relations legislation; and sometimes a hybrid of the two, with the general labor relations legislation covering certain aspects of bargaining, and special legislation covering other aspects. Hospital employees are usually covered by the general labor relations legislation that covers private sector employees—in some jurisdictions by the civil service legislation and in some jurisdictions by separate legislation. Teachers are covered by the general labor relations act in some jurisdictions, but more often by separate legislation.

Clearly, there is no uniform pattern to the statutory regimes that apply to the different elements of the public sector. The relevant statutes include separate statutes for the particular sector, the general labor relations legislation that governs private sector employees (often with separate sections dealing with the particular element of the public sector), civil service collective bargaining legislation, and hybrids of the above.

Dispute Resolution Procedures

In part reflecting these different statutory regimes, the dispute resolution procedures also differ dramatically across jurisdictions and across the different elements of the public sector. Although there are variants within each of the different procedures, the main dispute resolution procedures are: (1) the right to strike (STR)[6]; (2) the limited strike (LST) which gives the right to strike only to employees who are not designated as essential; (3) binding arbitration (ARB) when strikes are not allowed; (4) arbitration at the request of either party (RAR); and (5) choice of procedure (COP), where the union is allowed to choose in advance of negotiation between strikes or arbitration. Arbitration at the request of either party is often thought of as the equivalent of regular binding arbitration, because it essentially eliminates the strike from the arsenal of the union. It is also true that it essentially eliminates the threat of a lockout on the part of the employer; but since lockouts are rarely evoked, this right to choose arbitration is of little use to unions.

As discussed subsequently, even when the strike or limited strike is allowed, back-to-work legislation is commonly invoked, with arbitration being required. Such back-to-work legislation, therefore, may be considered a sixth dispute resolution procedure that has become institutionalized in the Canadian public sector.[7] Also, some would argue that a seventh dispute resolution procedure has emerged—unilateral determination of contract terms by the public sector employer—either through wage controls or more recently through abrogation of the existing collective agreement (both discussed subsequently).

Table 2 highlights the main dispute resolution procedures that exist across the different jurisdictions and elements of the public sector in Canada. As the bottom panel indicates, the right to strike (STR) is the most common procedure, existing in over half (40 of the 77 cases). (The 77 cases represent 11 jurisdictions times 7 elements of the public sector.) The limited strike (LST) exists in about 10% of the cases (8 of 77). Binding arbitration (ARB) is required only in about 12% of the cases (9 of 77). Hybrids between the right to strike and arbitration are involved in the other 26% of cases, with the choice of procedure (COP) being involved in 5 cases (all in the federal jurisdiction), and the right for either party to request arbitration (RAR) being the procedure in 20% of cases (15 of 77). Considering that all but the nine binding arbitration

requirements can involve the potential for the legal use of the strike, it
can be said that the overwhelming majority of the public sector elements in the different jurisdictions in Canada involve the possibility of
the legal use of strikes as the ultimate dispute resolution procedure.

TABLE 2

Dispute Resolution Procedures by Jurisdiction
and Element of Public Sector, Canada, 1994

Jurisdiction	Munic- ipal	Gov't Enter- prise	Civil Service	Police	Fire- fighter	Hospital	Teachers
Federal	STR	STR	COP	COP	COP	COP	COP
Br. Columbia	STR	STR	STR	STR	STR	STR	STR
Alberta	STR	ARB	ARB	ARB	ARB	ARB	STR
Saskatchewan	STR	STR	STR	STR	RAR	STR	STR
Manitoba	STR	STR	RAR	STR	RAR	STR	RAR
Ontario	STR	LST	LST	RAR	RAR	ARB	STR
Quebec	STR	STR	STR	RAR	RAR	LST	STR
New Brunswick	STR	LST	LST	RAR	RAR	LST	STR
Nova Scotia	STR	STR	RAR	STR	STR	STR	STR
PEI	STR	RAR	RAR	ARB	ARB	ARB	RAR
Newfoundland	STR	STR	LST	RAR	STR	LST	STR
Total (77)	11	11	11	11	11	11	11
STR (40)	11	7	3	4	3	4	8
LST (8)	0	2	3	0	0	3	0
COP (5)	0	0	1	1	1	1	1
RAR (15)	0	1	3	4	5	0	2
ARB (9)	0	1	1	2	2	3	0

Source: Adapted from Swimmer and Thompson (1995) and Thompson and
Ponak (1992).

Key: STR = right to strike; LST = limited right to strike for employees who are
not designated as essential; COP = choice of procedure whereby union chooses
either strike or arbitration; RAR = arbitration at the request of either party (and
sometimes by the Minister's order); ARB = arbitration.

Note: Police in the city of Winnipeg in Manitoba have arbitration at the request
of either party (RAR), and firefighters in the city of St. John's Newfoundland have
arbitration. For police in the federal jurisdiction, the RCMP have no collective bargaining rights.

This image must be tempered—indeed many would argue it is a
false image—by various qualifications. In many situations (in British
Columbia, for example) even when the strike is allowed, general legislation often exists stipulating that employees providing essential services

may be required to continue working during a strike. While this is somewhat less restrictive than the limited strike where such designated employees *will* be required to continue working during a strike, it does restrict the unfettered right to strike. The strike possibility also can be limited by the fact that in many of the cases either party can request arbitration (RAR), or the union may choose arbitration (COP). Similarly, restricting the right to strike to only nondesignated employees, as under the limited strike (LST), can effectively emaciate the union's bargaining power, depending upon how many employees are so designated. Furthermore, as discussed subsequently, having the right to strike can mean little, if in fact the government constantly invokes back-to-work legislation, wage controls, or the suspension of the collective agreement.

As indicated by the variation across columns, the dispute resolution procedures vary considerably across the different elements of the public sector. Being covered by the private sector labor relations legislation of their particular jurisdiction, municipal workers have the right to strike, although they can obviously be subject to back-to-work legislation. Teachers and workers in government enterprises also usually have the right to strike. At the other end of the spectrum, police and firefighters often do not have the strike weapon, either because binding arbitration is required or (more commonly) because either party can request arbitration, in which case the employer is effectively protected from a strike possibility. For hospital workers and civil servants, the dispute resolution procedures are more varied. Strikes or limited strikes are allowed in slightly over half of the jurisdictions.

As indicated by the variation across rows, there is considerable variation in the dispute resolution procedures across the different jurisdictions. It is, of course, extremely difficult to rank the jurisdictions by their degree of liberalism with respect to allowing the use of strikes, in part because of the various restrictions that exist when it is used, and in part because the severity of the strike differs by sector. Nevertheless, a crude ranking is possible based on information in Table 2. British Columbia, Saskatchewan, and Nova Scotia appear to be the most "liberal" in allowing the right to strike in all or almost all of their sectors, although in British Columbia general legislation exists indicating that workers performing essential duties may be prohibited from striking. Newfoundland and Quebec seem the "next most liberal" in allowing the strike or limited strike in most of the elements of the public sector. Manitoba, New Brunswick, Ontario, and Prince Edward Island, in roughly that order, fall in between, utilizing a wider range of dispute resolution procedures. Alberta is the most restrictive, requiring arbitration in five of the seven elements of the public sector. It is difficult to categorize the federal jurisdiction. While it appears the most liberal in that it allows the strike or the union to choose between the strike or arbitration in all cases, over time it has severely restricted the effectiveness of the strike through the designation of large numbers of employees as essential and, hence, not having the right to strike.

Clearly there is some pattern to the use of dispute resolution procedures by jurisdiction and element of the public sector. Some jurisdictions appear to more consistently grant the right to strike while others require arbitration. As well, there is some tendency to allow strikes in the less essential sectors (municipal, government enterprises, and teachers) and to restrict them in the more essential sectors (police and firefighters). Nevertheless, the patterns are by no means universal, and there appear to be some "minor inconsistencies" with respect to allowing strikes for more essential sectors, while prohibiting them for less essential sectors. For example, Saskatchewan, Manitoba (outside of Winnipeg), and Nova Scotia all allow strikes in their police sectors (which would generally be considered as essential). Yet Saskatchewan and Manitoba effectively have arbitration by allowing it at the request of either party for firefighters (which would generally be considered as equally essential). Furthermore, Manitoba and Nova Scotia have the same arbitration procedure in their civil service (which would generally be considered as less essential).

In all likelihood these variations reflect events, political pressures, bargaining power, and historical circumstances that are peculiar to each jurisdiction. In many cases the public sector dispute resolution procedures were established as a means of addressing illegal strikes or job actions such as work to rule. Certainly, it is hard to discern the results of a rational evolution of public sector dispute resolution procedures reflecting differential degrees of hardship imposed by strikes in the different jurisdictions. Nevertheless, it would be interesting to determine if there has been some convergence in that direction, in that the "gross inconsistencies" have been eliminated and the pattern increasingly reflects how the costs and benefits associated with the different dispute resolution procedures may vary across jurisdiction and elements of the public sector.

Choice of Procedures and the Designation of Employees in the Federal Government

One of the more innovative dispute resolution procedures involves the choice of procedures[8] as exists in the federal civil service since 1967.

Here the union gets to choose in advance of each new negotiation whether the ultimate dispute resolution procedure will be arbitration or strike (with conciliation). Initially, bargaining units (especially the weaker ones) often chose arbitration, hoping they would be granted the same awards as the stronger units that tended to choose the strike route. Over time, however, unions have moved away from the arbitration route and more often have chosen the strike route, obviously feeling they could win more through the ultimate strike threat. While the choice of procedure has remained intact in the federal jurisdiction, it has not been utilized in other provinces, except for a few short experiments where it was tried and abandoned (Ponak and Thompson 1995).

In the federal jurisdiction when the strike route is chosen, it is often a limited strike only for those employees who are not designated as essential. As such, the designation of essential employees is an important weapon of the employer, since if a large portion of the bargaining unit is designated, then the employer can carry on with the essential functions in the case of a strike. The designation of employees is negotiated by the parties, with disputes settled ultimately by a conciliation board. The proportion of employees designated as essential ranges from zero (e.g., in a bargaining unit of librarians) to 100% (e.g., for correctional officers). Prior to 1982, an average of about 37% of employees in the different bargaining units were designated as not having the right to strike.[9] In the post-1982 period that portion rose to 58%. The increase was a defensive reaction on the part of the federal employer to the increase of the strike route chosen by the union. This was facilitated by a Supreme Court of Canada decision (*CATCA v. The Queen*) that upheld the right of the employer to determine the level of service that was to be provided—a determination that effectively would dictate the designation of employees. Furthermore, designated employees were required to perform *all* of their normal duties, not just their essential duties as was previously the case. As stated by Swimmer (1995:381), the "government apparently succeeded in removing the right to strike by the back door."[10]

Arbitration and Arbitration Criteria

When the right to strike is prohibited by statute or by ad hoc back-to-work legislation, arbitration is invariably required to determine the terms and conditions of the new collective agreement. Conventional arbitration tends to be used in Canada, with any of the variants of final offer selection being rare (O'Grady 1992; Ponak and Falkenberg 1989).

Final offer selection can induce the parties to settle prior to arbitration so as to avoid the risk of having to live with an "all-or-nothing" settlement, and it can encourage them to submit reasonable demands so as to enhance the probability of their being accepted. On the negative side, it can lead to potentially unworkable settlements if the offers do not come together, and it fosters an adversarial climate since there is a clear "winner and loser."[11] These negative consequences, however, can be mitigated through "inter-temporal compromise" as subsequent awards are likely to compensate for unusual previous awards (Swimmer 1975).

In Canada as in the United States (Belman and Heywood, this volume), the dominant criteria used by arbitrators in determining their awards is comparability. The comparison group is usually settlements elsewhere, especially in the private sector, albeit the lack of comparable groups in the private sector often means that other public sector settlements are emulated. This can lead to a de facto form of pattern bargaining, with key settlements being emulated throughout the system. As in the private sector, however, such patterns are often breaking down, with settlements tending to reflect local conditions.

While comparability is by far the dominant criteria used by arbitrators, other criteria include cost-of-living adjustments, especially with respect to inflation; the employer's ability to pay; aggregate productivity increases in the economy as a whole; and minimum living standards, especially for low-wage groups (Gunderson 1983; O'Grady 1992). In earlier years arbitrators often awarded wage increases equal to the inflation rate plus some measure of aggregate productivity in the economy. With very low inflation rates and stagnant productivity growth, these criteria have become less prominent. The employer's ability to pay is a more common consideration, often prompted by legislative requirements that reflect political concern over tax increases. Arbitrators are often reluctant to adhere to ability to pay, however, especially if comparability suggests a wage increase is in order. There is still a strong belief that public employees should not be required to subsidize taxpayers by being paid wages below prevailing rates so as to avoid tax increases.

Wage Controls of the Early 1980s[12]

Although obviously not a formal dispute resolution procedure, wage controls have been a prominent feature of recent public sector bargaining. By eliminating one of the key items over which collective bargaining occurs, such controls effectively abrogate the purpose of any dispute resolution procedure, be it the strike or arbitration or any variants. In effect, wage controls selectively applied to the public sector means that the employer unilaterally decides the wage increase.

Earlier wage control programs, instituted in 1975 throughout Canada, applied to both the private and public sector, although they had features that made their impact more prominent in the public as opposed to the private sector. These included exemptions for low-wage workers, ceilings for high-paid workers, exemptions for wage increases that were designed to reduce gender discrimination or recruiting problems, and exemptions for firms employing fewer than 500 employees in the private sector.

While earlier wage control programs had features that indirectly made them more effective in the public sector, the wage control programs of the early 1980s were overtly aimed at the public sector—indeed they were restricted to that sector. In 1982 the federal government imposed its "6 and 5" program, limiting wage increases in the public sector to 6% in 1982 and 5% in 1983. Five other provinces adopted the same program, and Quebec instituted a 20% rollback. The other five provinces reduced their spending programs overtly to limit public sector pay.

Freezes, Rollbacks, Unpaid Leaves and Suspended Bargaining of the Early 1990s[13]

The public sector wage controls of the early 1980s were followed by even more draconian measures in the early 1990s. As Fryer (1995) points out, however, a wide range of different approaches were followed: imposed wage freezes and rollbacks, hard-nosed bargaining under the threat of imposed rollbacks, and bargaining under an altered bargaining agenda that involved joint efforts by labor and management for cost cutting.

In 1991 the federal government again took the lead, this time freezing wages and ultimately suspending collective bargaining for two years (subsequently extended until 1997). Seven other provinces[14] followed with their own programs of wage freezes and sometimes mid-contract rollbacks. As part of a "social contract," some provinces also instituted mandatory unpaid days of leave, typically ranging from 5 to 12 days per year. Such mandatory worksharing spread over the larger public sector workforce was touted as an alternative to layoffs that would otherwise fall on a smaller segment of the workforce. The employees would be given some time off in return for the pay reduction.

In two other jurisdictions (Saskatchewan and Alberta) the wage restraint or rollbacks were voluntarily negotiated with the unions, albeit this was obviously done under the threat of the more unilateral actions that were happening in the other provinces. British Columbia also negotiated voluntary agreements with their unions, also with an eye to what was happening elsewhere. As Fryer (1995) emphasized, however, the BC procedure involved a number of important characteristics: extensive consultations with all the parties; collective bargaining over an extended period of time; a sectoral approach for seven different subsectors of the public sector; job security often guaranteed in return for flexibility and cost saving; and bringing to the bargaining table a wide array of issues, including restructuring, human resource practices, and public sector service delivery mechanisms. The interesting question here is whether the BC experiment will work and whether it is an aberration (reflecting the labor orientation of its social democratic provincial government and the fortunes of a strong provincial economy) or a harbinger of a new model of public sector bargaining—one that involves joint problem solving over a wide range of issues to effect cost cutting and enhance efficiency without simply cutting wages and employment.

Strikes and Dispute Resolution Outcomes

The wide array of dispute resolution procedures that prevail in the different elements of the public sector were clearly designed to minimize strikes or to mitigate their impact given their potentially adverse consequences to the general public. The services in varying degrees are essential, and the public often has few alternatives. As such, it is not surprising that there is considerable interest in public sector strike activity. That interest has also been fostered more recently by the importance of public infrastructures in enhancing competitiveness. If such infrastructures are disrupted by strikes, the consequences can have broader spillover effects to the private sector. The increased scrutiny being paid to the cost effective delivery of public services in general also draws attention to the role of strikes. Strikes in the public sector are also of interest since they are subject to a degree of policy control, for example, through the array of dispute resolution procedures previously discussed.

Strike Days Lost[15]

Figure 1 illustrates the recent time pattern of strike activity in the public and private sectors, as measured by strike days lost as a percent of days worked. Three conclusions emerge: (1) there is considerable annual variation in strike activity in both sectors, (2) there is a decline in strike activity in both sectors, and (3) the decline is greater in the private sector than the public sector.

FIGURE 1

Strike Days as Percentage of Days Worked
Public and Private Sectors, 1978-94

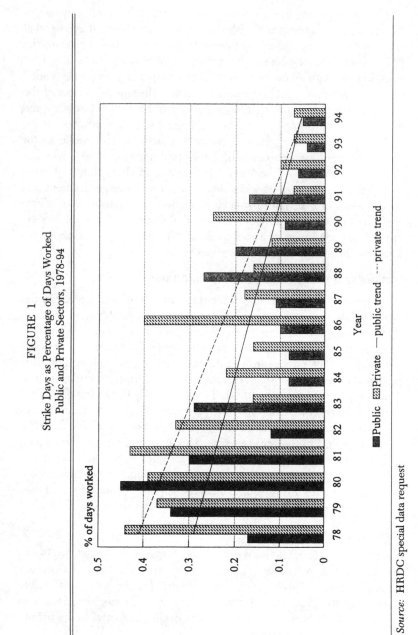

Source: HRDC special data request

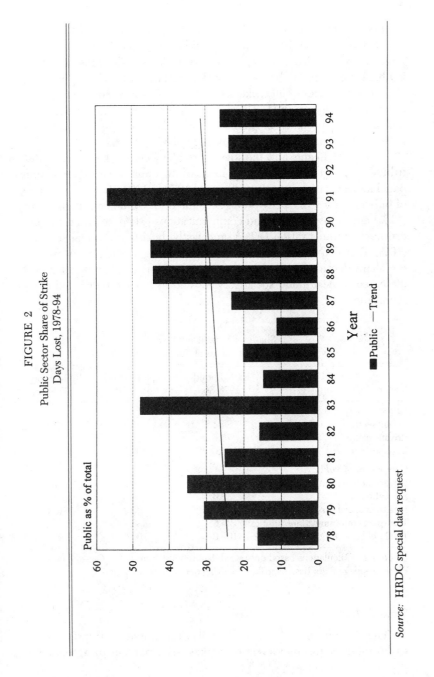

FIGURE 2
Public Sector Share of Strike
Days Lost, 1978-94

Source: HRDC special data request

Because the decline of strike activity has been greater in the private sector than the public sector, the public sector has accounted for a larger share of strike activity in recent years. This is illustrated in Figure 2 which shows that public sector strikes accounted for a trend value of almost one-quarter of all strike activity in 1978, and almost one-third of all strike activity by 1994. There is, however, wide annual variation in the relative importance of public sector strikes, ranging from a low of 11% of all strike activity in 1986 to a high of 57% in 1991.

Table 3 highlights how the share of public sector strike activity is distributed across the various components of the public sector. The bottom panel indicates that, over the full period 1978 to 1994, the greatest share of public sector strike activity was accounted for by the education sector (31%) and transportation and communications (31%), followed by government administration (22%), and lastly, health and social services (16%). Between the earlier 1978-86 and the more recent 1987-94 period, the share decreased in education and government administration and increased in health and social services and in transportation and communication.

TABLE 3

Shares of Strike Days Lost,
Private and Various Elements of Public Sector, 1978-94

Sector	Early Period 1978-86	Later Period 1987-94	Full Period 1978-94
Public as % of Total			
Public sector	24.4	32.5	26.8
Private sector	75.6	67.5	73.2
Both sectors	100.0	100.0	100.0
Component of Public			
Government administration	25.4	16.1	22.1
Education	35.0	24.5	31.2
Health & social services	12.8	20.7	15.6
Transport/communications/utilities	26.8	38.7	31.1
Total public sector	100.0	100.0	100.0

Source: Calculations based on special data request from Labor Canada, based on Work Stoppage Data Base of strikes involving one or more employees.

Strike Rates[16]

The decline in strike activity is also illustrated by the decline in strike rates or the incidence of strikes—the percent of agreements signed after a strike or lockout. As illustrated in Figure 3, the incidence of strikes is consistently lower in the public sector than in the private sector, obviously reflecting in large part the fact that strikes are often banned in the public sector, with arbitration being the required dispute resolution procedure. Between 1978 and 1994, strike rates have declined steadily from a trend value of about 17% to 8% in the private sector and 6% to 2% in 1994 in the public sector. In essence, the propensity of a collective agreement to be signed after a strike or lockout has been cut by half or more over the past 17 years in both the public and private sectors. The decline in strike rates has been slightly more rapid in the private sector than in the public sector.

Table 4 highlights the variation in strike rates across the different elements of the public sector. As indicated in the second to last row, strike rates in the private sector averaged 13% over the full 1978-94 period, declining from 15% in the first half to 11% in the second half of the period. In the public sector, strike rates averaged 3.4% over the full period, declining from 4.1% in the first half to 2.6% in the second half. For the different elements of the public sector, strike rates tended to be considerably below average in federal administration and to a lesser extent in the large education, health, and welfare sector. The most notable changes were the large decreases in strike activity for all three levels of government.

Settlement Stages

Table 5 gives the various different stages at which collective agreements tend to be settled in the public and private sectors in Canada. Over the full period 1978-1994, almost half of the agreements in the public and private sectors were settled by direct negotiation. The proportion of agreements signed after direct bargaining or some additional stage of conciliation or mediation (but short of an impasse involving arbitration or a strike) was 85% in the private sector and 72% in the public sector (i.e., the sum of the first five rows). Clearly, voluntary settlement rates are considerably higher in the private sector than in the public sector, albeit often with some form of third-party assistance such as conciliation or mediation. In the public sector the threat of arbitration or legislative intervention does seem to chill the negotiation process, leading to fewer voluntary settlements.

Arbitration is extremely rare in the private sector (less than 1% of agreements). In the public sector slightly over 8% of agreements required arbitration, which is over twice the 3.4% that involved a strike. Dispute

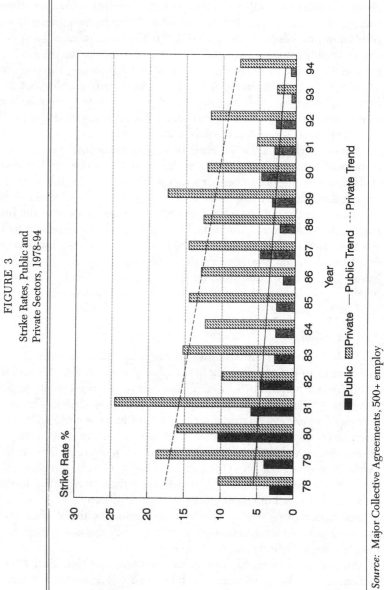

FIGURE 3
Strike Rates, Public and
Private Sectors, 1978-94

Source: Major Collective Agreements, 500+ employ

TABLE 4

Strike Rates for Various Elements of
Public Sector, 1978-94
(% of agreements signed after a strike)

Public Sector Level or Function	Early Period 1978-86	Later Period 1987-94	Full Period 1978-94
Federal administration	1.6	0.5	1.1
Provincial administration	6.8	1.6	4.5
Local administration	7.9	2.0	5.5
Education/health/welfare	3.0	3.1	3.0
Utilities	5.8	2.2	4.2
Crown corporations	5.0	4.2	4.6
Total public	4.1	2.6	3.4
Private	14.9	10.7	13.3
Ratio private/public	3.6	4.1	3.9

Source: Calculations based on special data request from Labor Canada's Major Wage Settlements data base, for major collective agreements, usually of 500 or more employees. Strikes refer to both strikes and lockouts.

TABLE 5

Settlement Stages, Major Collective Agreements,
Public and Private Sectors, 1978-94
(Proportion of Agreements Signed at Each Stage)

Settlement Stage	Early Period 1978-86		Later Period 1987-94		Full Period 1978-94	
	Public	Private	Public	Private	Public	Private
Direct bargaining	43.0	42.9	51.2	53.5	46.8	47.0
Conciliation	12.2	19.9	8.6	15.1	10.5	18.0
Post-conciliation	4.0	8.4	2.4	5.7	3.3	7.3
Mediation	10.0	12.2	9.8	11.6	9.9	11.9
Post-mediation	1.4	0.7	2.5	0.6	1.9	0.7
Arbitration	10.7	0.4	5.1	1.2	8.1	0.7
Strike	4.1	14.9	2.6	10.7	3.4	13.3
Legislated	14.0	0.3	8.8	1.2	11.6	0.7
Other, unknown	0.6	0.2	0.3	0.0	0.5	0.1
Social contracts	0.0	0.0	8.6	0.5	4.0	0.2
Total	100.0	100.0	100.0	100.0	100.0	100.0

Source: Calculations based on special data request from Labor Canada's Major Wage Settlements data base, for major collective agreements, usually of 500 or more employees. Totals may not sum to 100.0 because of rounding.

rates (arbitration plus strikes) are fairly similar, at 14% in the private sector and 11.5% in the public sector. Almost 12% of the agreements in the public sector were signed after some form of legislated intervention, sometimes a back-to-work requirement but usually the imposition of the agreement through wage control legislation. This form of dispute resolution procedure is more prominent than arbitration or the strike—indeed, it is as common as both combined. About 4% of the public sector agreements (8.6% in the 1987-94 period) were also part of a legislated social contract.

These figures highlight the prevalence of some form of legislation (back-to-work, wage controls, social contracts) as a dispute resolution procedure in the public sector. Such legislated procedures are more important than strikes and arbitrations combined, and they are growing in importance. Clearly, our conventional focus on strikes and arbitrations as the main dispute resolution procedures in the public sector seems somewhat misguided, given the prominence (and growing importance) of legislated settlements of some form. This growing importance of legislated resolutions to public sector disputes is also occurring in the United States (Lund and Maranto, this volume).

Overall, the pattern of strike activity suggests the following key generalizations:

- Strikes have recently declined in both the private and public sectors, with the decline being greater in the private sector. As a result, the public sector has accounted for an increasing share of total strike days lost.
- Dispute rates (strikes plus arbitrations) are fairly similar in both sectors: at 14% for the private sector and 11.5% for the public sector. While arbitration is almost nonexistent in the private sector, it is used in almost three-quarters of the disputed settlements in the public sector.
- Legislated intervention, such as wage controls, back-to-work legislation, or "social contracts," are now more common means of dispute resolution in the public sector than are arbitration and the strike combined.

Impact of Alternative Dispute Resolution Procedures

In spite of the considerable cross-section and time series variation in the different dispute resolution procedures in Canada, there is a dearth of empirical work on the impact of the different procedures. Most studies and reviews[17] of the impact of binding arbitration conclude that arbitration imparts a slight upward bias to wage settlements, but the impact is small. As well, it chills negotiations, leading to lower negotiated settlement rates (shown previously in Table 5).

Based on Canadian data over the period 1964-87, Currie and McConnell (1991) find that prohibiting public sector workers from striking does lead to fewer strikes (albeit many still occur) and to more arbitrations. This reduces total dispute costs (strikes plus arbitrations),[18] since the cost of a strike is considerably higher than the cost of an arbitration. However, from the public's perspective, this reduction in dispute cost is more than offset by the higher wage costs that occur under arbitration. Hence, from the perspective of the public, total costs (dispute cost plus wage cost) would be lower if the right to strike is prohibited.[19]

In Currie and McConnell (1991), dispute costs are limited to the costs of strikes and arbitrations. Restricting the right to strike reduces dispute costs because the reduction in the use of costly strikes more than offsets the larger increase in the use of less costly arbitrations. Hebdon (1992), however, provides Canadian evidence indicating that restricting the right to strike also redirects conflict to other costly forms such as grievances.[20]

Public Sector Compensation

Considerable attention has been paid in Canada to the issue of public sector compensation. This has been prompted by a variety of questions. To what extent are public sector workers paid more (or less) than comparable workers or workers in comparable positions in the private sector? To what extent has this changed over time? To what extent does the gap vary by such factors as gender, level of pay, and union status? How is the gap affected by fringe benefits? Are there spillover effects to the private sector? Is wage determination less responsive to market forces in the public sector than in the private sector?

Figure 4A illustrates that aggregate average base wage increases in major collective agreements (500 or more employees) have been fairly similar since 1978 in both the public and private sectors. In shorter intervals within that period of time, wage increases may be slightly higher in the public sector than the private sector, but this usually reflects a catch-up for earlier smaller increases, and the larger increases are usually dissipated in subsequent periods. In essence, the public sector wage line periodically dips below and then above the private sector line. This raises the interesting question of whether the slower public sector increases that have prevailed since 1990 will be followed by a

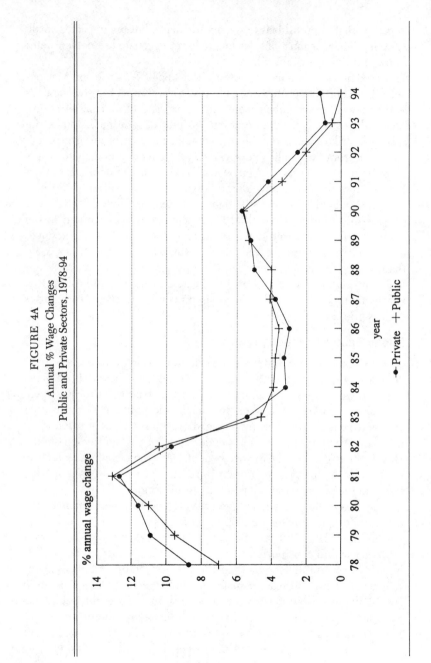

FIGURE 4A
Annual % Wage Changes
Public and Private Sectors, 1978-94

catch-up or whether this is a more permanent transformation associated with fundamental restructuring.

Figure 4B illustrates a similar pattern for the three levels of government, although there is more annual variation in the increases. Of particular note, increases in the federal government have generally been smaller than for the provincial and local governments since 1981. Figure 4C illustrates a similar pattern of wage increases with considerable annual variation in the broader public sector components of education, health, government enterprises, and utilities.

The fact that short-run periods of "excessive" public sector settlements usually reflect a catch-up for previous periods of falling behind and the gains are usually dissipated in subsequent periods is more clearly illustrated in Table 6, which gives the cumulative wage increases in the private sector and the various components of the public sector since 1978. Over that time period, the cumulative increase in base wages was actually slightly less in the public sector than in the private sector. Within the different components of the public sector, it was lowest in the federal government, followed by education, health and welfare, and then utilities. Cumulative wage increases were slightly above the private sector in provincial and local government and for crown corporations.

Econometric studies[21] that relate these base wage changes to aggregate economic conditions suggest that wage settlements in both the private and public sector have been responsive to aggregate demand and market pressures. In essence, public sector wage settlements are not immune to market forces such as unemployment. Furthermore, there is no evidence that there are significant spillover effects whereby public sector settlements would influence private sector settlements, independent of other market forces that affect wages in both sectors.

The previous analysis, based on aggregate base wage changes, suggests that such *changes* are fairly similar in the public sector as in the private sector, at least over longer periods of time. Because they utilize base wages in major collective agreements, these studies implicitly control for differences in the type of worker or position, since the base wages are usually those paid in the starting positions. Nevertheless, it is possible that the *levels* of pay for the same positions or people could be different in the public and private sectors, and these differences in levels are perpetuated by similar increases in both sectors. Furthermore, starting positions could change, and it is not clear whether base wages in major collective agreements are representative of wages throughout the public and private sectors.

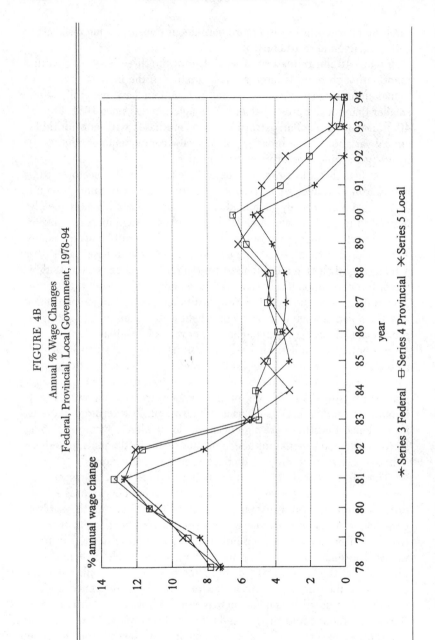

FIGURE 4B
Annual % Wage Changes
Federal, Provincial, Local Government, 1978-94

✳ Series 3 Federal   ⊟ Series 4 Provincial   ✳ Series 5 Local

FIGURE 4C
Annual % Wage Changes
Education, Health, Crown, Utility, 1978-94

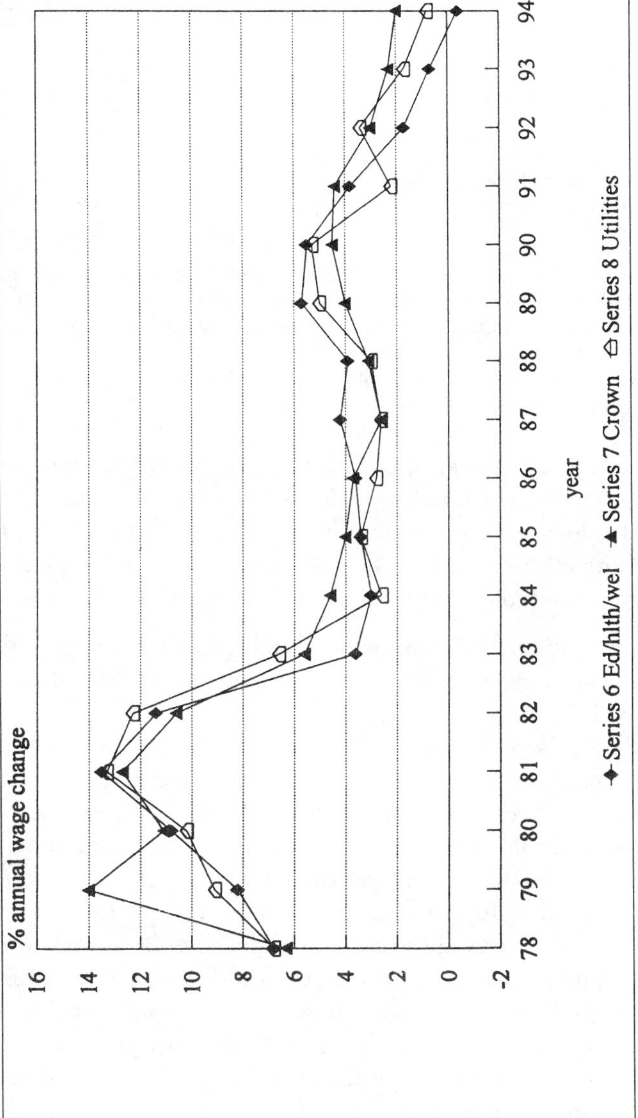

Source: Department of Finance (1995)

TABLE 6

Cumulative Percent Wage Increase,
Private and Public Sectors, 1978-94
(1978 = 100)

Sector	Cumulative % Wage Increase
Private	234
All public	226
Federal government	211
Provincial government	240
Local government	241
Education, health and welfare	221
Crown corporations	242
Utilities	225

Source: Calculated from the average annual base wage increases, given in Department of Finance (1995, p. 81, 82). The calculations were based on setting 1978 equal to 100 and then cumulating the average annual base wage increase for each year, as reported in the publication. The data refer to base wages in major collective agreements of 500 or more employees. The base wages is typically the lowest wage rate in the collective agreement.

Empirical studies in Canada that compare public and private sector wages in the same narrowly defined positions or econometric studies that compare the wages of individual workers in the public and private sectors after controlling for differences in human capital and other determinants of earnings[22] yield the following generalizations:

- A pure public sector wage advantage tends to prevail, although it is not large, probably in the neighborhood of 5% to 10% and at most 15%.
- It is larger for females than for males and for low-wage as opposed to high-wage employees. In fact, for higher-wage professionals and executives, a public sector wage disadvantage prevails.
- Over time, the public sector wage advantage tends to be declining, especially for males, although it appears to be increasing for females. In the short run, public sector settlements are quite volatile, with unusually high settlements dissipating over time and often reflecting a catch-up to earlier private sector settlements. In the longer run, aggregate wage changes in the public sector are remarkably similar to those in the private sector, with both being responsive to market forces and aggregate demand and with no significant spillover effects from the public to the private sector.

- Although the evidence is extremely limited, it does suggest that fringe benefits are higher in the public than in the private sector, thereby increasing the gap slightly on the basis of total compensation.
- The evidence is consistent with the hypothesis that public sector compensation often occurs in the form of deferred compensation, whereby current wage settlements are somewhat lower in return for the expectation of higher future compensation in such forms as pensions, job security, and seniority-based wage increases.
- The union wage impact is smaller in the public sector than in the private sector, but the proportion of workers who are covered by collective agreements is larger in the public sector than in the private sector. The latter effect slightly outweighs the former, so that on net, unions contribute to the public sector wage advantage.
- Wage settlements under arbitration tend to be slightly higher than under right-to-strike regimes.

A number of important policy implications follow from these empirical generalizations. First, there are some grounds for continued vigilance given the pure public sector compensation advantage. Second, extreme reactions are not merited for various reasons: The compensation advantage appears to be small, it is likely declining over time, unusually high public sector settlements tend to reflect catch-up and to dissipate over time, and the pay advantages tend to go to women and low-wage workers who are otherwise disadvantaged in the labor market. Third, the public sector wage disadvantage that likely prevails for executive and higher-paying personnel suggests that recruiting problems may develop at that level. This is especially of concern if such personnel are important in guiding the restructuring that is occurring in that sector. Fourth, the fact that wage settlements tend to be higher under arbitration than under the right to strike suggests that more attention could be paid to expanding "economic rationality" and the use of market criteria in this process.[23] Fifth, policy attention should be directed to reduce the incentive for current taxpayers to try to save on current public sector labor costs by shifting them onto future generations of taxpayers by granting deferred wage increases in such forms as liberal pensions, job security, and seniority-based wage increases. Sixth, facilitating public sector unionization and granting the right to strike may not be as "costly" as it first seems for various reasons: The public sector union wage premium is small, wage settlements tend to be more moderate when unions have the right to strike as opposed to being subject to arbitration, and compulsory arbitration may simply redirect conflict into other costly forms such as grievances during the life of the contract.

Concluding Observations and Emerging Issues

Phases of Canadian Public Sector Employment Relations

Employment relations in the Canadian public sector can be characterized as developing in four overlapping but somewhat distinct phases. The first phase, prior to the 1960s, involved employee associations engaging in a consultative process with their employers—often cynically termed "collective begging."

The second phase, from the mid-1960s to the mid-1970s, involved the establishment of collective bargaining, often by legislative decree. A crazy-quilt pattern emerged across the different jurisdictions and elements of the public sector. Legislative regimes differed (e.g., coverage under the private sector statute or separate statute or hybrids) as did the dispute resolution procedure (e.g., strikes, arbitration, limited strikes, choice of procedures). Unionization became extensive—indeed, it has almost reached a saturation level in many parts of the Canadian public sector. The main bargaining issues, especially during the 1970s, were money and bargaining rights.

The third phase, in the 1980s and early 1990s, could be labeled as "collective regulation"—by some it is thought of as "collective repression." It involved extensive government regulation and overriding of the process of collective bargaining through various mechanisms: wage controls, designations of employees as essential and not having the right to strike, back-to-work legislation, and social contracts that often reopened collective agreements and subjected them to wage freezes or even rollbacks. The main bargaining issues, especially in the 1980s, were retention of bargaining rights and, to a certain degree, money.

A fourth phase is emerging in the mid-1990s. It is an open question as to whether it will be characterized as "collective cooperation" or "collective cooption"—or whether the "collective" modifier will be dropped altogether, and a variant of the third phase involving unilateral employer determination of the terms and conditions of employment will be continued. The main—indeed, overriding—bargaining issue is job security.

The emerging fourth phase is part and parcel of the process of "reinventing government" (Osborne and Gaebler 1992) that is occurring elsewhere[24] and that is more slowly being introduced into Canada. The process of reinventing government involves a number of interrelated ingredients: trimming bureaucracy; customer and service orientation; emphasis on efficiency, cost-effectiveness, accountability, and incentives; privatization and subcontracting; user charges and vouchers; decentralization and local delivery; and performance appraisals and budgeting on the basis of performance. In the minds of many, it is also simply a code word for downsizing and reducing the role of government, not reinventing the role. Clearly, reinventing government—whatever its motives and mechanisms—will require reinventing employment relations in the public sector.

Features of Public Sector Model That Inhibit Change

Warrian (1995a, 1995c) has cogently argued that certain key features of the current public sector bargaining model in Canada have made it ill-suited to meet these new challenges. These features stem from the fact that public sector bargaining in Canada incorporated many features of the industrial, adversarial Wagner model. While that model may have been well suited to the blue-collar, industrial workforce, it is questionable as to whether it is well suited to today's private sector, and it is certainly doubtful that it is well suited to the new challenges facing the public sector.

First, it has encouraged a proliferation of fragmented bargaining units that make it difficult to negotiate over the broader issues pertaining to such factors as multiskilling, work reassignment, wage restraint, job security, job classification, transfers, and budget cuts. Internal rivalries are common, and it is difficult for the unions to speak with one voice. Individual bargaining units understandably are reluctant to engage in concessions for a common goal, not knowing how other units will respond.

Second, the current public sector model fosters an adversarial mentality and a separation of employer and employee interests, inhibiting cooperative solutions to common problems. Management rights clauses in collective agreements and lack of information sharing, for example, make it difficult for employees to have a meaningful input into areas where they have considerable expertise and could contribute to restructuring.

Third, the current public sector model emphasizes job control unionism with narrow job classification and rigid seniority and other work rules. These can inhibit the multi-tasking, cross-training, transfers, and workplace flexibility that may be necessary to meet the new public sector challenges in more creative ways than simply downsizing in response to budget cuts. Warrian (1995c:14), for example, provides evidence indicating that during the 1980s there was actually an increase in the number of narrowly defined job classifications and seniority-based work rules in the public sector. This is in contrast to the private sector, where the opposite occurred (O'Grady 1992).

Emerging Challenges

Clearly, the pressures posed by public sector retrenchment and reinventing government will create new challenges for public sector employment relations. The challenges involve modifications of the existing system with its proliferation of small bargaining units, adversarial mentality and separation of employer and employee interests, and narrow job classifications, and rigid seniority and other work rules.

Certainly there will be a continued search for wage determination and dispute resolution procedures to find that elusive balance between the public interest in maintaining essential services at reasonable cost and public employee interests in their terms and conditions of employment, especially job security. That search will increasingly involve alternative dispute resolution procedures and cooperative efforts. However, there will also be a need to refocus from conventional public sector issues of dispute resolution and wage arbitration to the new issues emanating from restructuring and reinventing government. The public sector bargaining agenda will increasingly shift from conventional wage issues to issues of employment security. The challenge will be to find that elusive balance between a degree of employment security, on the one hand, and dynamic restructuring for efficiency gains and customer service orientation, on the other hand.

As Warrian (1995a, 1995b) points out, government funding and budget allocations in broader public sector areas such as health and education will increasingly be tied to performance measures. Since employees in those sectors clearly influence productivity and performance, this poses a challenge for both the organization and its employees to enhance performance to ensure their mutual survival and to survive budget cuts. The demand for public sector labor is derived from the demand for public services. Since the demand for public services is being dramatically influenced by interrelated forces such as restructuring, retrenchment, privatization, and contracting-out, then this will have important feedback effects to public sector labor markets. Issues of employment security, job classification, relocation, retraining, and work rules are becoming more important than conventional bargaining over wages.

Within the narrow civil service, performance measures are also increasingly being used. Furthermore, with privatization and subcontracting, the function of civil servants is increasingly changing from one of delivering the service to one of policy provision and managing and monitoring the performance of the subcontractors and private providers. Obviously, this has important implications for a wide range of industrial relations functions, including training, relocation recruiting, and dispute resolution procedures, as well as procedures with respect to subcontractors and private providers.

Since the public sector issues differ across the different elements of the public sector, sectoral strategies are likely to be in order. This can facilitate using the expertise from both employers and employees in each sector and perhaps circumvent the problems associated with the proliferation of small bargaining units. The sectoral strategies can involve sectorwide bargaining. This can facilitate bargaining over the broader restructuring issues within a sector, although it may not be conducive to issues pertaining to the performance of different organizations within each sector. The sectoral strategies can also be modeled after the labor-management cooperation "councils" that have been established in a number of private sector industries in Canada to deal with the labor adjustment and human resource problems associated with restructuring (Warrian 1995c).

The whole issue of restructuring within the public sector is giving rise to a wide range of industrial relations and human resource management issues. These include job classification, multi-tasking, transfer rights, successor rights, relocation issues, retraining, work rules, workplace practices, and worksharing as a possible alternative to layoffs. These issues are certainly not conducive to being handled by interest arbitration, nor are they likely to be well handled by conventional collective bargaining in the public sector, at least as it is currently structured. Nevertheless, modifications and adaptations can certainly lead to success stories. Borins (1995) and Hebdon and Hyatt (1996), for example, provide evidence of how a number of public sector organizations successfully have been able to modify their practices to deal with the emerging challenges in four key areas: information technology, case management (one-stop, single-wicked service provision), decentralization of operational decision making, and the accommodation of diversity and changing preferences.

Clearly, there are a wide range of new challenges facing employment relations in the public sector in Canada, as in most other developed nations. These challenges ensure that public sector employment relations will remain in the forefront of public debate in Canada as elsewhere. They also imply the need for a fundamental rethinking of public sector employment relations. Issues include not only wage determination and dispute resolution but also restructuring and the employment relations issues associated with the human resource management and workplace practice emanating from the changing role of governments and the broader public sector. The impending transformation of the public sector implies a concomitant transformation of public sector employment relations and the strategic choices associated with that transformation.

Acknowledgments

Financial support from the Social Sciences and Humanities Research Council is gratefully acknowledged. The authors are grateful for helpful discussions with Dale Belman, Bob Hebdon, Allen Ponak, Gene Swimmer, Mark Thompson, Anil Verma, and Peter Warrian.

Endnotes

[1] As is evident in the citations, the writing of this chapter has benefited immensely from a recent and thorough compendium on public sector collective bargaining in Canada (Swimmer and Thompson 1995). That volume contains chapters on the history of public sector unionism, the relationship with the Charter of Rights and Freedoms, pay and employment equity, compensation, strikes, privatization, special issues in the different elements of the public sector (federal, provincial, municipal, health, education, police and fire), as well as the special issues of Quebec and the international context.

[2] More detail on public sector employment in Canada is given in Ponak and Thompson (1995), Thompson and Ponak (1991, 1992), and Swimmer and Thompson (1995).

[3] Figures for this paragraph and more detailed information on unionization in the Canadian public sector are given in Ponak and Thompson (1995), Riddell (1993) and Rose (1995).

[4] More detail on the history and evolution of collective bargaining in the Canadian public sector, from which this material draws, is given in Finkelman and Goldenberg (1983), Goldenberg (1973,1988), Ponak and Thompson (1995), Rose (1995), Swimmer (1995), and Thompson and Ponak (1992), as well as in references to earlier material cited in those studies.

[5] See Swan (1985), Swimmer and Thompson (1995), and Ponak and Thompson (1995).

[6] In situations where the right to strike exists, the parties always have the right to agree to voluntary interest arbitration, although such agreements tend to be rare in the public sector as in the private sector.

[7] Ponak and Thompson (1995:440) indicate that back-to-work legislation has been invoked 62 times to end public sector strikes between 1965 and 1993. Obviously, these tend to be prominent strikes if they invoke such a legislative response.

[8] See Ponak and Thompson (1995), Subbarao (1985), Swimmer (1978, 1989, 1995), and Swimmer and Winer (1993).

[9] These are unweighted averages from bargaining units that opted for the strike route—33 in the pre-1982 period, and 47 in the post-1982 period. They are calculated from figures given in Swimmer (1995:379-80).

[10] This does raise the puzzle of why unions have increasingly used the strike route when its efficacy has been reduced by the designation of larger portions of employees. This may be explained, in part, by the fact that coalition bargaining has been practiced in the federal public sector, and this requires the ultimate right to strike, even though by mutual agreement that right will not be exercised.

[11] It is somewhat of a puzzle that final offer selection is so rare in Canada when it is common in the United States. Presumably, the pros and cons prevail in both countries. It is not obvious why the cons seem to outweigh the pros so much in Canada relative to the United States.

[12] Labor relations issues pertaining to the application of wage controls in the Canadian public sector are discussed in Fryer (1995), Panitch and Swartz (1984), Ponak and Thompson (1995), Thompson (1988), and Thompson and Ponak (1991).

[13] The measures discussed here are documented in detail in Fryer (1995) and summarized in Ponak and Thompson (1995).

[14] Newfoundland, Nova Scotia, New Brunswick, Prince Edward Island, Quebec, Manitoba, and Ontario.

[15] The information on strike days lost is based on special data provided by Human Resources Development Canada from their "Work Stoppage" File for strikes of any size. The working time data are from Statistics Canada, *Labor Force Annual Averages*, annual, and special data requests for the most recent year (Gunderson and Reid 1995).

[16] Information on strike rates is based on a special data request to Human Resource Development Canada (HRDC), based on their "Major Wage Settlements" data base of major collective agreements of 500 or more employees.

[17] Anderson (1981), Currie and McConnell (1991), Downie (1979), Gunderson (1983), Gunderson and Riddell (1993), Gunderson, Hebdon and Hyatt (1996), O'Grady (1989), Ponak and Falkenberg (1989), and Saunders (1986).

[18] Dispute costs refer to such factors as lost time and legal fees, but not the cost of the wage settlement or other terms of the contract.

[19] Gunderson, Hebdon, and Hyatt (1996) reanalyze that data based on what they argue are more appropriate categorizations of the dispute resolution procedures. Although this results in a reclassification of about 30% of the contracts, this does not substantially alter their main conclusion with respect to the impact of compulsory arbitration and the right to strike on dispute rates and the probabilities of strikes and arbitrations.

[20] His econometric analysis is based on 8,859 public sector bargaining units in Ontario in 1988.

[21] Such studies—termed "augmented Phillips curves"—include Auld, Christophides, Swidinsky, and Wilton (1980); Auld and Wilton (1985); Cousineau and Lacroix (1977); Riddell and Smith (1982); Swimmer and Winer (1993), and Wilton (1986).

[22] Daniel and Robinson (1980), Gunderson (1978, 1979, 1995), Gunderson and Riddell (1991, 1995), and Shapiro and Stelcner (1989).

[23] This is expanded upon, for example, in Gunderson (1983), which discusses the theoretical and practical issues associated with greater use of "disequilibrium" measures on the quantity side, such as queues and shortages. O'Grady (1992) provides a critique of the use of such measures.

[24] Warrian (1995c) discusses this process in the United States, the United Kingdom, New Zealand, and Australia and relates it to industrial relations and human resource management practices.

References

Anderson, John. 1981. "The Impact of Arbitration: A Methodological Assessment." *Industrial Relations*, Vol. 20 (Spring), pp. 129-48.

Auld, Douglas, and David Wilton. 1985. "Wage Settlements in the Ontario Public Sector and the Ontario Controls Program." In D. Conklin, T. Courchene, and W. Jones, eds., *Public Sector Compensation*. Toronto: Ontario Economic Council, pp. 80-108.

Auld, Douglas, Louis Christofides, Robert Swidinsky, and David Wilton. 1980. "A Microeconomic Analysis of Wage Determination in the Canadian Public Sector." *Journal of Public Economics*, Vol. 13 (June), pp. 369-88.

Borins, S. 1995. "Public Sector Innovation: The Impacts of New Forms of Organizationed Work." In B. Peters and D. Savoie, eds., *Governance in a Changing Environment*. Montreal: McGill-Queen's University Press, pp. 260-87.

Cousineau, Jean-Michel, and Robert Lacroix. 1977. *Wage Determination in Major Collective Agreements in the Private and Public Sectors*. Ottawa: Economic Council of Canada.

Currie, Janet, and Sheena McConnell. 1991. "Collective Bargaining in the Public Sector: The Effect of Legal Structure on Dispute Costs and Wages." *American Economic Review*, Vol. 81 (September), pp. 693-718.

Daniel, M., and W. Robinson. 1980. *Compensation in Canada: A Study of the Public and Private Sectors*. Ottawa, Conference Board.

Downie, Bryan. 1979. *The Behavioral, Economic and Institutional Effects of Compulsory Interest Arbitration*. Ottawa: Economic Council of Canada.

Finkelman, Jacob, and Shirley Goldenberg. 1983. *Collective Bargaining in the Public Service: The Federal Experience in Canada*. Montreal: Institute for Research on Public Policy.

Fryer, John L. 1995. "Provincial Public Sector Labor Relations." In G. Swimmer and M. Thompson, eds., *Public Sector Collective Bargaining in Canada*. Kingston: IRC Press, pp. 341-67.

Goldenberg, Shirley B. 1973. "Collective Bargaining in the Provincial Public Services." In J.F. O'Sullivan, ed., *Collective Bargaining in the Public Service*. Toronto: Institute of Public Administration of Canada.

_____. 1988. "Public-Sector Labor Relations in Canada." In B. Aaron, J. Najita, and J. Stern, eds., *Public Sector Bargaining*, 2d ed. Washington, DC: Bureau of National Affairs, pp. 266-313.

Gunderson, Morley. 1978. "Public-Private Wage and Nonwage Differentials in Canada: Some Calculations from Published Tabulations." In D. Foot, ed., *Public Employment and Compensation in Canada*. Toronto: Butterworths, pp. 167-88.

_____. 1979. "Earnings Differentials between the Public and Private Sectors." *Canadian Journal of Economics*, Vol. 12 (May), pp. 228-42.

_____. 1983. *Economic Aspects of Interest Arbitration*. Toronto: Ontario Economic Council.

_____. 1995. "Public Sector Compensation." In G. Swimmer and M. Thompson, eds., *Public Sector Collective Bargaining in Canada*. Kingston: IRC Press, pp. 103-34.

Gunderson, Morley, and Frank Reid. 1995. "Public Sector Strikes in Canada." In G. Swimmer and M. Thompson, eds., *Public Sector Collective Bargaining in Canada*. Kingston: IRC Press, pp. 135-63.

Gunderson, Morley, and Craig Riddell. 1991. "Provincial Public Sector Payrolls." In M. McMillan, ed., *Provincial Public Finances*. Toronto: Canadian Tax Foundation, pp. 164-92.

_____. 1995. "Estimates of the Current Public-Private Sector Wage Differentials in Canada." Governments and Competitiveness Series, School of Policy Studies, Queen's University.

Gunderson, Morley, Robert Hebdon, and Douglas Hyatt. 1996. "Collective Bargaining in the Public Sector: Comment." *American Economic Review*. Vol. 86 (March), pp. 315-26.

Hebdon, Robert. 1992. "Ontario's No Strike Laws: A Test of the Safety-Valve Hypothesis." *Proceedings of the 28th Conference of the Canadian Industrial Relations Association*, pp. 347-57.

Hebdon, Robert, and Douglas Hyatt. 1996. "Workplace Innovation in the Public Sector: The Case of the Office of the Ontario Registrar General." *Journal of Collective Negotiation in the Public Sector*, Vol. 25, no. 1, pp. 63-81.

O'Grady, John. 1992. "Arbitration and Its Ills." Paper prepared for Governments and Competitiveness Research Program, Institute of Policy Studies. Queen's University.

Osborne, D., and T. Gaebler. 1992. *Reinventing Government*. Reading, MA: Addison-Wesley.

Panitch, Leo, and Don Swartz. 1984. "From Free Collective Bargaining to Permanent Exceptionalism: The Economic Crisis and the Transformation of Industrial Relations in Canada." In M. Thompson and G. Swimmer, eds., *Conflict or Compromise: The Future of Public Sector Industrial Relations*. Montreal: Institute for Research on Public Policy, pp. 403-35.

Ponak, Allen, and Loren Falkenberg. 1989. "Resolution of Interest Disputes." In A. Sethi, ed., *Collective Bargaining in Canada*. Scarborough: Nelson Canada, pp. 260-97.

Ponak, Allen, and Mark Thompson. 1995. "Public Sector Collective Bargaining." In M. Gunderson and A. Ponak, eds., *Union-Management Relations in Canada*, 3d ed. Toronto: Addison-Wesley, pp. 415-54.

Riddell, Craig. 1993. "Unionization in Canada and the United States: A Tale of Two Countries." In D. Card and R. Freeman, eds., *Small Differences That Matter: Labor Markets and Income Maintenance in Canada and the United States*. Chicago: University of Chicago Press, pp. 109-48.

Riddell, Craig, and Phillip Smith. 1982. "Expected Inflation and Wage Changes in Canada." *Canadian Journal of Economics*, Vol. 15 (August), pp. 377-94.

Rose, Joseph B. 1995. "The Evolution of Public Sector Unionism." In G. Swimmer and M. Thompson, eds., *Public Sector Collective Bargaining in Canada*. Kingston: IRC Press, pp. 20-51.

Saunders, George. 1986. "The Impact of Interest Arbitration on Canadian Federal Employees' Wages." *Industrial Relations*, Vol. 25 (Fall), pp. 320-27.

Shapiro, David, and Morton Stelcner. 1989. "Canadian Public-Private Sector Earnings Differentials." *Industrial Relations*, Vol. 28 (Winter), pp. 72-81.

Subbarao, A. 1985. "Impasse Choice in the Canadian Federal Service: An Innovation and an Intrigue." *Relations Industrielles*, Vol. 40, pp. 567-90.

Swan, Ken. 1985. "Differences among Provinces in Public Sector Dispute Resolution." In D. Conklin, T. Courchene, and W. Jones, eds., *Public Sector Compensation*. Toronto: Ontario Economic Council, pp. 49-75.

Swimmer, Gene. 1975. "Final Position Arbitration and Intertemporal Compromise: The University of Alberta Compromise." *Relations Industrielles*, Vol. 30, no. 3, pp. 533-36.

_____. 1978. "The Impact of the Dispute Resolution Process on Canadian Federal Public Service Wage Settlements." *Journal of Collective Negotiations in the Public Sector*, Vol. 16, no. 1, pp. 53-61.

_____. 1989. "Critical Issues in Public Sector Industrial Relations." In A. Sethi, ed., *Collective Bargaining in Canada*. Scarborough: Nelson, pp. 400-21.

_____. 1995. "Collective Bargaining in the Federal Public Service of Canada: The Last Twenty Years." In G. Swimmer and M. Thompson, eds., *Public Sector Collective Bargaining in Canada*. Kingston: IRC Press, pp. 368-406.

Swimmer, Gene, and Mark Thompson. 1995. "Collective Bargaining in the Public Sector: An Introduction." In G. Swimmer and M. Thompson, eds., *Public Sector Collective Bargaining in Canada*. Kingston: IRC Press, pp. 1-19.

Swimmer, Gene, and Stanley Winer. 1993. "Dispute Resolution and Self-Selection: An Empirical Examination of the Federal Public Sector, 1971-82." *Relations Industrielles*, Vol. 48, no. 1, pp. 146-62.

Thompson, Mark. 1988. "Public Sector Industrial Relations in Canada: The Impact of Restraint." *Proceedings of the Annual Spring Meeting of the Industrial Relations Research Association*. Madison, WI: IRRA.

_____. 1995. "The Industrial Relations Effects of Privatization: Evidence from Canada." In G. Swimmer and M. Thompson, eds., *Public Sector Collective Bargaining in Canada*. Kingston: IRC Press, pp. 164-79.

Thompson, Mark, and Allan Ponak. 1991. "Canadian Public Sector Industrial Relations: Theory and Practice." *Advances in Industrial and Labor Relations*, Vol. 5, pp. 59-93.

_____. 1992. "Restraint, Privatization and Industrial Relations in the 1980s." In R. Chaykowski and A. Verma, eds., *Industrial Relations in Canadian Industry*. Toronto: Dryden Press, pp. 284-322.

Warrian, Peter. 1995a. "Performance-based Government and the Crisis of the 'Industrial Union' Model in the Public Sector." Mimeo, University of Toronto, Center for International Studies.

_____. 1995b. "Matching Performance Measurement and Transfer Funding System: The Ontario Hospitals' Funding Reallocation Formula." Mimeo, University of Toronto, Center for International Studies.

_____. 1995c. "The End of Public Sector 'Industrial' Relations in Canada?" Toronto: KPMG Center for Government Foundation.

Weiner, N. 1995. "Workplace Equity." In G. Swimmer and M. Thompson, eds., *Public Sector Collective Bargaining in Canada*. Kingston: IRC Press, pp. 78-102.

Wilton, David. 1986. "Public Sector Wage Compensation." In W.C. Riddell, ed., *Canadian Labor Relations*. Toronto: University of Toronto Press, pp. 257-84.

Chapter 8

Public Sector Industrial Relations in Europe

Phillip B. Beaumont
University of Glasgow

The basic purpose of this chapter is to set some of the North American material of the other chapters in a larger context by looking at recent developments in public sector industrial relations in Europe. The nature of the material to be presented here can usefully be viewed and interpreted in the light of the following two observations: Industrial relations arrangements within individual countries are currently characterized by a combination of change and continuity; across countries, one sees common pressures and developments but also diversity—the latter deriving from the differing historical traditions and institutional arrangements of the systems concerned. The general conclusion reached here is that currently there is considerable validity and value in these two observations when considering public sector industrial relations developments in Europe. This being said, it is likely that change and increasingly common pressures and developments will be the "wave" of the future.

The basic structure of the chapter is as follows. Initially, the role of budgetary pressures as a stimulus for change in public sector industrial relations is examined. The role and strength of this source of pressure is viewed as common to many countries, particularly the member countries of the European Union (EU). These budgetary pressures have resulted in the introduction of larger reform programs designed to change the basic structure and operating arrangements of the public sector in a number of countries. An integral element of these larger programs of organizational change is a series of measures that have both direct and indirect effects on the nature of public sector industrial relations. Such measures are not, however, a homogeneous set as regards their content—a fact that will be illustrated by three examples of public sector industrial relations and human resource management change. The theme of diversity is then introduced by examining the "extreme case" of Britain in somewhat more detail. The argument to be presented is that the motivation for change, the substantive nature of change, and the processes of change in the public sector in Britain differ in kind, rather than simply in degree, from much of the rest of Europe. Finally, the theme of commonality is returned to by examining some of the implementation difficulties experienced in introducing new practices into the highly unionized public sector with particular attention being given to the occurrence of industrial action and strike activity.

At this stage a small point of clarification and explanation is in order. The material presented in the tables in the chapter is generally for countries in the Organization for Economic Cooperation and Development (OECD), a grouping which is broader than that of simply Europe. However, the discussion in the text very much concentrates on Europe, particularly the member countries of the EU.

The Key Role of Budgetary Deficit Pressures

The size, nature, and role of the public sector in the economies of the OECD countries varies a great deal. This fact is well illustrated by the figures set out in Table 1. What is common to most OECD countries at the present time is the poor state of public finances with the general government deficit being around 3%–3.5% of GDP for the area as a whole in 1995 and 1996 (OECD 1995:8–9). Governments are attaching increased priority to tackling the size of these deficits as part of their larger concerns about national competitiveness in an increasingly integrated global economy. However, as Oxley and Martin (1991) observed, such concerns and attempts are not simply a feature of the mid-1990s:

> The 1980s witnessed a sharp shift in policy priorities with respect to the public sector away from the objectives espoused in the previous two decades. After the second oil price shock in 1979, expansionary fiscal policy was generally eschewed, and most OECD countries embarked on medium-term strategies to reduce their budget deficits. Concern over the effects of a continuing expansion of the public sector on private sector performance and a greater appreciation of the social costs of higher taxation produced broad agreement that the brunt of this strategy should be borne by reductions in expenditure rather than tax increases (p. 146).

However, governments' attempts at fiscal adjustment have frequently only produced short-run, temporary improvements. To some economists this has been because expenditure cuts have not sufficiently concentrated on transfer payments and the compensation of government employees (Alesina and Perotti 1995). In the light of the latter observation

TABLE 1

The Scale of the Public Sector
OECD Countries, 1990

Country	Government Employment/Total Employment (%)	Public Expenditure/ GDP (%)
Norway	32.0	54.8
Sweden	31.9	61.4
Denmark	30.5	58.4
France	22.6	49.9
Austria	20.8	46.7
Finland	20.8	40.9
Canada	20.6	46.9
United Kingdom	19.4	42.1
New Zealand	18.6	—
Iceland	17.7	37.9
Italy	17.2	53.3
Ireland	17.1	43.6
Australia	16.1	37.6
United States	15.5	36.1
Germany	15.1	46.0
Portugal	14.7	42.9
Netherlands	14.7	55.6
Spain	13.4	41.9
Switzerland	10.5	30.7
Greece	10.2	50.9
Turkey	9.3	—
Japan	8.1	32.4
Belgium	—	55.2

Source: OECD, *Public Management Developments: Survey 1993*, Paris, p. 11.

it is useful to examine some recent information for both public sector employment and wage levels. As Table 2 indicates, the rate of public sector employment growth in the 1980s was certainly less than in the 1970s. However, the annual growth rate of public sector employment still exceeded 2% in nine countries in the second half of the 1980s, while in most countries the public sector share of employment actually rose during the 1980s. Only the United Kingdom experienced a sizeable and sustained decline in public sector employment throughout the 1980s.

As to public sector wages, Chan-Lee, Coe, and Prywes (1987) have noted that,

almost all OECD countries introduced public sector pay restraint over the past several years. Pay freezes (the United

TABLE 2

Public Sector Employment,* OECD Countries, 1979-90

	Annual Rate (%) 1979-84	Average Growth (%) 1984-90	Share in Total Employment (%)		
			1979	1984	1990
United States	0.1	2.3	16.1	15.3	15.5
Japan	0.7	0.2	8.8	8.7	8.1
Germany	1.0	1.5	14.7	15.5	15.6
France	1.8	1.0	19.9	22.1	22.8
Italy	1.4	1.3	15.8	16.6	17.4
United Kingdom	-0.3	-0.2	21.2	21.8	19.6
Canada	2.4	2.2	19.5	20.8	20.6
Australia	2.7	1.3	16.2	17.4	15.6
Austria	1.9	2.7	17.6	19.1	21.1
Belgium	0.9	0.7	18.3	19.9	19.9
Denmark	2.5	0.7	26.9	30.2	30.1
Finland	3.2	2.2	17.2	18.9	20.6
Greece	2.2	2.5	9.1	9.4	10.1
Ireland	1.9	-0.8	16.1	18.3	17.9
Luxembourg	1.5	3.0	10.6	11.3	11.4
Netherlands	0.7	0.3	14.7	16.1	15.1
Norway	3.7	2.8	24.3	28.1	29.3
Portugal	6.2	3.4	10.5	13.3	14.6
Spain	2.9	4.0	10.0	12.8	13.7
Sweden	2.2	0.0	29.9	32.9	31.8
Switzerland	1.4	0.9	10.1	10.2	10.5
Unweighted average	2.0	1.5	16.5	18.0	18.2
Weighted average	0.8	1.4	15.3	15.6	15.6

* These figures exclude employees in public enterprises.

Source: Howard Oxley and John P. Martin, "Controlling Government Spending and Deficits: Trends in the 1980s and Prospects for the 1990s," *OECD Economic Studies*, No. 17, Autumn 1991, Table 5, p. 168.

States and New Zealand) or reduced indexation coverage (France, Italy, Belgium, Denmark and the Netherlands) have been common. In a substantial number of countries, public sector pay increases were held systematically below those in the private sector (Japan, Germany, the United Kingdom, Austria, Denmark, Ireland, Greece, Spain, and Sweden). In the Netherlands, public sector wages were even cut in nominal terms (by 3% in 1984) (p. 132).

One can compare the wage movements of the public and private sectors across countries in recent years, although it needs to be recognized that such sector comparisons, even for a single country, involve difficulties of both measurement and interpretation; the results are highly sensitive, for example, to compositional changes in the sectors and to the base year and particular time period chosen for comparison purposes. This being said, some relevant information is set out in Table 3.

TABLE 3

Average Wages of Public Sector Employees,[*]
Selected OECD Countries, 1979-90

| | Average Annual Growth Rate in Percentage | |
	Real Wages[1]	Relative Wages[2]
United States		
1979-84	1.5	1.4
1984-90	0.5	0.4
Japan		
1979-84	-0.6	-1.1
1984-90	2.5	0.4
Germany		
1979-84	-0.3	0.1
1984-90	-0.1	-1.8
France		
1979-84	0.0	-0.7
1984-90	0.3	-1.0
Italy		
1979-84	-0.3	-1.1
1984-90	1.3	-0.8
United Kingdom		
1979-84	0.0	-1.6
1984-90	0.5	-3.1
Canada		
1979-84	-0.1	0.0
1984-90	-0.2	-1.3
Austria		
1979-84	-0.3	-0.3
1984-90	0.3	-1.9
Belgium		
1979-84	-0.2	-0.1
1984-90	0.4	-0.2
Denmark		
1979-84	0.0	0.5
1984-90	0.0	-0.8
Finland		
1979-84	1.5	-0.5
1984-90	3.5	-0.5
Ireland		
1979-84	0.2	-0.8
1984-90	-0.1	-1.9
Netherlands		
1979-84	-0.1	1.3
1984-90	0.4	-0.7

TABLE 3 (*Continued*)
Average Wages of Public Sector Employees,[*]
Selected OECD Countries, 1979-90

| | Average Annual Growth Rate in Percentage | |
	Real Wages[1]	Relative Wages[2]
Norway		
1979-84	-1.0	-1.0
1984-90	0.1	-0.5
Spain		
1979-84	0.3	0.0
1984-90	0.2	-0.7
Sweden		
1979-84	-3.0	-0.3
1984-90	1.5	-0.5
Switzerland		
1979-84	1.1	0.8
1984-90	0.8	-2.0

[1] Relative to the private consumption deflator.

[2] Relative to the average private sector wage.

[*] These figures exclude employees in public enterprises.

Source: Howard Oxley and John P. Martin, "Controlling Government Spending and Deficits: Trends in the 1980s and Prospects for the 1990s," *OECD Economic Studies*, No. 17, Autumn 1991, Table 4, pp. 166-67.

The overall impression to emerge from Table 3 is that, generally, public sector employees experienced a wage loss relative to their private sector counterparts through the 1980s. The basic thrust of these findings is generally consistent with the results of more detailed studies for individual countries (Beaumont 1992). Broad public/private sector wage comparisons appear to be, at least in some countries, of declining value because of the increased intra-public sector variation in wage movements in recent times. For example, a recent study for the U.K. public sector covering the years 1970–92 revealed that doctors, police, nurses, and teachers enjoyed significantly greater real earnings growth than other public sector employee groups (Elliott and Duffus 1995).

For the post-1990 years, information on public sector employment and wage movements is much more scattered and fragmentary in nature for the group of OECD countries. However, what is available tends to point to considerable variation between countries. For example, total public sector employment fell in the U.K. between 1992 and 1993 (i.e., 4,890,000 to 4,616,000) and in Sweden (a 48,000 reduction), while it rose in Ireland (i.e., 268,832 to 270,045) and Portugal (i.e., 705,300 to 715,200) in the same period of time. New initiatives to limit the size of public sector wage increases have also been a feature of the 1990s in some countries. For example, in the U.K. a freeze on operating costs in 1994–95 meant that civil service departments were to keep pay budgets to the 1993–94 level. And in Germany, pay awards in the public sector in 1994 were less than half of the average increase of 2%.

The role of budgetary deficit pressures in stimulating public sector reform programs has been particularly important for the member countries of the EU. This is because the Maastricht Treaty lays down four minimum ("convergence") criteria for economic and monetary union, including the requirements that government deficits must not exceed 3% of GDP and government debt must not exceed 60% of GDP. These are clearly going to be relatively demanding criteria for many member states to meet, as indicated by Table 4.

Table 4 shows that among the fifteen EU countries, by 1996 only six are expected to have deficits below the Maastricht limit of 3% of GDP and only four to have debt-to-GDP ratios below 60%. These figures suggest a rather different picture to the relatively optimistic views of Sir Leon Brittan, a well-known member of the European Commission (Brittan 1994:56–60).

Moreover, these budgetary deficit pressures in stimulating public sector reform appear to transcend the role of political parties to a considerable extent. That is, they are not pressures that produce only reform measures from conservative, right-wing governments which are not generally well disposed toward the public sector and the union movement. The case of Sweden is likely to be a particularly interesting one to monitor in this regard. In the years 1991–94, Sweden had a four-party, center-right coalition government in office. This administration launched a number of public sector initiatives that broke radically with past practice including a sizeable reduction in public sector employment, a proposal to privatize some 34 wholly or partially state-owned companies, and the introduction of a new system of government grants to local authorities. However, the Social Democrats were returned to power in October 1994, although the extent to which they will be prepared to reverse the previous administration's public sector change program seems open to considerable question given Sweden's decision to join the EU and the current size of their budget deficit (i.e., some 11% of GDP).

Furthermore, for the OECD group these fiscal adjustment pressures are unlikely to decrease in the future. Indeed, they are forecast to

TABLE 4

Progress toward Maastricht Fiscal Targets

(General government financed balances and general government gross debt [Maastricht basis] as a percentage of nominal GDP)

Country	Financial Balances				Gross Debt			
	1993	1994	1995	1996	1993	1994	1995	1996
Austria	-4.1	-4.0	-4.5	-3.9	62.8	64.5	65.9	66.9
Belgium	-6.6	-5.3	-4.3	-4.0	137.2	136.2	134.5	132.6
Denmark	-4.5	-3.9	-2.1	-1.6	80.3	75.6	75.8	75.4
Finland	-7.9	-5.5	-5.0	-3.3	57.1	60.1	66.5	70.8
France	-6.1	-6.0	-5.0	-4.1	45.8	48.5	51.2	52.6
Germany	-3.3	-2.5	-2.3	-2.2	48.2	50.1	58.0	58.1
Greece	-13.2	-12.5	-11.4	-10.0	115.1	113.6	114.0	114.0
Ireland	-2.3	-2.2	-2.5	-2.4	96.9	90.9	86.3	82.1
Italy	-9.6	-9.0	-7.8	-6.9	119.4	125.4	124.9	123.3
Luxembourg	1.1	1.2	—	—	6.8	7.0	—	—
Netherlands	-3.2	-3.0	-3.3	-2.7	81.4	78.3	78.6	78.7
Portugal	-7.1	-5.7	-5.4	-5.0	66.5	69.5	69.9	69.9
Spain	-7.5	-6.6	-6.2	-5.5	59.9	62.2	65.3	67.4
Sweden	-13.4	-10.4	-9.2	-6.4	74.7	79.1	84.2	86.0
United Kingdom	-7.9	-6.5	-4.2	-2.6	48.3	52.5	54.3	53.7

Source: OECD *Economic Outlook*, No. 47, June 1995, p. 10.

increase as a result of aging populations putting increased demands on pension payments and health care spending.

The OECD has attempted to forecast the budgetary impact of demographic trends on spending and receipts related to pensions, health care, and education over the period to 2030 (OECD 1995:3342). The results of this exercise pointed to the likely emergence of serious long-term problems in many OECD countries which will require governments to make in the report's view early and sustained fiscal consolidation efforts that give priority to expenditure reductions via public sector efficiency measures, privatization, cuts in state subsidies, and fundamental reassessments of social transfer payments. In short, the clear message is that budgetary pressures as a source of public sector change will increase rather than decrease in the immediate and longer-term future. For this reason it should occasion little surprise that proposals for expenditure cuts and social security reform are so prominent in the budget plans of many European countries in the mid-1990s. For instance, state expenditure on social security and pensions in Italy is forecast to be 19.7% of national income by 2000; currently, the government there is proposing to phase out state earnings-related pensions and replace them with a contributions-related scheme.

Larger Public Sector Reform

What sort of tangible changes have occurred in the public sector as a result of these budgetary pressures? This question has been examined in a series of reports on public management developments in the 1990s with major surveys being carried out in 1990 and 1993 and updates in other years. In essence these reports divide the reform measures as follows: (1) attempts to adjust the size and structure of the public sector by seeking to make it leaner, more competitive, less centralized, and able to provide more choice; and (2) efforts to improve public sector management by enhancing the effectiveness of, in particular, the financial, personnel, performance, and regulatory management functions.

Table 5 indicates the relative importance attributed by (the national correspondents of) member countries to different types of public sector reform initiatives during 1994. The contents suggest that limiting the size of the public sector is the major structural issue being addressed with financial resources management also being a priority reform area.

In order to provide some more detail for the nature of the measures taken under these various headings, Table 6 lists some recent illustrative examples for a number of countries. Table 6 indicates a number of

TABLE 5

New Public Sector Management Initiatives: OECD Countries, 1994°

	Limits to the size of the public sector	Privatization	Commercialization/corporatization of public bodies	Decentralization to sub-national government	Deconcentration within central government	Use of market-type mechanisms	New roles for central management bodies	Other restructuring/"rationalization"
Australia	1	1	1	1	2	1	1	1
Austria	2	2	0	1	1	1	0	2
Belgium	2	1	1	1	0	0	1	2
Canada	2	1	1	1	1	1	2	2
Denmark	0	0	2	0	0	1	0	1
Finland	2	1	2	2	1	1	1	0
France	0	2	1	1	2	0	1	1
Germany	2	2	2	2	1	2	1	2
Greece	1	0	0	2	2	0	2	1
Iceland	2	2	2	1	0	2	0	0
Ireland	2	0	0	1	2	0	2	2
Italy	2	2	2	2	2	1	2	2
Japan	1	1	0	2	0	0	0	0
Luxembourg	1	0	0	0	0	0	0	0
Mexico	2	2	1	2	1	0	2	0
Netherlands	1	0	0	1	0	0	0	0
New Zealand	0	1	1	0	2	1	0	2
Norway	1	0	2	1	0	1	0	0
Portugal	1	1	1	0	1	0	0	0
Spain	0	0	0	2	0	2	0	2
Sweden	2	1	2	1	0	1	2	1
Switzerland	2	1	1	1	2	0	1	1
Turkey	1	2	1	0	0	1	1	1
United Kingdom	1	1	1	0	2	1	0	2
United States	2	2	2	2	2	1	2	1

TABLE 5 (*Continued*)

New Public Sector Management Initiatives: OECD Countries, 1994[*]

	Management of policy-making	Performance management	Financial resources management	Personnel management	Regulatory management and reform	Improving relations with citizens/enterprises	Management of information technology	Other
Australia	1	2	1	1	1	1	0	2
Austria	1	2	2	2	2	2	2	1
Belgium	0	1	1	2	2	2	1	2
Canada	2	1	2	1	2	2	2	1
Denmark	1	0	2	0	0	2	1	1
Finland	2	2	2	2	1	1	2	1
France	1	0	1	1	1	1	1	0
Germany	1	2	2	1	2	2	2	0
Greece	2	0	2	2	1	2	1	0
Iceland	0	2	2	1	1	0	0	0
Ireland	2	1	2	1	2	1	1	2
Italy	2	2	2	2	2	2	2	2
Japan	0	1	1	2	2	0	2	2
Luxembourg	0	1	1	0	1	1	0	0
Mexico	2	2	0	0	1	2	1	0
Netherlands	0	2	2	2	2	1	0	0
New Zealand	1	2	2	1	0	1	0	0
Norway	2	1	1	1	1	1	2	1
Portugal	0	0	1	0	0	2	2	2
Spain	0	2	2	2	1	2	0	1
Sweden	1	2	2	1	1	0	2	0
Switzerland	1	2	1	2	1	1	1	2
Turkey	0	0	1	1	0	1	1	1
United Kingdom	0	0	2	2	2	1	1	2
United States	1	2	2	2	2	2	2	2

Source: OECD *Public Management Developments: Update 1995*, Paris, pp. 14-15.
[*] Ratings have been made by national correspondents where 2 = major initiative; 1 = less important measure; and 0 = no significant steps taken.

TABLE 6

Recent Public Sector Reform Initiatives in OECD Countries

1. Limits to size and spending (i.e., centrally imposed constraints on public sector pay and recruitment)
   - Greece: A continuing freeze on appointments and recruitment.
   - U.K.: Departmental pay budgets (which represent 60% of total running costs) were to be kept at 1993-94 level in 1994-95.

2. Decentralization to subnational government and deconcentration within central government
   - Sweden: A new system of government grants to local authorities was introduced and numerous earmarked grants discontinued.
   - Finland: Structural changes and a redefinition of the roles of each level of government.

3. Improving relations with citizens and enterprises
   - Belgium, France, Portugal, and U.K.: Further development of citizens' charters.

4. Performance management
   - Denmark: A new concept of "service standard statements" is being developed by the Ministry of Finance for organization-specific application across the public sector.
   - Finland: The Ministry of Finance has set up a "Quality and Productivity Project" with several sectoral pilot projects and guidelines on quality management and cost control methods.

5. Financial resources management
   - Belgium: The use of multi-year budgeting as a management tool has been strengthened.
   - Finland: The Budget Decree has been completely rewritten to include instructions on ministerial management of agencies by results.

6. Human resources management
   - Italy: Measures have been introduced to put public sector employment on a more competitive footing with the private sector and European counterparts.
   - Netherlands: The privatization of the Civil Servants Superannuation Fund was agreed upon by the Minister for Home Affairs and the unions (in principle from January 1, 1996).

7. Regulatory management and reform
   - Ireland: A task force has been set up by the Minister for Enterprise and Employment to draw up a charter for small business.
   - Norway: The Ministry of Government Administration has prepared a draft checklist for assessing new regulations.

Source: OECD, *Public Management Developments: Update 1994*, Paris, 1994, pp. 7–9.

larger structural changes in the public sector which are likely to have important, albeit rather indirect, effects on the nature of industrial relations arrangements. At the same time, however, there are examples of

TABLE 7

Major Public Sector Initiatives
in the Netherlands, 1982–92

1982-86	Comprehensive government reorganization project including decentralization measures, especially in personnel management.
1984	Provision made to award bonus payments in recognition of special effort.
1984-86	Central steering committee on personnel policy monitors project for reorganization of all personnel management.
1988	A market-related allowance or bonus to recruit and retain certain categories of civil servants (with skills in demand) was introduced in order to respond to specific needs.
1988-90	Targets set for job reductions for each ministry with a 1988 target of 3,500 cuts and a total target of approximately 20,000 full-time equivalents.
1989	A system of pay differentials introduced across the public service to reward performance with approximately 23 million guilders earmarked for civil service funding.
	The requirement to reach an agreement on labor conditions for civil servants (pay, pensions, etc.) institutionalized in a "Protocol."
1990	Preparations start for introducing the concept of "labor productivity in the public sector."
	Ministerial committee formed to steer a "greater efficiency operation" aimed at reducing government tasks, improving structural organization and a cost reduction of 300 million guilders by 1994.
	"Small-scale efficiency operation" launched with the aim of increasing labor productivity in the public sector by the same percentage as in comparable private sector activities.
1991	Government adopts recommendation of a working group reviewing management rules. Proposals include introduction of agencies to widen range of forms of self-management.
	Renewed government attention to decentralization with an extensive package of proposals to devolve responsibilities and resources to lower level of government aimed at saving 50 million guilders.
	"Core business" operation attempts to define each ministry's central tasks aimed at reducing personnel expenditures by 600 million guilders and a proportional reduction in numbers of personnel.
	Significant steps taken to "normalize" further the status of government employees through proposals to codify staff consultation procedures and the right to strike in conformity with private sector arrangements, except for defense personnel.
	Performance-related pay scheme evaluated.

TABLE 7 (*Continued*)

Major Public Sector Initiatives
in the Netherlands, 1982–92

1992	Decentralization impulse continues with agreement between central government and representatives of local government in transfer to tasks amounting to 800 guilders.
	As part of its continuing "greater efficiency operation," government adopts specific measures for each ministry, including privatization and staff reductions.
	Central government and trade unions agree to the privatization of the general pension fund for public employees by 1996.

Source: OECD Public Management Developments: Survey 1993, par. 5, pp. 124-5.

other initiatives more directly aimed at existing industrial relations arrangements. The contents of Table 7 provide a listing of some of the major public sector changes over time in the Netherlands which have impacted both directly and indirectly on industrial relations.

Table 7 usefully illustrates the fact that the public sector reform movement in the Netherlands, as in many OECD countries, stretches back into the 1980s, albeit the pace of change has considerably accelerated in more recent years. The mixed nature of the various changes listed also indicates the likelihood of varying responses to individual initiatives by the public sector unions.

To help focus more specifically on the nature of public sector industrial relations and human resource management changes in Europe, it is useful to employ an increasingly used generic phrase, namely, "making the public sector more like the private sector." This is the subheading for the next section, although there I consider three very different lines of development: (1) privatization involving the transfer of public sector operations to the private sector; (2) transferring private sector collective bargaining practices to the public sector by moving away from the traditional notion of the sovereign employer doctrine in the public sector; and (3) importing private sector human resource management practices into the public sector, most notably performance-related pay arrangements.

Making Public Sector Industrial Relations More Like the Private Sector

Privatization

Privatization involves the transfer of public sector operations to the private sector. Within Europe the scale of the privatization program has been much greater in the U.K. than elsewhere, with some 930,000 jobs being transferred from the public to the private sector since 1979. Table 8 lists the major corporations transferred to the private sector in the U.K. in the period 1982–94.

TABLE 8

Public Corporations Transferred to the Private Sector, 1982–94

Corporation	Date of Transfer	Number of Employees (if reported)
National Freight Company	February 1982	28,000
Britoil	October 1982	14,000
Associated British Ports (formerly Transport Docks Board)	February 1983	
Gas Corporation	June 1984	
British Telecom	November 1984	250,000
British Shipbuilders	July 1984	
British Gas plc	December 1986	89,000
British Airways plc	February 1987	36,000
Royal Ordnance	April 1987	17,000
BAA plc	July 1987	7,200
National Bus Company subsidiaries	July 1986-April 1988	
British Steel	December 1988	53,000
Local authority bus companies (25)	September 1988	
General Practice Finance Corporation	March 1989	
Regional Water Authorities and Water Authorities Association	December 1989	40,000
Scottish Transport Group subsidiaries	August 1990	
Liverpool Airport	June 1990	
Girobank	July 1990	6,700
Regional Electricity Board and National Grid Company	December 1990	119,000
National Power and Powergen	March 1991	26,400
Scottish Power (formerly the North of Scotland Hydro Electric Board)	June 1991	9,800
British Technology Group	April 1992	
Northern Ireland Electricity Service	June 1993	5,000
East Midlands International Airport	August 1993	

Source: A. Hughes. 1995. "Employment in the Public and Private Sectors. *Economic Trends*, no. 495 (January), p. 21.

The transfer of these organizations to the private sector has been associated with a number of notable industrial relations changes (Beaumont and Harris 1995). Perhaps the most well-known change is the movement away from industry-level bargaining arrangements to single employer bargaining structures in industries such as water and electricity. Other changes include sizeable employment reductions, reductions in the number of individual pay grades, the introduction of performance-related pay arrangements for managers, and a growing interest in establishing single-table bargaining arrangements. Furthermore, some recent research (Beaumont and Harris 1995) has examined the impact of privatization on the level of union organization and the extent of collective bargaining arrangements. The major findings reached were that: (1) the extent of management recognition of unions for collective bargaining purposes has changed little although, (2) an above-average decline in the level of union organization had occurred largely as a result of sizeable employment reductions and the ending of closed-shop arrangements.

In addition to the privatization of corporations, there has been legislation requiring compulsory competitive tendering of various services in certain parts of the public sector (e.g., health service, local government) in the U.K. For example, the Local Government Planning and Land Act 1980 required local authorities to seek competitive tenders for most building and highways work. This process was extended by the Local Government Act 1988 to cover further manual work areas such as cleaning of buildings, school catering, vehicle maintenance, refuse collection, and street cleaning. Most recently, compulsory competitive tendering is being further widened to a range of white-collar and professional services in local government, including architecture, engineering, property management, information technology, legal, financial, personnel, and housing management. In general, most tenders to date have been awarded to the "in-house" bid, but this outcome has involved the extensive undermining of industrywide, collectively bargained terms and conditions of employment—an outcome very much favored and sought by the Conservative government. In addition to privatization and contracting out, the U.K. public sector reform program has involved various related measures, such as: (1) the extensive transfer of civil service jobs from ministries to more freestanding executive agencies (which can negotiate their own terms and conditions of employment), (2) the "market testing" of many civil service jobs to see if they can be performed more cheaply or efficiently in the private sector, (3) schools opting out of local authority control, and (4) the creation of internal markets in the health service and local government by distinguishing between the purchaser (e.g., doctors) and provider of public services (e.g., hospitals). The general thrust of these changes has been to try and enhance the decentralization of industrial relations arrangements in the British public sector.

In France a dozen or so major industrial and financial groups were sold off to the private sector in the years 1986–88, while in 1993 an industrial company and two banks were also privatized. Slowly, perhaps reluctantly, privatization has begun to figure more prominently on the agendas of other European countries in recent years. This fact is illustrated by the contents of Table 5 which was presented earlier. In short, the small number of "token" privatizations in other European countries involving only partial government sell-offs of nonstrategic organizations to date seems likely to change in the future. Arguably, Italy and Germany are two of the most important countries to watch in this regard.

Transferring Private Sector Collective Bargaining Arrangements to the Public Sector

Private sector collective bargaining arrangements have been introduced into the public sector of a number of European countries. As indicated in Table 7, for instance, public sector employees in the Netherlands acquired the right to go on strike in 1981. Subsequently, the principle of collective bargaining was introduced there in 1989. In 1994 the bargaining arrangements were decentralized, and most recently, legislation on works councils is to be extended to the public sector except in education and defense. Similarly, in late 1994 it was announced by the government that civil servants in Greece were to gain collective bargaining rights. Italian legislation in 1993 placed employment contracts in the public sector on the same legal basis as those in the private sector, established a new bargaining agent for the state as employer, and proposed a dialogue to determine the representativeness of individual unions at the national level in the public sector. The first collective agreements in the Italian public sector since the employment relationship was "privatized" were concluded by the unions and the new public sector bargaining agency in early 1995. Their contents (designed to more closely align public administration employment conditions with those of the private sector) included changes in disciplinary procedures, reduced holiday entitlements for new recruits, and changes in special paid leave and sickness absence arrangements. Moreover, public sector wage negotiations have assumed a more prominent and independent role in a number of systems traditionally characterized by highly coordinated, national-level bargaining arrangements. Indeed, in the Swedish system the increasingly assertive role of the public sector has played a not inconsiderable role in undermining the traditional wage bargaining arrangements (Wise 1993).

Transferring Private Sector Human Resource Management Practices to the Public Sector

The increased presence in the public sector of more individual employee-oriented human resource management practices is well illustrated by the increased adoption of performance-related pay arrangements. In the U.K., for example, by 1989 some 400,000 civil servants (out of a total of 585,000) had some part of their pay determined by performance appraisal. A recent survey of 65 local authorities in Britain also revealed that one-third of these had performance-related pay for one or more groups of employees. Developments along these lines are far from being unique to the U.K. For example, 1989 saw more funds allocated to flexible salaries in Denmark, a performance bonus experiment initiated in Finland, and performance-related pay introduced for some senior management grades in Ireland. In 1991 initiatives to strengthen the pay–performance linkage occurred in Norway and Switzerland. In 1994 a government report proposed the introduction of performance-related pay bonuses in the German civil service. Many of these arrangements are largely confined to upper management grade employees, although the precise details of the schemes tend to vary quite considerably across countries. An OECD study (1993) noted the major features of these public sector schemes and identified the following problems with their operation:

1. A lack of differentiation in performance ratings.
2. A clustering of managers at the top of the salary range in merit pay schemes where they are no longer eligible for merit increments.
3. Dissatisfaction among staff who are rated fully satisfactory, but who under quotas and other restrictive guidelines for some schemes either receive a smaller performance pay award than their colleagues or no award at all in a given year.
4. Relatively low levels of funding which make schemes highly competitive and, in some countries, cut-backs in funds during times of economic restraint.

5. A narrowing of the range and reduction in the average size of bonuses paid.

The report went on to raise the question of whether the inadequate operation of many of these schemes derived from their poor design and implementation or whether the assumptions underpinning such schemes were not valid for the public sector. Although no firm conclusions were reached in these matters, the report contained a number of recommendations such as the need for regular monitoring, increased funding, and improved appraisal training.

British Exceptionalism?

Looking across Europeanwide changes in public sector industrial relations, there is a general perception that the British case is an exceptional one involving differences in kind rather than simply in degree. As Ferner (1994) has put it:

> The divergences in approach are as striking as the similarities. The Thatcherite program in Britain represents one extreme of the spectrum: an ideologically propelled political project of hacking the state down to size, and with it the allegedly overpowerful public sector trade unions. Nowhere else has there been such enveloping animosity to what the post-war public sector stands for; or such a thorough dismantling of the old ways of doing things in industrial relations; or such far-reaching reform of the remaining administrative apparatus. In other European countries, modernization of the state has been pragmatic, gradualist, accomplished with labor rather than against it, often going hand-in-hand with the consolidation of pluralist industrial relations institutions within the state (p. 65).

In short, it is widely held that the motivation for change, the substance of change, and the process of change in the public sector in Britain is very different to that in the rest of Europe. In Britain the motivation for public sector change is seen as deriving in large measure from a right-wing conservative administration which is highly critical of the notion of "big government" on ideological and economic grounds. The strong "anti-public sector" stance of the government is also intimately tied to its more general opposition to and criticism of trade unions and collective bargaining arrangements which has manifested itself in a major program of antiunion legislation which is unique in Europe (Taylor 1994:43–8).

As to the substance of change, the contention is that certain changes have gone much further in Britain than elsewhere. The scale of the privatization program, the extent of "market testing" for civil service jobs, and the fact of *compulsory* competitive tendering in the health service and local government are among the leading examples cited in this regard. Finally, fundamental differences in the processes of change have been emphasized with the particular contention being that an already highly centralized state has become increasingly centralized in nature as the government has driven through a program of change with little attention being given to the processes of consultation and discussion with the other stakeholders concerned. The very different conception of the role and value of the public sector in Britain compared to other parts of Europe (e.g., Germany), the limited tradition of national-level government-union consultations in Britain, and the relatively greater capacity of the party in power to dominate the state apparatus in Britain have been among the major reasons given for explaining this variation between Britain and the rest of Europe (Ferner 1994:74–5).

The major observation to make about the program of public sector change in Britain is to recognize its highly controversial nature with many different verdicts being rendered on its success and effectiveness. For instance, some commentators have argued that the scale of change can easily be exaggerated, others have emphasized its success, while yet a third group has pointed to its negative effects. This variation in perception and judgment seems to be a function of precisely which particular indicators of change individual commentators choose to examine and emphasize (i.e., "selective perception").

For example, an advocate of the "limited change" school of thought might choose to emphasize the fact that twenty-five years ago the ratio of general government expenditure to GDP in Britain was 41.25%; in 1995–96 it is forecast to be 41.75%. More specifically in the industrial relations area, one might argue that the breakup of industrywide collective bargaining arrangements in local government and the health service has been very slow and limited to date, despite considerable government encouragement to this effect. In contrast, however, if one chose to look at the civil service, one would find much more evidence of the growth of decentralized bargaining arrangements: In 1990, for instance, half a million civil servants were covered by five central agreements, whereas in 1995 there are just 140,000 covered by four national deals. In contrast to the limited change view, a number of political commentators (Hutton 1995:4–5; Jenkins 1995) have placed great emphasis on the loss of democratic accountability as the change program has given more and more decision-making authority to appointed, rather than elected, individuals in the public sector.

In the absence of a systematic and comprehensive monitoring of the overall public sector change process, it is virtually impossible to say with any degree of confidence which school of thought paints the more accurate picture. However, those emphasizing limited change and the counter-productive effects of change have performed a most useful service by emphasizing some important tensions and potential contradictions in the program of change. For example, Jenkins (1995) strongly emphasizes that the increased role and concern of the Treasury with the total size of the public sector wage bill does not sit comfortably with government encouragement of decentralized industrial relations arrangements in the public sector.

An Anglo-Irish Comparison

The exceptional nature of the British public sector change program can be usefully highlighted by a comparison with the position in Ireland. This is potentially a most instructive comparison because of (1) the traditional similarity of industrial relations arrangements in the two countries and (2) the identification of Ireland as the leading example of successful fiscal adjustment in the latter part of the 1980s (Alesina and Perotti 1995:239). As regards the latter point, Ireland had a central government deficit as a percentage of GNP of 13.8% in 1985 (the largest among the OECD countries), a figure which was substantially reduced to 2.6% by 1990. This adjustment process was associated with a number of public sector changes such as those listed in Table 9.

Ireland, like the U.K., is one of the most highly centralized states in Europe, which clearly facilitates the government's ability to carry through a change program. However, in contrast to the hostile Conservative government attitude to the public sector in the U.K., the position in Ireland has been characterized as a "mixture of ambivalent benevolence to the public sector, [a] pragmatic reaction to events and a tendency for governments to give priority to what will carry us through to the next election—in other words, just muddling through" (McGinley 1994:208).

This very different government attitude toward the public sector has been manifested in a number of ways in Ireland. First, the scale of privatization has been relatively limited (e.g., the Irish Life and the Irish Sugar Company, employing together about 4,000 people) and driven largely by budgetary rather than ideological considerations. Second, the

TABLE 9
Some Leading Public Sector Changes in Ireland, 1987–92

1987	Budget goals defined to contain public expenditure in real terms at or below 1986 levels as a percentage of GNP.
	Government accepts in principle a report by an Independent Review Body on Higher Remuneration in the Public Sector which recommends that the pay of a senior management grate (assistant secretary) be performance related.
1988	Comprehensive three-year agreement with public service unions negotiated.
1989	In budget statement, Minister for Finance announces new system of budgetary allocations for administration or running costs based on a three-year period and on delegated spending authority.
1990	Filling of essential posts authorized but no general resumption in public service recruitment.
	Performance-related pay scheme introduced to assistant secretary grade.
1991	Program for Economic and Social Progress signed by the government and the social partners to provide a strategic framework for development over the next decade and specific proposals to 1993.
	Three-year administrative budgets for 1991-93 introduced in most (23) departments aimed to reduce running costs by 2% in 1992 and to improve efficiency and effectiveness by delegating more expenditure authority to line departments and line managers.
	A strategic initiative is launched to base staff development on needs analysis and guidelines of best practice.
	Two commercial state enterprises privatized.
1992	A monitoring committee including representatives of the Department of Finance is set up in each department covered by the administrative budget program to review progress.
	Steady privatization of commercial state enterprises continues.

Source: OECD, *Public Management Developments: Survey 1993*, Paris, p. 96.

public sector employment reductions of the late 1980s have not been maintained over time. For example, total public sector employment declined from 303,135 in 1985 to 267,277 in 1990 but rose to 270,002 in 1993. Third, the extent of tangible public sector industrial relations reform has been relatively limited to date. The government has, for instance, long been critical of public sector pay determination arrangements on two major grounds, namely, the excessive use of: (1) internal wage comparisons within the public sector itself, and (2) third-party dispute settlement procedures. Extensive consultations with public sector unions have taken place on these matters, but little change has resulted to date; the government's desire to ensure the successful negotiation of national agreements has clearly limited the pace of change in these matters.

It is, of course, possible to argue that other European countries, such as Ireland, will be forced under budgetary pressures to follow more of the British approach in the future. If this does in fact occur, then what one would be observing at the present moment is simply a time lag between Britain and the rest of Europe which could well shrink in the future. This is a possible line of development that cannot be completely ruled out. However, concerns about the effectiveness of the public sector change program in Britain are likely to limit the incentive of some European countries to go fully down this route. Moreover, the very different nature of the state in other European countries (i.e., a more decentralized, multiple stakeholder notion) is likely to limit the ability of governments to fully do so.

Implementation Difficulties: The Union Response

Various OECD reports (1993:16) on public sector reform initiatives have been highly critical of the relative absence of formal and systematic arrangements for monitoring and evaluating the impact of these change programs in many countries. The need for such arrangements was held to derive from the existence of possible constraints on the processes of implementing the reforms. One potentially important constraint in this regard would seem to be the relatively high rate of unionization in the public sector in many European countries (OECD 1990). By the late 1980s, the public sector accounted on average for about 40% of union membership in the OECD countries, while in some European countries, notably Norway, Sweden, and Finland, collective bargaining coverage was virtually 100% in the public sector.

What has been the response to injecting the sort of changes discussed here into a relatively highly unionized sector of employment? Perhaps predictably there has been considerable evidence of disputes and strike activity. Arguably the most high-profile instance of such recent activity was the three weeks of public sector strike activity in France in December 1995 in response to government proposals for fiscal adjustment deemed necessary to help meet the Maastricht convergence criteria. The 1995 bargaining rounds in Sweden and Norway were also seriously disrupted by instances of strike action in the public sector. In the same year, following the privatization of the local bus line in Esbjerg (Denmark), a very bitter dispute over pay lasted over seven months despite police intervention and numerous mediation attempts.

The 1990s in Ireland has witnessed a number of very high-profile strikes in the semi-state commercial sector, many of which have involved union rejection of management agendas developed in response to certain European deregulation initiatives (Hastings 1994).

The general perception of enhanced strike activity in the public sector is not simply a phenomenon of the last couple of years. Indeed, one recent study (Shalev 1992) has documented the fact that in nine of the sixteen countries OECD examined, the share of public service strikes in the total volume increased in the 1980s, in some cases quite notably. In the light of our earlier discussion, it is hardly surprising to find such a tendency in Britain. For instance, the largest single dispute in each year in Britain over the period 1978–94 occurred in the public sector in ten out of these years. In 1993, for example, a strike by civil servants over market testing, privatization, and cuts in service accounted for 42% of all workers on strike and 25% of all days lost. Further relevant evidence can be cited for Ireland where the following has been reported (Brannick and Doyle 1994): (1) the proportion of strikes in the public sector was 18.3% for 1970–79, 29.1% for 1980–89, and 47.5% in 1990–92; and (2) the proportion of workers involved in strike activity in the public sector was 22.6% for 1970–79, 68.9% in 1980–89, and 67.1% for 1990–92. The increased "commercialization" of state enterprise companies, employment reductions in the late 1980s, and the deferred implementation of special public sector wage increases within the context of national wage agreements have been cited as some of the leading factors involved in this changed pattern of strike activity in Ireland.

Conclusions

The central argument advanced here is that budget deficit pressures have provided the major stimulus for changes in the public sector across European countries with these changes including ones that both directly and indirectly impact on industrial relations structures, processes, and outcomes.

The extent and nature of these changes have been very considerable, frequently resulting in adverse employee and union reactions in a relatively highly organized sector of employment. To date, these changes have gone furthest in Britain, where the success of the change program is subject to intense debate and disagreement. However, some substantive steps in the British direction in other European countries cannot be entirely ruled out in the future as the strength of budget deficit pressures increase, particularly as the process of European integration and competitiveness concerns gather pace. This being said, the all-important processes of change are likely to remain relatively divergent between countries.

Acknowledgments

I am most grateful to Mark Carley and Paul Thompson of Industrial Relations Services and Paddy Gunnigle at the University of Limerick for the provision of information.

References

Alesina, A., and R. Perotti. 1995. "Fiscal Expansions and Adjustments in Countries." *Economic Policy*, Vol. 21, pp. 207–48.

Beaumont, P.B. 1992. *Public Sector Industrial Relations*. London: Routledge.

Beaumont, P.B., and R.I.D. Harris. 1995. "Privatized Organizations and Industrial Relations Change." *Policy Studies*, Vol. 16, no. 4, pp. 18–28.

Brannick, T., and L. Doyle. 1994. "Industrial Conflict." In T.V. Murphy and W.K. Roche, eds., *Irish Industrial Relations in Practice*. Dublin: Oak Tree Press.

Brittan, L. 1994. *Europe: The Europe We Need*. London: Hamish Hamilton.

Chan-Lee, J., D.T. Coe, and M. Prywes. 1987. "Microeconomic Changes and Macroeconomic Wage Disinflation in the 1980s." *Economic Studies*, Vol. 8, pp. 121–57.

Elliott, R.F., and K. Duffus. 1995. "What Has Been Happening to Pay in the Public Service Sector of the British Economy? *Treasury Occasional Paper No. 3*. London: HM Treasury.

Ferner, A. 1994. "The State as Employer." In R. Hyman and A. Ferner, eds., *New Frontiers in European Industrial Relations*. Oxford: Blackwell, pp. 52–79.

Hastings, T. 1994. *Semi-States in Crisis*. Dublin: Oak Tree Press.

Hutton, W. 1995. *The State We're In*. London: Jonathan Cape.

Jenkins, S. 1995. *Accountable to None*. London: Hamish Hamilton.

McGinley, M. 1994. "Industrial Relations in the Public Sector." In T.V. Murphy and W.K. Roche, eds., *Irish Industrial Relations in Practice*. Dublin: Oak Tree Press, pp. 206–50.

Organization for Economic Cooperation and Development (OECD). 1990. *Employment Outlook*. Paris: OECD.

_____. 1993a. *Public Management Developments: Survey*. Paris: OECD.

_____. 1993b. *Private Pay for Public Work: Performance Related Pay for Public Sector Managers*. Paris: OECD.

_____. 1995. *Economic Outlook*. Paris: OECD.

Oxley, H., and J.P. Martin. 1991. "Controlling Government Spending and Deficits: Trends in the 1980s and Prospects for the 1990s." *Economic Studies*, Vol. 17, pp. 145–89.

Shalev, M. 1992. "The Resurgence of Labor Quiescence." In M. Regini, ed., *The Future of Labor Movements*. London: Sage, pp. 102–32.

Taylor, R. 1994. *The Future of Trade Unions*. London: Deutsch.

Wise, L.R. 1993. "Whither Solidarity? Transitions in Swedish Public-Sector Pay Policy." *British Journal of Industrial Relations*, Vol. 31, pp. 75–95.